CREDIT DERIVATIVES

⊠ Wharton School Publishing

In the face of accelerating turbulence and change, business leaders and policy makers need new ways of thinking to sustain performance and growth.

Wharton School Publishing offers a trusted source for stimulating ideas from thought leaders who provide new mental models to address changes in strategy, management, and finance. We seek out authors from diverse disciplines with a profound understanding of change and its implications. We offer books and tools that help executives respond to the challenge of change.

Every book and management tool we publish meets quality standards set by The Wharton School of the University of Pennsylvania. Each title is reviewed by the Wharton School Publishing Editorial Board before being given Wharton's seal of approval. This ensures that Wharton publications are timely, relevant, important, conceptually sound or empirically based, and implementable.

To fit our readers' learning preferences, Wharton publications are available in multiple formats, including books, audio, and electronic.

To find out more about our books and management tools, visit us at whartonsp.com and Wharton's executive education site, exceed.wharton.upenn.edu.

CREDIT DERIVATIVES

A PRIMER ON CREDIT RISK, MODELING, AND INSTRUMENTS

George Chacko
Anders Sjöman
Hideto Motohashi
Vincent Dessain

Wharton
UNIVERSITY *of* PENNSYLVANIA

Vice President, Editor-in-Chief: Tim Moore
Wharton Editor: Yoram (Jerry) Wind
Executive Editor: Jim Boyd
Editorial Assistant: Susie Abraham
Development Editor: Russ Hall
Associate Editor-in-Chief and Director of Marketing: Amy Neidlinger
Cover Designer: Chuti Prasertsith
Managing Editor: Gina Kanouse
Project Editor: Michael Thurston
Copy Editor: Kelli Brooks
Indexer: Lisa Stumpf
Senior Compositor: Gloria Schurick
Manufacturing Buyer: Dan Uhrig

© 2006 by Pearson Education, Inc.
Publishing as Wharton School Publishing
Upper Saddle River, New Jersey 07458

Wharton School Publishing offers excellent discounts on this book when
ordered in quantity for bulk purchases or special sales. For more information,
please contact U.S. Corporate and Government Sales, 1-800-382-3419,
corpsales@pearsontechgroup.com. For sales outside the U.S.,
please contact International Sales at international@pearsoned.com.

Printed in the United States of America

First Printing: June 2006

ISBN 0-13-146744-1

Pearson Education LTD.
Pearson Education Australia PTY, Limited.
Pearson Education Singapore, Pte. Ltd.
Pearson Education North Asia, Ltd.
Pearson Education Canada, Ltd.
Pearson Educatión de Mexico, S.A. de C.V.
Pearson Education—Japan
Pearson Education Malaysia, Pte. Ltd.

Library of Congress Cataloging-in-Publication Data
Credit derivatives : understanding credit risk and credit instruments / George Chacko ... [et al.].
    p. cm.
  ISBN 0-13-146744-1 (alk. paper)
  1. Credit derivatives. 2. Risk. I. Chacko, George.
HG6024.A3C75 2006
332.64'57—dc22

                                                    2005036789

CONTENTS

About the Authors   vii

Acknowledgments   ix

Part I: What Is Credit Risk?   1

1   INTRODUCTION   3

2   ABOUT CREDIT RISK   9

Part II: Credit Risk Modeling   61

3   MODELING CREDIT RISK: STRUCTURAL APPROACH   63

4   MODELING CREDIT RISK: ALTERNATIVE APPROACHES   119

Part III: Typical Credit Derivatives   145

5   CREDIT DEFAULT SWAPS   147

6   COLLATERALIZED DEBT OBLIGATIONS   191

INDEX   247

ABOUT THE AUTHORS

George C. Chacko is an associate professor at Harvard Business School (HBS) in the finance area, which he joined in 1997. He is also a managing director at IFL in New York, which he joined in 2005. Professor Chacko's work has focused on three areas: (1) transaction costs and liquidity risk in capital markets, particularly in the fixed income markets; (2) portfolio construction by institutions and individuals; and (3) the analysis and application of derivative securities. Professor Chacko holds a Ph.D. in business economics from Harvard University and dual master's degrees in business economics (Harvard University) and business administration (University of Chicago). He holds a bachelor's degree in electrical engineering from the Massachusetts Institute of Technology.

Senior researcher **Anders Sjöman** joined Harvard Business School at its Paris-based Europe Research Center in 2003. Mr. Sjöman works across management disciplines throughout Europe, conducting research and developing intellectual material for HBS. Prior, Mr. Sjöman worked five years in Boston for Englishtown.com, the world's largest online English school and an initiative by the EF Education Group. As director of production, he developed Englishtown's web services and built the company's European reseller network. A M.Sc. graduate of the Stockholm School of Economics in his native Sweden, and initially specialized in information management and international business, Mr. Sjöman speaks Swedish, English, French, and Spanish.

Hideto Motohashi is a manager in the Financial System Division at NTT COMWARE Corporation. He is currently consulting with financial institutions to help them introduce risk management systems. Previously, also for NTT COMWARE, Mr. Motohashi worked two years in the Boston office as a senior researcher in financial risk management. His experience at NTT COMWARE also includes systems analysis for the financial and telecommunications industries. Mr. Motohashi completed the Advanced Study Program at Massachusetts Institute of Technology as a fellow. He holds a master's degree in international management from Thunderbird, the Garvin School of International Management, and a bachelor's degree in chemistry from Keio University, Japan.

Vincent Dessain was appointed executive director of the Europe Research Center for Harvard Business School, based in Paris, in November 2001. The center he runs works with HBS faculty members on research and course development projects across the European continent. Prior, he was senior director of corporate relationships at INSEAD in Fontainebleau and on the school's board of directors. Mr. Dessain has been active as a management consultant with Booz-Allen & Hamilton in New York and Paris in the financial services field. His field of consulting was international market entry strategies, financial products, strategy, negotiation and implementation of cross-border alliances, financial restructuring, mergers, and acquisitions. He has also been active as a foreign associate with the law firm Shearman & Sterling in New York in banking and finance and as an advisor to the president of the College of Europe in Bruges, Belgium. A speaker of five European languages (French, English, German, Dutch, and Italian), Mr. Dessain holds a law degree from Leuven University (Belgium), a business administration degree from Louvain University (Belgium), and an MBA from Harvard Business School. Mr. Dessain is an avid mountain climber, marathon runner, and tennis player, and will not miss a good art exhibition.

ACKNOWLEDGMENTS

We could not have completed this book without the generous assistance from colleagues at Harvard Business School and other academic institutions, students in our courses, practitioners in the field, and numerous other people. As a group we are particularly indebted to Penelope Fairbairn for her sharp proofreading eyes and precise content questions. We owe any success this book might have to the kind participation of all these people. Any errors remain naturally our own.

In addition, **George** would like to thank his friends and family for mental support, and the Harvard Business School Division of Research for financial support.

Anders embraces Lotta, Vilgot, Liselotte, and Johannes.

Hideto would like to thank his wife Lin-an and his son Keiya.

Finally, **Vincent** gives thanks from the bottom of his heart to Stéphanie.

Part I

WHAT IS CREDIT RISK?

Chapter 1   Introduction   3

Chapter 2   About Credit Risk   9

1

INTRODUCTION

A Disease Known as Credit Risk

The following situation may sound familiar: A while ago, you lent money to a friend and the time has come for the friend to pay you back. You already worry, though, that your friend won't be able to pay back the loan. The idea that you might have to remind him is unpleasant; it makes you uneasy, queasy, almost to the point of nausea. Well, we are here to inform you that you have just been infected with the Credit Risk virus. And you won't be cured until the money is safely returned.

In the modern world, this is a virus as ordinary as the common cold. It does not limit itself to you or your friends. Credit risk touches anyone that extends a loan or has money due. It affects banks that offer loans to individuals, companies that give credit lines to their customers, and investors that buy corporate bonds from companies. In each of these examples, the credit taker—the individual, the clients, or the company— may not return the money or pay back the loan.

Put simply, credit risk is the risk that a borrower won't pay back the lender.

Of course, this should be expected when lending money—and it should be just as expected that the lender wants to evaluate how "safe" or credit worthy the borrower is. Banks run background checks on borrowers to avoid ending up with—in industry terms—a **non-performing** or **bad loan**. For instance, if an individual applies for a house purchase loan, the bank will automatically verify the applicant's history of bank loans. This check of a person's credit worthiness answers several questions: Has he taken loans earlier, how big were they, and did he pay them back on time? Furthermore, are there assets that the bank can use as substitutes for payment—also known as **guarantees** or **collateral**—if the person does not pay back the loan? How valuable is the collateral, or rather, how much of the bank loan can the collateral pay back (sometimes referred to as the **recovery rate**)?

The same type of evaluation takes place if the borrower is a company. Picture a corporation that wants to build a new steel factory and applies for a loan to finance the factory. The bank will want to learn the history of the company. Is it knowledgeable about the steel industry? Has it built steel factories before? Does it have a credit rating from an external agency, such as Standard & Poor's or Moody's? What guarantees can it provide? A good bank will discuss all these issues before deciding whether to grant the steel factory a loan.

Credit risk is not limited to banks and their borrowers. Companies themselves are exposed to credit risk when they trade with customers and suppliers. In business, almost all companies are exposed to credit risk, simply because they do not ask for direct payments for products or services. Think of the standard payment program for a new car: The car dealership carries a credit risk, which slowly diminishes until the car is paid in full. Or, think of the typical company that ships its products with a bill specifying 30 days net payment: During those 30 days, and until payment has been made, the company is exposed to credit risk. As a result, companies often have to rely on its clients and trust their credit worthiness.

Companies also have to pay attention to their *own* credit risk. If the actors in the financial markets—such as banks and bond investors—believe that a company's credit worthiness has dropped, they will charge more for lending money to that firm, because they now have to factor in a higher perceived uncertainty and risk. For the firm, this means that its borrowing cost rises, as lenders demand a higher interest on loans than before. In other words, credit risk is a "disease" that can hit a company both as a lender and as a borrower.

Curing Credit Risk: Credit Derivatives

Several methods and instruments for handling credit risk have been developed over the years. Of course, the easiest way to avoid credit risk is to refuse making a loan. Although this may be a pretty infallible method of credit enhancement, it eliminates the possibility of making any kind of a profit. Other methods are less drastic. Some of them involve changing a company's business practices—for instance, asking for payment *before* the service or product is delivered. This is more natural for some businesses than others; popular examples include magazine subscriptions, health club memberships, or travel. If the company cannot manage this change in cash flow, it can still improve its credit exposure. For instance, the company mentioned earlier with a 30-days net payment practice can simply tighten the payment terms to, for example, 15 days. It can apply this practice across the board for all customers, or just for troubled clients with a history of paying late or not at all. Companies can also sign up for insurance products or ask for guarantees or letters of credit from their counterparts.

More advanced methods involve financial instruments known as **credit derivatives**.[1] Initially created by actors in the financial sector, such as banks and insurance companies, these tools are now also commonly used by regular commercial businesses. Credit derivatives include instruments such as total return swaps, credit spread options, and credit linked notes. They all serve the same primary purpose: to help companies and institutions reduce credit risk by separating out the credit risk part of an investment or asset and sell it onward. As an example, let's return to the bank that was considering making a loan to a steel factory. The bank believes in the project, and wants to grant the loan. However, it already has a number of loans outstanding to other steel factories, and worries about its overall exposure to the steel industry. If the steel sector were to experience economic difficulties, the bank would have a number of borrowers that might be unable to pay their interests or repay their loans. Therefore, to be able to grant the loan to the new steel factory, the bank (let's call it Bank A) turns to another bank (Bank B) and enters into an agreement using a credit derivative mechanism.

The agreement says that if the steel company stops its loan payments (or **defaults** on them, to use the industry jargon), Bank B will pay Bank A the amount in the place of the steel company. For this service, Bank A will pay a monthly fee to Bank B. Hopefully, the steel company will never default on its loan payments, but if it does, Bank A is now insured against the effects of that eventuality. On the one hand, Bank A's credit exposure improves. On the other, Bank B earns a monthly fee and wagers that the steel factory will probably not default on its loan.

This basic agreement is an example of a credit derivative (in this case, a **credit default swap**). Credit derivatives are financial instruments or contracts that allow a participant to decrease (Bank A in the preceding steel example) or increase (Bank B) its exposure to a particular type of credit risk for a specified length of time.

Who Suffers from Credit Risk?

This book is for anyone who suffers from credit risk, wants to understand the disease better, and wants to learn what there is to do about it. It is an introductory book—hence the word *Primer* in its title—and thus is not meant for the seasoned credit risk manager with years of credit experience. However, it is still a practitioner's book, written for the working professional and not for the academic researcher.

The book is a guide for industry, service, or finance professionals with an interest in credit risk and credit instruments. It is meant for investing institutions on the buy-side of the financial markets, such as mutual funds, pension funds, and insurance firms, as well as sell-side retail brokers and research departments. Our reader can be, for example, the chief financial officer (CFO) who wants to assess a proposal for a new credit derivative—or the investment banker who sits down to prepare the proposal.

How to Read This Book

Investors face all sorts of risk and not just credit risk. Grouping risks into different "baskets" helps investors choose which type(s) of risk to accept and which to leave for other investors. They might try to minimize **company-specific risk** through diversification, or use long-short strategies to cancel out **market risk** as they speculate on converging prices for individual securities. **Interest rate risk** is a common concern for anyone else looking to finance a large project. Investors who consume in one currency but invest in another are exposed to **currency risk**.

This book, however, addresses none of these risks. Instead, it focuses on another important risk that is often borne by investors, namely the risk that a company or individual cannot meet its obligations or liabilities on schedule: **credit risk**.

Part I, "What Is Credit Risk?," covers the basics of credit risk. It defines what credit is, what facing credit risk might entail, and also gives a short overview of some common credit derivative tools that transfer credit risk from those investors who do not want to bear it to those investors who are willing to accept it. The two chapters also discuss concepts such as default probabilities, recovery rates, and credit spreads.

After the introduction, Part II, "Credit Risk Modeling," then goes into detail on how credit risk models can be used to describe and predict credit risk events. It covers three different approaches to modeling credit risk: the structural, empirical, and reduced-form approaches. Chapter 3 focuses on structural models. It features the Merton model as an example of the approach, and also discusses the Black and Cox, and Longstaff and Schwartz models. Chapter 4 looks at empirical models, especially the Z-model, and reduced-form models, such as the Jarrow-Turnbull model.

Part III, "Typical Credit Derivatives," concludes the book by discussing in detail two specific credit derivative instruments used to transfer credit risk. Chapter 5 looks at credit default swaps (CDSs) and Chapter 6 at collateralized debt obligations (CDOs).

Endnotes

1 In financial jargon, a derivative is a financial instrument whose value is based on, or **derived from**, another security such as stocks, bonds, and currencies. For instance, a typical derivative is a stock option, which gives the holder the right but not the obligation to buy a company's stock at a future date. Derivatives can also be seen as contracts between two parties; its value then normally depends on a risk factor such as a credit event, an interest rate level, bond prices, currency changes, or even weather data. A credit derivative thus derives its value from a credit note, such as a corporate bond, just as a currency forward contract derives its value from currency exchange rates.

2

ABOUT CREDIT RISK

In this chapter, we start by discussing what credit actually is and why people and organizations may not live up to their credit engagements. This will help us define credit risk properly. We will then look at the credit risk market, its size, and its origins. We will finally give an overview of the financial instruments available to adjust or mitigate credit risk. These so-called credit derivatives will be covered in detail in Part II, "Credit Risk Modeling," of this book, but are introduced here for your understanding.

The Building Blocks of Credit Risk

We stated rather cursorily in the introduction that credit risk is "the risk that a borrower won't pay back the lender." To fully understand what this means—and to come up with a more encompassing definition of credit risk—let's first define the underlying concept of credit.

What Is Credit?

The short and seemingly simple word *credit* represents a powerful economic concept. Credit stands for the idea that a person or company can use somebody else's money to support their own finances. They may use this money for a shorter or longer time, and normally for a fee. Modern society has developed around the idea of credit, because it enables people to have or invest in the things they want today, but can't afford to pay for until tomorrow, possibly as a result of the initial investment itself. To a large degree, credit is the oil that greases the cogwheels of the world economy.

Just think of a very common type of credit: a loan. An individual wants to buy or build a house. She can't afford to pay for it all at once on her own, but if she builds it, she will generate work for constructors, builders, and decorators in her hometown. A financial institution, such as a bank, could help her build the house by granting her a loan. Before lending the money, the bank verifies that she is likely to pay it back. The loan has to be paid back at a certain point in the future, and until that point, the loan taker has to pay a fee to the bank—the interest—at regular intervals. The bank extends a credit, is paid for parting with its money, and enables the individual to go about investing in her house.

As the example shows, financial institutions such as banks normally take on credit risk by granting loans. They also take on the debt of other companies in the form of corporate bonds or the debt of governments in the form of government bonds. By contrast, commercial companies normally acquire credit risk by delivering products and services in exchange for future payments. If you bought a new dishwasher and were given a payment plan of 10 payments over 12 months, you in fact received a credit. You probably have to pay a fee for this, meaning your total payment at the end of 12 months may end up being higher than if you had paid for the new dishwasher all at once. The fee covers the company's risk for extending the credit, and you pay it because it gives you the opportunity not to have to make the full payment all at once.

Let's restate what we have been describing in slightly more technical terms: Credit is money granted by a **creditor** or lender to a **debtor** or borrower (sometimes even referred to as the **obligor**, because he or she has an obligation). In exchange for the credit, the lender is paid a fee or **interest**. In the case of bonds, the fee is more commonly known as the **coupon**. If the credit is tied to a loan, the lender is then returned the full amount or the **principal** at the end of the loan period.

The Importance of Interest

Interest is an important component of credit. Creditors want compensation for providing a service to obligors, and also for having to part with their funds. The interest is the fee they charge for their services. The borrower gets money to use today, whereas the creditor, through the interest, receives more money in the future than he lent.

The interest component should also cover more than just the fee element. Because the value of money decreases over time due to inflation—one normally talks about money's **time value**—the interest has to take into consideration this decline. Suppose a creditor lends $100 today for a year, and that he seeks a 10 percent interest return in a year. Assume further that inflation rates in the economy during this year run at around 5 percent. The creditor then sets the interest rate at 15 percent so that by the time the loan expires, he will receive $115. Adjusted for 5 percent inflation, his return is really only 10 percent.

Typical Types of Credit

Practically, credit can come in several shapes and forms. Let us look at three of the ways that a person or company can use somebody else's money to support their own finances.

CURRENCY

A loan is just one type of credit. There is another much more common type of credit that we all enjoy, often without thinking about it: currency. We all seem to agree, for instance, that a $100 bill is worth exactly $100, although the bill itself, as the saying goes, is not worth the paper it is printed on. However, the value of the bill is backed by the country's credit. It enjoys the full faith and credit of the country's government. The government sustains the value of the currency and people use it based on the country's credit or **sovereign debt**.

LOANS

Loans are a very clear-cut case of credit. In the most typical case, the lender (a bank, a company, or an individual) gives money or property to a borrower. The borrower agrees to return the fund or property at some future point in time, and for the use of the money, the borrower has to pay the lender a fee or interest.

A specific type of loan is a mortgage, used to finance the purchase of real estate. The borrower normally uses the real estate as collateral for the loan, meaning that if the borrower should default on the loan payments, the lender can claim the real estate in lieu of payment.

DEBT OBLIGATIONS: GOVERNMENT AND CORPORATE BONDS[1]

Debt obligations are a way for both companies and governments to raise money. They issue debt in the form of bonds, which are purchased by institutions and individuals. The bond issuer promises to return the initial sum or principal at a determined future date, otherwise known as the **expiration** or **maturity date**. The issuer also normally agrees to pay interest or the coupon at a fixed or floating rate on various, fixed dates.

In its simplest form, a bond is a contract between a lender and a borrower under which the borrower promises to repay a loan with interest. Bonds, however, come with many additional features, based on who issued the bond, for how long the bond is valid, what type of coupon rate is used, and if there are any redemption features attached to the bond. These features help buyers evaluate the risk-and-reward profile of individual bonds. Figure 2-1 classifies bonds according to these features.

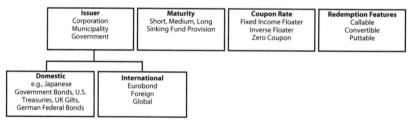

Figure 2-1 Bond classification

Source: George Chacko, Peter Hecht, Vincent Dessain, and Monika Stachowiak. "Note on Bond Valuation and Returns." Harvard Business School Note No. 205–008. Boston: Harvard Business School Publishing, 2004.

Naturally, the issuer of the bond is a major determinant of a bond's expected return and risk. It is easy to understand that companies are seen as riskier providers of debt than governments: Companies are more likely to go bankrupt than countries. In the international debt markets, securities issued by the U.S. government are considered to have the lowest default risk of all. It is seen as so low that U.S. Treasury Bonds are generally referred to as **risk-free bonds** or **default-free bonds.**

Government bonds go by different names depending on their origin. In the U.S., they are called Treasury Bonds, because they are issued by the U.S. Treasury. Japanese government bonds are normally referred to by their abbreviation, JGBs, whereas British bonds are called Gilts.

In addition to issuing bonds in their local currency, governments can also issue them in foreign currencies. Examples are Eurobonds (denominated in a currency other than that of the country in which they are issued; note that the notation is related to neither the continent Europe nor the currency euro), foreign bonds (when the issuer is not domiciled in the country in which the bond is sold and traded), and global bonds (which are both foreign bonds and Eurobonds).

As mentioned previously, bonds are loans, and like most loans they have a final expiration date, or a **term-to-maturity**. At this date, the issuer redeems the bond buyer by paying back the principal investment (also known as **retiring the bond**). In the case of government debt, bonds with a maturity shorter than one year are generally considered short term. Bonds with a maturity between 1 and 10 years are viewed as intermediate term, and long-term bonds are those with a maturity of 10 years or more. Using the U.S. as an example, short-term bonds are known as Treasury Bills (or T-Bills), intermediate-term papers as Treasury Notes, and long-term debt as Treasury Bonds.

In the case of corporate debt, short-term bonds between 2 and 270 days are usually referred to as **commercial papers**, whereas intermediate- and long-term bonds are simply known as **corporate bonds**.

Corporate bonds may also carry a **sinking fund provision**, a condition requiring the company to pay off the principal of the bond over time. According to this provision, in contrast to the one-time bullet payment of retiring a bond, the issuer makes periodic payments to compensate the bond holders. The payments are often made to an independent trustee who then buys back bonds that are available on the market.

In addition to paying back the principal at maturity, the bond issuer normally compensates the buyer by periodic interest payments, known as **coupon payments**. Worth noting is that if the bond does not make coupon payments, and only pays back the principal value at maturity, it is known as a **zero-coupon bond**. Most coupons are based on a fixed rate, although floating rates can also be used, where the coupon rate varies according to the movements of an underlying benchmark such as the LIBOR.[2]

Finally, bonds can come with specific redemption features. For example, they can be callable (the bond issuer has the right to redeem, or call back, the bond prior to its maturity date, normally for a higher price) or puttable (the opposite of callable, meaning the bondholders have the right to sell their bonds back to the issuer at a predetermined price). Convertible bonds also exist, which give bondholders the right but not the obligation to convert their bonds into a predetermined number of equity shares at or prior to the bond's maturity. (Of course, this only applies to corporate bonds.)

Who Defaults?

As we have already stated, not paying back your loan is known as defaulting on the loan. As history shows us, it can happen to all types of borrowers: individuals, companies, and governments alike.

INDIVIDUALS

Excessive credit card use, poor investment management, and lowered real estate value are common causes for bringing individuals to the brink of personal bankruptcy. Figure 2-2 shows that the number of personal bankruptcy filings in the U.S. steadily increased between 1992 and 2003. In 2003, there were more than 400,000 compared to 250,000 in 1992.

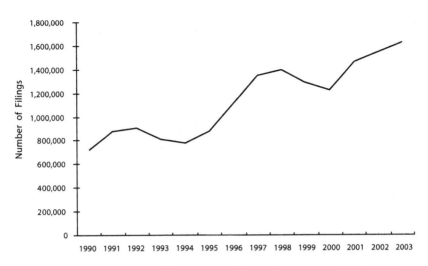

Figure 2-2 U.S. personal bankruptcy filings by quarter (1990-2003)

Source: "The 2004 Bankruptcy Yearbook & Almanac." Edited by McHugh and Sawyer. Boston:
2004. Taken from page 6 (column for nonbusiness filings).

COMPANIES

Just like individuals, companies file for bankruptcy when their costs
exceed their revenues and available capital. One of the sure-tell signs of
an upcoming corporate default is when a firm stops paying coupons on
the bonds they have issued. Unable to meet this financial obligation, the
actual default is not far away. Table 2-1 details business bankruptcies,
along with other measurements of U.S. business between 1990 and 2003.

Table 2-1 U.S. Business Measures, 1990-2003

End of Year	Real GDP* (Billions of 2000 $)	USD Index (1973 = 100)	Number of Public Bankruptcies	Assets of Public Bankruptcies (mn USD)
1990	7,113	85.37	115	82,781
1991	7,101	84.15	123	93,624
1992	7,337	91.37	91	64,226
1993	7,533	92.49	86	18,745
1994	7,836	87.13	70	8,337
1995	8,032	85.26	85	23,107
1996	8,329	88.48	86	14,201
1997	8,704	97.99	83	17,247
1998	9,067	94.61	122	29,195
1999	9,470	95.63	145	58,760
2000	9,817	102.79	176	94,786
2001	9,867	110.32	257	258,490
2002	10,083	100.08	195	382,683
2003	10,398	84.75	143	97,404

Note: * = Real GDP is adjusted by year 2000's value of the U.S. dollar.

Source: Compiled from Small Business Association. "Small Business Economic Indicators for 2003." August 2004. Taken from page 14, www.sba.gov/advo/stats/sbei03.pdf, accessed June 2005. And from "The 2004 Bankruptcy Yearbook & Almanac." Edited by McHugh and Sawyer. Boston: 2004. Taken from page 40 for Number of Public Bankruptcies and Assets of Public Bankruptcies and public currency data.

As an overview, the data in Table 2-1 is shown graphically in Figure 2-3.

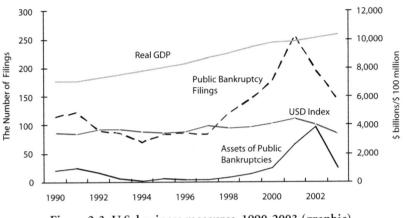

Figure 2-3 U.S. business measures, 1990-2003 (graphic)

Source: Same as Table 2-1.

Note: As the table and the graphic both show, bankruptcies of U.S. public companies have grown
between 1996 and 2001, although real GDP—gross domestic product, an indicator of a
region's financial wealth—has continued to grow. Peaks in bankruptcies can be observed in
2001 for filings and 2002 for asset value, reflecting the large-scale bankruptcies of companies such as Enron, WorldCom, and Parmalat.

COUNTRIES

For the most part, bonds issued by governments are immune from
default. If the government needs more money to pay its debt, it can just
print more. However, municipalities and sometimes whole countries
do occasionally default on their debt. For instance, in 1978, the city of
Cleveland, Ohio defaulted on $15 million in loans it owed to six differ-
ent banks, after refusing to sell the city's electric plant to solve its acute
cash shortage. On a national level, Mexico suspended all its debt payments in 1914, and then again in 1982. More recently, Russia defaulted
on loans in 1998, Turkey in 2001, and Argentina in 2002, in what was
the biggest sovereign default in history at $141 billion of public debt
owed to national and international banks and financial institutions.[3] In
situations like those, the International Monetary Fund (IMF) typically
works with the country government to develop a partial repayment
plan. Such was the case in July 1997, when a dramatic 30 percent drop
in the Thai baht against the U.S. dollar and Japanese yen brought with
it several other Asian currencies. At the end of the year, Thailand, South
Korea, and Indonesia used IMF support to reconstruct their economies.

What Causes Defaults: Credit Events

Not having enough money to pay your loans is an easy-to-understand reason for defaulting on a loan. Any obligor might default for this reason. There are several other so-called **credit events** that might lead to default. Commercial and financial contracts normally specify credit events in more detail. Typical credit events mentioned in such contracts include the following:

- **Bankruptcy**, when a company or organization is dissolved or becomes insolvent and is unable to pay its debts.

- **Failure to pay** within a reasonable amount of time after the due date and after reminders from the receiver.

- **Significant downgrading of credit rating**, meaning the credit rating provided by an external company, such as Fitch or Standard & Poor's (S&P), falls below a specified level.

- **Credit event after merger**, which renders the new merged entity financially weaker than the original entity.

- **Government action or market disruptions**, typically confiscation of assets or effects of wars.

Credit events are often categorized as being driven by either market risk or company-specific risk. Market risk can be a change in overall interest-rate levels or industry dynamics; company-specific risk relates to events concerning only the firm itself.

Among events that do *not* qualify as credit events are falling share prices, smaller than anticipated share dividends, non-significant reductions in the company's credit rating, failures by the company to pay for products or services, or accidental failures by the company to make a payment on time, provided the payment is eventually made within a suitable time period.

Default Process

Although a country can default on selected loans without declaring bankruptcy, as Argentina did in 2002, most companies that default on a bond almost automatically go into full bankruptcy. When a company declares bankruptcy and defaults on all its due loans and credits, the liquidation process gathers whatever can be saved in the form of financial assets. How much that can be gathered relative to all outstanding debt is known as the **recovery rate**. All debt—bank loans, bonds, credit lines, and so on—is then ranked by **seniority** to decide which debtors to pay back first. (A useful comparison is dividend distribution: Holders of preference shares receive dividends before holders of normal shares, preference shares being senior to normal shares.) The debt is traditionally broken up into two major parts: senior and junior debt, with senior debt ranked ahead of junior. For any new debt contract, such as a bond, a company is required to indicate if the new debt is junior or senior to already outstanding debt. Creditors with junior debt do not get paid until the senior debt holders have been paid in full. Senior corporate bonds thus carry less risk for investors than junior bonds, but also have a lower profit potential. An investor that plans to purchase a bond from an issuer that issues several types of bonds needs to consider the seniority of each bond, as this affects the recovery rate.

If bankruptcy should take place, debt holders have priority over stock and equity holders. The company's suppliers and providers should be paid first, and only after that should the company's owners be given whatever might be left. This rhymes with the general investment philosophy that investing in a company's equity (its stock) comes with higher risk and return than investing in its debt, such as bonds.

The seniority of debt and the resulting cascade of cash flow are often referred to as the **debt waterfall**. Figure 2-4 shows a typical debt waterfall. Note that this is a simplified waterfall and that debt waterfalls can be much more complicated and include many more types of debt. For instance, there may be variations on senior and junior debt involved, such as so-called senior mezzanine debt (which normally is ranked ahead of junior debt but after senior debt), hybrid debt, or convertible debt. In addition, collateralized or securitized debt, such as collateralized loan obligations or collateralized mortgage obligations, are always senior to general bond and debt holders.

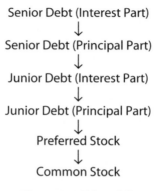

Senior Debt (Interest Part)
↓
Senior Debt (Principal Part)
↓
Junior Debt (Interest Part)
↓
Junior Debt (Principal Part)
↓
Preferred Stock
↓
Common Stock

Figure 2-4 Waterfall

Credit Risk Definition

Now that we know *what* credit is, *who* it is that can default on his credit obligations, and *how* the default process is carried out, we have the foundation for actually defining credit risk.

We stated previously, in layman's terms, that credit risk is the risk that you won't be paid back money that you lent. Using the terminology we've developed in this chapter, we can now say

> *Credit risk is the risk of loss arising from some credit event with the counterparty.*

We have also seen that there are many types of counterparts (individuals, companies, and sovereign governments) and many types of obligations (customer credit to financial derivatives transactions), which means that credit can take many forms. Common to all forms of credit, though, is the risk of default: that an obligor does not honor her payment obligations. As you've noticed, the word default is closely tied to the idea of credit risk, and credit risk is also often referred to as **default risk**.

Credit analysts often talk about how much **credit exposure** a given organization faces. Also known as exposure at default (EAD), credit exposure is a measurement of how much the creditor would lose if the counterparty defaulted on its obligation. Credit exposure can also be defined as the risk that one's exposure to a given counterparty exceeds *a* *given threshold*. Because a small exposure at a low level may not be that damaging to a creditor, this definition helps companies focus on their larger exposures. EAD is often used by regulators of financial institutions, which require credit issuers to measure exposure.[4] The regulators' guidelines require exposure measurements to reflect current as well as future risk, both of which take into account the cost of replacement if the counterparty defaults. These measurements are primarily for derivative instruments, which we will discuss in more detail later in the book, and are based on the fact that current credit positions might not represent future credit risks. When credit derivatives such as swaps are involved, the potential change in value of the swap must also be included.[5]

Measuring Credit Risk Through Credit Spread

Credit risk is commonly broken down into smaller, more manageable components in order to facilitate its measurement. Professional credit risk managers spend their careers working out ways to do this—developing credit risk models. However, most models are based on two fundamental concepts: **default probability** and recovery rate. Together, these give a good measurement of a debt's quality. Combined as one measurement, they are often referred to as **credit spread**. Let's dive into all three concepts a bit further.

Default Probability

The probability of default is exactly what it sounds like: the likelihood that the counterparty will default on its obligation. When debt holders and lenders calculate this probability for all obligations, they can do it either for the life of the obligation or for some specific time period, such as a month or year. (When calculated for a year, a common benchmark is the expected default frequency of various obligations.)

Estimating the default probability of a counterpart can be done in several ways, but is traditionally achieved using the party's credit history, its credit rating with rating agencies, and an evaluation of its finances. Lenders to commercial companies need to estimate the dynamics of the counterparty's business—such as its industry, competitors, production cycle, marketing plan (in short, its business drivers)—in order to fully comprehend how the company would react to changes in its environment. For instance, how would the firm's capability to pay back loans be affected by a sudden drop in interest rate levels? Modeling a company's possible reactions to such macroeconomic changes and to other econometric factors is known as running **stress scenarios** on the debt.

Recovery Rate

The recovery rate measures the extent to which the market value of an obligation may be recovered if the counterparty defaults. For instance, if a corporation with large bank loans declares bankruptcy, its banks will be able to recover some of the debt during the liquidation process. Exactly how much depends on different variables, such as the debt's seniority (discussed earlier in the section "Default Process" when we discussed debt waterfalls).

Combining the default probability and recovery rate with the credit exposure of a given debt, companies can calculate the **expected loss** of any given obligation, using the following formula:

Expected Loss = Default Probability × Credit Exposure × (1 – Recovery Rate) [1]

Credit Spread: Putting a Value on Credit Risk

For investors in credit, and especially in bonds, an important concept is credit spread. Credit spread incorporates both the default probability and recovery rate concepts, and becomes a quick way for bond traders to quote prices.

Credit spread is the difference between a bond's yield[6] and the yield of a risk-free government bond, such as a U.S. Treasury Bond. Next, we'll go through an example of how to calculate credit spread. Let's first remind ourselves, however, that risk- or default-free bonds are bonds that have virtually no risk of defaulting, because they are backed by the full faith and credit of a country's government. The difference in yield between the risk-free and the riskier bonds—their spread—reflects how much risk is embedded in the risky bond, and how much extra yield the investor wants as a compensation for buying the higher risk bond (also known as the investor's **risk premium**). Quoting the credit spread helps investors understand how risky the bond is; the higher the spread, the riskier the bond. The riskier the bond (or conversely, the lower its credit quality), the higher the yield the investor will demand.

Let's exemplify. We'll start with (1) a risk-free government bond, compare it to (2) a corporate bond of comparable maturity without a risk premium, and then compare it to (3) one with a risk premium. Finally, we'll (4) compare the yields for the last two bonds to come up with the credit spread, or risk premium.

1. Risk-Free Government Bond

Suppose you buy a government bond: a U.S. Treasury Bond with a one-year maturity. Because U.S. Treasury Bonds are guaranteed by the U.S. government, they are considered to be virtually risk free. An investor in such a bond should only expect compensation for the opportunity cost of the going general interest rate, sometimes called the **default-free rate**. The bond you buy is a zero-coupon bond, meaning there are no regular payments. When the bond expires at the end of the year, you are repaid the principal.

Suppose further that the return you seek on the investment is 5 percent, and (to simplify our calculations) that at the end of the year you want the full payback to be $100. How much do you want to pay for the bond when you buy it at the beginning of the year?

The straight-forward calculation is as follows: Divide the return you seek ($100) by 1 plus the interest (1 + 5%). Because there are no coupon payments, and because the bond is risk-free, there are no other considerations to make. The price you would be willing to pay is then as follows:

$$\$100 / 1.05 = \$95.24 \qquad [2]$$

2. Corporate Bond Without Risk Premium

Now, imagine you want to buy a corporate bond instead of the government bond. The new bond has the same maturity of one year, but being a corporate bond, it is inherently riskier. You estimate that there is a 10 percent risk that this particular corporate bond might default. However, you do *not* seek extra compensation for this default risk; you are not looking for a risk premium. You further estimate that if the bond defaults, you will actually be able to recuperate all but 30 percent of its value; in other words, the recovery rate is $70. You can then calculate the expected value of the bond by combining what you assume the bond will pay off if it doesn't default ($100 with a 90 percent chance) with what it will be worth to you if it does default ($70 with a 10 percent chance). Using numbers, this can be expressed as the following:

$$\$100 \times 90\% + \$70 \times 10\% = \$97.00 \qquad [3]$$

So, for an estimated payment value of $97, how much would you be willing to pay? Just divide the return with the risk-free rate of 5 percent we used above:

$$\$97 / 1.05 = \$92.38 \qquad [4]$$

3. CORPORATE BOND WITH RISK PREMIUM

Let's now take the same corporate bond, but assume that you do want to be compensated for the extra risk the bond carries compared to a risk-free government bond. You want the corporate bond's expected value to be higher than the risk-free bond's expected value. In our example here, you want it to be higher than $97—but how much higher is up to your own preference as an investor. You might look at the profit potential of other investments, at transaction costs involved, and so on to determine how much this particular investment should potentially bring you. For now, let's just find the maximum price you'd be willing to pay. To do that, we need a discount value for the 5 percent investment return we've been seeking all along:

$$1 / 1.05 = 0.9523 \qquad [5]$$

We then subtract the discount value from the value of the bond that we just calculated:

$$\$92.38 - 0.9523 = \$91.43 \qquad [6]$$

$91.43—This is how much you are willing to pay for the bond with a risk premium.

4. CALCULATE THE CREDIT SPREAD

Credit spread is a variable that incorporates both the probability of default and recovery rate. Instead of having to use both variables, credit traders just have to work with one value. As a tool for the traders to quote prices, the credit spread facilitates the comparison of spreads between two investments in credit. In other words, one can avoid going through the full features of recovery rates, default probabilities, discount rates, and so on—these are all effectively "summarized" in the credit spread.

Let's use our two corporate bonds to calculate and compare credit spreads. The following formula can be used:

$$\frac{100}{1+r+s} = EPV \qquad [7]$$

where

- r = risk-free rate

- s = spread

- EPV = expected payment value

We have all those values for our two bonds, except the spread, which is what we are looking for. Substituting what we know in the formula for the bond with no risk premium gives us the following:

$$\frac{100}{1+5\%+s} = \$92.38$$
$$s = 3.25\% \qquad [8]$$

So, the spread for that first bond is 3.25 percent. For the bond *with* a risk premium, the spread is

$$\frac{100}{1+5\%+s} = \$91.43$$
$$s = 4.38\% \qquad [9]$$

It is natural for the spread to be higher for the bond with a risk premium than for the risk-free bond. Although the two bonds have the same risk, investors of the second bond are looking for a higher return—they want to be compensated for the risk they take on. But exactly how much more compensation do they want? Just take the difference between the two spreads to get an actual value for the risk premium they seek:

$$4.38\% - 3.25\% = 1.13\% \text{ (or 113 Basis Points)}^{7} \qquad [10]$$

To summarize, credit risk quickly measures how much riskier a bond is compared to a risk-free government bond. It also incorporates the risk premium that investors seek. As such, it becomes a quick way for traders to compare investment opportunities in credit instruments, such as bonds.

Evaluating Default Probability: Credit Rating Agencies

As we established in the preceding section, credit spread is based on the two components default probability and recovery rate. Evaluating default probability is a particularly important task for professionals in the credit industry. The task is easy to understand (assess the capability of a counterparty to pay back debt) but hard to carry out. Many banks, investment managers, and financial companies employ their own credit analysts to evaluate the probability of default. However, the same service can be purchased from professional rating agencies such as Moody's, S&P, and Fitch. These agencies evaluate the financial strength of companies, assign them ratings, and rate the debt they issue. They also rate municipal and sovereign governmental debt. In fact, companies with publicly traded debt hire one or more of these agencies to prepare credit ratings of their debt.

Different rating agencies use different rating systems. Normally, however, debt with a high rating is collectively known as **investment grade** debt. This is appropriate for good credit quality for investments even though it always contains a certain level of credit risk. Obligations with a lower rating are known as **non-investment grade** or **speculative grade**. The higher default risk is then compensated by a higher possible return. Really poor quality debt is summarily referred to as **junk bonds**.

The ratings serve as a reference, helping investors match their strategies and risk preferences with investment opportunities. Table 2-2 gives a high-level overview of the systems used by S&P and Moody's.

Moody's rating scheme looks similar to that of S&P, with some differences in nomenclature. For instance, the highest Moody's rating is

Aaa and the lowest is C. The lowest investment grade rating is Baa, and anything below Baa is deemed speculative grade.

Table 2-2 Credit Rating System for S&P and Moody's

S&P	Moody's	Description
AAA	Aaa	Best credit quality—Extremely reliable with regard to financial obligations
AA	Aa	Very good credit quality—Very reliable
A	A	More susceptible to economic conditions—Still good credit quality
BBB	Baa	Lowest rating in investment grade
BB	Ba	Caution is necessary—Best sub-investment credit quality
B	B	Vulnerable to changes in economic conditions—Currently showing the ability to meet its financial obligations
CCC	Caa	Currently vulnerable to nonpayment—Dependent on favorable economic conditions
CC	Ca	Highly vulnerable to a payment default
C	C	Close to or already bankrupt—Payment on the obligation currently continued
D	-	Payment default on some financial obligation has actually occurred

Source: Compiled from www.riskglossary.com/articles/credit_risk.htm and www.b2breport.info/metod_en.htm. Accessed June 2005.

Credit Ratings and Default Data

Although credit rating agencies continuously improve and update their models, their ratings offer no guarantees. The agencies themselves are quick to point out that even top-rated companies, which are extremely reliable with regard to financial obligations, do still default, albeit very, very rarely. Credit rating systems help to inform investors, but are not an insurance against default.

To illustrate this point in numbers, let's see how much debt actually defaulted over time for various levels of credit ratings. Using data from Moody's, Table 2-3 shows annual default rates for each rating level between 1970 and 2004. As one would expect, more speculative grade debt defaults more often than investment grade debt.

Table 2-3 Annual Global Issuer-Weighted Default Rates by Whole Letter Rating, 1970-2004

Year	Aaa	Aa	A	Baa	Ba	B	Caa-C	IG	SG	All Corporate
1970	0.00	0.00	0.00	0.27	4.12	20.78	53.33	0.14	8.78	2.64
1971	0.00	0.00	0.00	0.00	0.42	3.85	13.33	0.00	1.10	0.29
1972	0.00	0.00	0.00	0.00	0.00	7.14	40.00	0.00	1.88	0.46
1973	0.00	0.00	0.00	0.46	0.00	3.77	44.44	0.23	1.24	0.45
1974	0.00	0.00	0.00	0.00	0.00	10.00	0.00	0.00	1.31	0.28
1975	0.00	0.00	0.00	0.00	1.02	5.97	0.00	0.00	1.73	0.36
1976	0.00	0.00	0.00	0.00	1.01	0.00	0.00	0.00	0.87	0.18
1977	0.00	0.00	0.00	0.28	0.52	3.28	50.00	0.11	1.34	0.35
1978	0.00	0.00	0.00	0.00	1.08	5.41	0.00	0.00	1.78	0.35
1979	0.00	0.00	0.00	0.00	0.49	0.00	0.00	0.00	0.42	0.09
1980	0.00	0.00	0.00	0.00	0.00	4.94	33.33	0.00	1.61	0.34
1981	0.00	0.00	0.00	0.00	0.00	4.49	0.00	0.00	0.70	0.16
1982	0.00	0.00	0.26	0.31	2.72	2.41	25.00	0.21	3.54	1.04
1983	0.00	0.00	0.00	0.00	0.91	6.31	40.00	0.00	3.82	0.97
1984	0.00	0.00	0.00	0.36	0.83	6.72	0.00	0.10	3.32	0.93
1985	0.00	0.00	0.00	0.00	1.40	8.22	0.00	0.00	3.67	1.01
1986	0.00	0.00	0.00	1.33	2.03	11.73	23.53	0.32	5.64	1.91
1987	0.00	0.00	0.00	0.00	2.71	6.23	20.00	0.00	4.23	1.51

Year	Aaa	Aa	A	Baa	Ba	B	Caa-C	IG	SG	All Corporate
1988	0.00	0.00	0.00	0.00	1.24	6.36	28.57	0.00	3.59	1.37
1989	0.00	0.00	0.00	0.59	2.98	8.95	25.00	0.15	5.79	2.27
1990	0.00	0.00	0.00	0.00	3.35	16.18	58.82	0.00	10.08	3.64
1991	0.00	0.00	0.00	0.27	5.35	14.56	36.84	0.07	10.40	3.28
1992	0.00	0.00	0.00	0.00	0.30	9.03	26.67	0.00	4.85	1.33
1993	0.00	0.00	0.00	0.00	0.56	5.71	28.57	0.00	3.52	0.95
1994	0.00	0.00	0.00	0.00	0.24	3.82	5.13	0.00	1.95	0.57
1995	0.00	0.00	0.00	0.00	0.69	4.81	11.57	0.00	3.33	1.04
1996	0.00	0.00	0.00	0.00	0.00	1.44	13.99	0.00	1.67	0.52
1997	0.00	0.00	0.00	0.00	0.19	2.12	14.67	0.00	2.06	0.66
1998	0.00	0.00	0.00	0.12	0.63	4.26	15.09	0.04	3.45	1.24
1999	0.00	0.00	0.00	0.10	1.01	5.85	20.54	0.04	5.65	2.16
2000	0.00	0.00	0.00	0.38	0.89	5.49	20.04	0.13	6.14	2.41
2001	0.00	0.00	0.16	0.19	1.57	9.36	34.37	0.13	10.58	3.82
2002	0.00	0.00	0.16	1.21	1.54	4.97	30.30	0.49	8.45	3.04
2003	0.00	0.00	0.00	0.00	0.95	2.66	21.53	0.00	5.27	1.70
2004	0.00	0.00	0.00	0.00	0.19	0.65	12.33	0.00	2.23	0.72

Note: Annual issuer-weighted default calculated by dividing the number of defaulted issuers per year by the number of total issuers.

Source: Moody's report. "Default and Recovery Rates of Corporate Bond Issuers, 1920–2004." January 2005. Taken from page 14, Exhibit 15.

Table 2-3 looks at annual default rates. However, investors usually have a longer time horizon than just one year. Table 2-4 therefore looks at the cumulative default rates over a longer time horizon (in this case, 11 years between 1994 and 2004). Not surprisingly, the longer the debt was held, the higher the default rate rose. Conversely, from an investor point of view, the longer you hold bonds, the higher the risk that they will default. This is intuitive, but the figure qualifies the argument with percentage levels. Worth noting is the dramatic jump in default rates between Baa-rated bonds (lowest investment grade rating) and Ba (highest speculative grade rating).

Table 2-4 Cumulative Global Issuer-Weighted Default Rates for 1994 Issued Debt

	1	2	3	4	5	6	7	8	9	10	11
Aaa	0.00	0.00	0.00	0.00	0.00	0.00	0.00	0.00	0.00	0.00	0.00
Aa	0.00	0.00	0.00	0.00	0.00	0.00	0.00	0.00	0.00	0.00	0.00
A	0.00	0.00	0.00	0.00	0.00	0.00	0.15	0.46	0.78	0.95	0.95
Baa	0.00	0.20	0.20	0.42	0.65	1.59	2.07	3.34	4.14	4.72	4.72
Ba	0.24	1.81	2.09	3.04	4.84	7.26	9.93	12.28	15.32	15.89	15.89
B	3.82	9.18	12.36	14.21	18.27	23.16	29.34	34.45	39.99	43.03	46.49
Caa-C	5.13	13.75	24.31	24.31	24.31	30.90	30.90	56.02	56.02	56.02	56.02
Investment Grade	0.00	0.06	0.06	0.12	0.18	0.44	0.64	1.12	1.48	1.71	1.71
Speculative Grade	1.95	5.38	7.28	8.54	11.08	14.49	18.28	22.07	25.86	27.28	28.45
All Corporate	0.57	1.57	2.08	2.44	3.07	3.99	4.89	6.00	6.99	7.42	7.62

Note: Annual issuer-weighted default calculated by dividing the number of defaulted issuers per year by the number of total issuers.

Source: Moody's report. "Default and Recovery Rates of Corporate Bond Issuers, 1920-2004." January 2005. Taken from page 30, Exhibit 26.

Companies, as well as bond issuers, can be up- or downgraded depending on changes in their activities and the economic environment. Table 2-5 shows how ratings change over a year, measured in percentage change from one rating to another. For example, it shows that an A-rated bond has a 2.25 percent probability of being upgraded to AA, or that the probability for an AAA-rated bond to keep its AAA rating is 93.66 percent.

Table 2-5 One-Year Ratings Transition Matrix (Based on Data from 1981–2000)

Original Rating	Probability of Rating at Year End (Percent)							
	AAA	AA	A	BBB	BB	B	CCC	Default
AAA	93.66	5.83	0.4	0.08	0.03	0	0	0
AA	0.66	91.72	6.94	0.49	0.06	0.09	0.02	0.01
A	0.07	2.25	91.76	5.19	0.49	0.2	0.01	0.04
BBB	0.03	0.25	4.83	89.26	4.44	0.81	0.16	0.22
BB	0.03	0.07	0.44	6.67	83.31	7.47	1.05	0.98
B	0	0.1	0.33	0.46	5.77	84.19	3.87	5.3
CCC	0.16	0	0.31	0.93	2	10.74	63.96	21.94
Default	0	0	0	0	0	0	0	100

Note: Based on bond rating data from 1981 to 2000. Data is adjusted for rating withdrawals. Based on raw data, no smoothing done. Statistical anomalies are present, such as a CCC-rated bond has 0.16 percent probability of upgrading to AAA, but a B-rated bond only has 0.00 percent probability.

Source: S&P. www.riskglossary.com/articles/default_model.htm. Accessed December 2004.

An Example of the Difficulty in Rating: WorldCom

Rating agencies normally look at balance sheet information, which gives a smoothed-out accounting version of the organization's financial health, or economic status, at a given point in time. Ratings based on such a snapshot sometimes lag behind new events. Using up-to-date economic and financial statements that change as new information arrives would lead to greater accuracy. Many large financial institutions and market players employ this alternative method in their internal rating departments.

To illustrate the problem with using balance sheet and other types of historical financial information as the basis for a credit rating (some observers even refer to them as **stale sources**), let's take the example of WorldCom, which right up until its spectacular bankruptcy in May 2002 showed very low credit spreads. As Figure 2-5 shows, WorldCom's credit spread stayed at the same level as that of comparative bonds from companies Ford and IBM. Then, two months before the bankruptcy filing, the credit spread started to increase, and it surged from 5 percent to 10 percent in the last month alone.

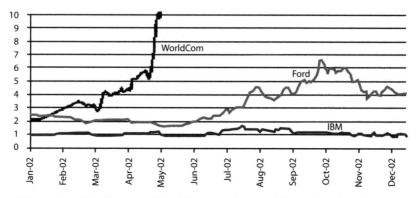

Figure 2-5 Credit spreads (%) in 2002 for WorldCom, Ford, and IBM

Source: Norges Bank (The Norwegian State Bank). www.norges-bank.no/english/petroleum_
    fund/articles/investment-creditmarket-2003/. Accessed June 2005.

Examples like WorldCom aside, it seems rating agencies are getting better and better at predicting defaults probabilities. Figure 2-6, which details the average rating of different debts just before they defaulted, shows that fewer high-rated companies default, and that the defaulting companies already had fairly low ratings as they went into default.

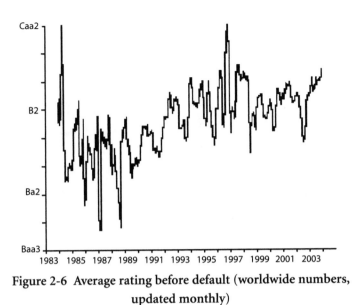

Figure 2-6 Average rating before default (worldwide numbers, updated monthly)

Source: Moody's report. "The Performance of Moody's Corporate Bond Ratings: March 2004 Quarterly Updates." April 2004. Taken from page 5, Figure 5.

Credit Risk Statistics

So far, we have talked primarily about the drivers behind credit risk, defaults, recovery, spreads, and so on. Let's add some more precision to these discussions by looking at actual credit risk statistics, primarily historical default and recovery rates.

We start by looking at the U.S. bond market and Figure 2-7, which shows the outstanding level of public and private bond market debt in the U.S. between 1995 and 2004.

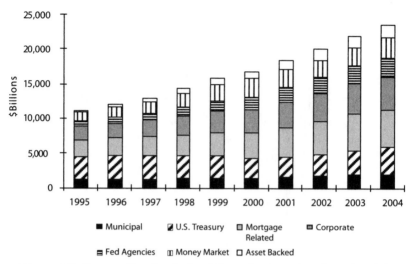

Figure 2-7 Outstanding level of public and private bond market debt

Sources: U.S Department of Treasury, Federal Reserve System, Federal National Mortgage
Association, Government National Mortgage Association, Federal Home Loan Mortgage
Corporation, and Thompson Financial. Obtained data from The Bond Market
Association, Research Statistical Data. www.bondmarkets.com/story.asp?id=323.
Accessed June 2005.

Figure 2-7 shows how the debt market in the United States has almost
doubled in 10 years. Debt in this graph is divided by public and private
issuers, as well as by the type of debt. Municipal and U.S. Treasury debt are
examples of clear-cut public debt. Debt that is mortgage related or issued
by fed agencies come from government-affiliated agencies, such as GNMA
(Ginnie Mae) or FNMA (Fannie Mae). (Some mortgage-related debt does
originate with private, nonpublic, issuers.) Corporate debt is issued in the
form of corporate bonds, whereas the money market specializes in very
short-term debt securities. Finally, asset-backed debt is a generic term for
debt backed by any sort of non-mortgage assets, such as auto loans,
credit card receivables, student loans, and so on.

Let's now take a closer look at the corporate bond market. Figure 2-8
shows the issuance of corporate bonds with a maturity of over one year
between 1995 and 2004.

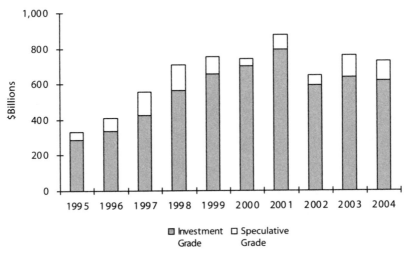

Figure 2-8 Corporate bond issuance (only bonds with maturity of more than one year)

Sources: Thomson Financial Securities Data. As presented by The Bond Market Association,
    Research Statistical Data. www.bondmarkets.com/story.asp?id=1720.
    Accessed June 2005.

Figure 2-8 shows that the clear majority of bonds issued are investment grade. It also shows that, despite fluctuations between years, issuance has grown over the 10-year period that the graph depicts. The volume in 2004 is approximately twice as large as that of 1995.

Default Rates

A key statistic for the debt markets are the actual default rates. How many companies default in a given year? Figure 2-9 looks at this question, showing the annual issuer-weighted default rates by bond grade and all corporate.

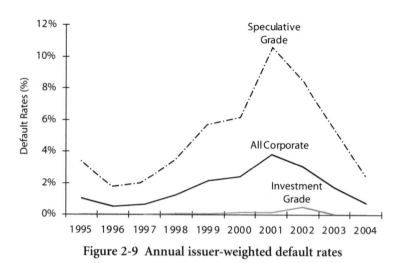

Figure 2-9 Annual issuer-weighted default rates

Note: Annual issuer-weighted default calculated by dividing the number of defaulted issuers per year by the number of total issuers.

Sources: Moody's report. "Default and Recovery Rates of Corporate Bond Issuers, 1920-2004." January 2005. Taken from page 13, Exhibit 14.

As the figure shows, only about 1 percent of investment grade debt ever defaults. However, speculative grade debt fluctuates between 2 percent and 10 percent. Taken together, the influence by the speculative grade debt on the overall corporate defaults is evident in the All Corporate debt line. Worth noting is that defaults peaked in 2001, a year marked by the September 11 events as well as the beginning of dot-com bankruptcies and several large-scale corporate defaults. This naturally affected bond issuance as well, which dropped in 2002 by $200 billion, as shown in the figure.

DEFAULT RATES BY GEOGRAPHY

Although the financial investment sector, like most business, is becoming increasingly global, there are still large regional differences between North America and the Asia-Pacific region, or between Latin America and Europe. It is often unforeseeable economic events that drive default rates—but the nature of these events differ from country to country and from region to region. Default rates will therefore naturally differ over time between geographical areas. Figure 2-10 illustrates this clearly, as it compares business bankruptcies in five major industrialized countries between 1990 and 2003.

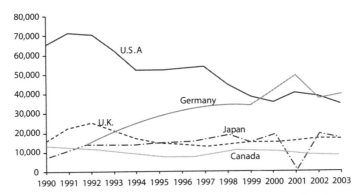

Figure 2-10 Geographical trends distribution of business bankruptcies in five major nations (graphic)

Source: "The 2004 Bankruptcy Yearbook & Almanac." Edited by McHugh and Sawyer. Boston: 2004. Taken from page 6 for U.S. Business Filings and pages 360 through 373 for other countries.

As the figure shows, the amount and trend of bankruptcy filings vary significantly between countries, even within the same region (compare U.K. and Germany, and U.S. and Canada). A similar comparison is done between regions in Figure 2-11, which shows defaulting corporate bond issuers by region between 1986 and 2004.

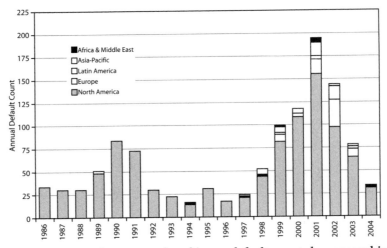

Figure 2-11 Annual corporate bond issuer default counts by geographical region, 1986-2004

Source: Moody's report. "Default and Recovery Rates of Corporate Bond Issuers, 1920-2004." January 2005. Taken from page 5, Exhibit 1.

Throughout the years of this time period, North America accounts for more than two-thirds of the annual default counts in the world. Again, we see the same spike in defaults for the years surrounding 2001 as we did in Figure 2-9.

DEFAULT RATES BY INDUSTRY SECTOR

Default rates can also be broken down by industry sector, as done in Table 2-6.

In 2003 and 2004, the telecommunications industry was the second and top defaulting sector respectively, driven by the liquidation of telecom giant WorldCom that started in 2002. Another traditionally stable segment, the energy and utilities sector, also experienced high default volumes, suffering the ripple effects of the Enron and DynaG bankruptcies. In the healthcare sector, Colombia Healthcare brought 2003 volume default numbers up, as it defaulted after suffering fraud allegations. Meanwhile, the textile sector saw a low default number in volume in both 2003 and 2004, but a high number in percentage of issuers, indicating that a large number of small debt issuers had to default during those two years.

Table 2-6 Distribution of 2003 Global Corporate Defaults by Industry Sector

Industry	2003		2004	
	Volume (% of Total)	Default Rate (% Issuers)	Volume (% of Total)	Default Rate (% Issuers)
Telecommunications	19.2%	5.1%	38.1%	1.26%
Metal & Mining	4.8%	6.9%	3.6%	3.92%
Utilities & Energy	21.6%	0.9%	8.7%	0.62%
Chemicals, Plastics, & Rubber	4.7%	3.9%	1.7%	0.63%
Printing, Publishing, & Broadcasting	4.5%	3.7%	5.7%	1.14%
Transportation	6.8%	3.1%	7.9%	3.64%
Beverage, Food, & Tobacco	6.4%	2.1%	1.7%	1.49%
Healthcare, Education, & Childcare	14.5%	2.7%	1.1%	0.89%
Textiles, Leather, & Apparel	3.7%	9.5%	1.6%	6.06%
Construction, Building, & Real Estate	1.4%	2.4%	2.6%	1.57%
Manufacturing	0.9%	2.7%	0.6%	2.08%
Retail	0.9%	2.9%	1.5%	0.02%
Financial (Nonbanking)	1.4%	0.3%	-	-
Electronics	1.0%	1.1%	2.1%	0.54%
Hotel, Casinos, & Gaming	1.0%	2.2%	12.1%	3.30%
Miscellaneous	0.5%	3.8%	3.1%	1.69%
Nondurable Consumer Products	0.4%	1.9%	0.7%	0.87%
Insurance	2.1%	0.4%	4.2%	0.33%
Forest Products & Paper	1.8%	1.3%	2.1%	1.32%
Aerospace & Defense	1.0%	2.2%	0.9%	2.00%
Machinery	0.9%	1.9%	-	-
Automobile	0.4%	1.0%	-	-
Total	$33.5 billion	1.7%	$16.0 billion	0.72%

Source: Compiled from Moody's report. "Default and Recovery Rates of Corporate Bond Issuers." January 2004. Taken from page 6, Exhibit 5. And from Moody's report. "Default and Recovery Rates of Corporate Bond Issuers, 1920-2004." January 2005. Taken from page 5, Exhibit 2.

Recovery Rates

Unlike default rates, recovery rates are traditionally difficult to value. Still, they can be estimated and are important to investors, who should not base their investment decisions solely on default rates. High default rates might be bad, but if the recovery rates are equally high, the investment situation changes considerably.

RECOVERY RATE BY SENIORITY

Recall our discussion on seniority among bond holders and the debt waterfall in Figure 2-4. Using seniority to break down recovery rates for defaulted bonds, Table 2-7 shows annual average issuer-weighted recovery rates. The recovery rate is defined as the observed recovery price per $100 at roughly 30 days after default time.

The data in the figure shows clearly that recovery rates are highly correlated with the defaulted instrument's seniority. As expected, senior bonds are more secure than subordinated junior ones. The figure also shows that recovery rates fluctuate over time.

Table 2-7 Annual Average Issuer-Weighted Defaulted Bond Recovery Rates by Seniority, 1982-2004

Year	Sr. Secured	Sr. Unsecured	Sr. Subordinated	Subordinated	Jr. Subordinated	All Bonds
1982	$72.5	$34.4	$48.1	$32.3	NA	$35.0
1983	$40.0	$52.7	$43.5	$41.4	NA	$50.1
1984	NA	$49.4	$67.9	$44.3	NA	$44.4
1985	$83.6	$60.2	$30.9	$42.7	$48.5	$39.9
1986	$59.2	$52.6	$50.2	$42.9	NA	$44.3
1987	$71.0	$62.7	$46.5	$46.2	NA	$61.7
1988	$55.3	$45.2	$33.4	$33.0	$36.5	$42.9
1989	$46.5	$43.8	$33.1	$26.8	$16.9	$32.8
1990	$35.7	$37.0	$26.7	$19.5	$10.7	$27.5
1991	$50.1	$38.9	$43.8	$24.1	$7.8	$39.1
1992	$62.7	$52.1	$47.9	$37.8	$13.5	$45.5
1993	NA	$37.1	$51.9	$43.7	NA	$48.0
1994	$69.3	$53.7	$29.6	$33.7	NA	$44.5
1995	$63.6	$47.6	$34.3	$39.4	NA	$45.8
1996	$47.6	$62.8	$43.8	$22.6	NA	$43.6
1997	$76.0	$55.1	$44.7	$38.4	$30.6	$51.8
1998	$51.8	$39.5	$44.2	$14.1	$62.0	$40.4
1999	$43.3	$38.3	$29.1	$35.5	NA	$37.6
2000	$41.7	$24.4	$20.3	$31.9	$15.5	$25.7
2001	$41.7	$23.1	$20.9	$15.9	$47.0	$34.3
2002	$49.3	$30.5	$25.3	$24.5	NA	$34.6
2003	$63.5	$41.4	$39.6	$12.3	NA	$43.1
2004	$80.8	$50.1	$44.4	NA	NA	$58.5
Mean	$57.4	$44.9	$39.1	$32.0	$28.9	$42.2
Median	$55.3	$45.2	$43.5	$33.4	$23.7	$43.1
Min	$35.7	$23.1	$20.3	$12.3	$7.8	$25.7
Max	$83.6	$62.8	$67.9	$46.2	$62.0	$61.7
Standard Deviation	$14.3	$11.2	$11.4	$10.5	$18.9	$8.7
N	251	1,207	478	485	22	2,443

Source: Moody's report. "Default and Recovery Rates of Corporate Bond Issuers, 1982-2004." January 2005. Taken from page 34, Exhibit 27.

Another way to break down statistics on recovery rates is by credit rating. Table 2-8 shows average issuer-weighted recovery rate by credit rating.

Table 2-8 Average Issuer-Weighted Recovery Rates by Credit Rating, 1982-2004

Rating	Years Prior to Default				
	1	2	3	4	5
Aaa	NA	NA	NA	$97.0	$74.1
Aa	$95.4	$62.1	$30.8	$44.4	$41.1
A	$49.8	$49.0	$43.1	$46.0	$45.2
Baa	$43.3	$41.3	$45.3	$42.2	$41.6
Ba	$40.7	$44.2	$43.8	$45.4	$44.0
B	$38.4	$38.1	$39.0	$40.0	$37.8
Caa-Ca	$36.4	$33.8	$31.0	$42.3	$12.3
Investment Grade	$46.0	$44.4	$44.1	$44.3	$43.2
Speculative Grade	$38.2	$38.6	$39.1	$41.7	$39.4
All Corporate	$39.0	$39.4	$40.2	$42.5	$40.7

Source: Moody's report. "Default and Recovery Rates of Corporate Bond Issuers, 1920-2004."
January 2005. Taken from page 34, Exhibit 28.

The preceding figure shows that one year before an Aa-rated bond defaulted, its recovery rate was $95.40 for every $100 issued. Overall, the figure shows that issuers that were higher rated one year prior to default than lower-rated issuers saw higher recovery rates. It also shows that the difference between investment-grade and speculative-grade bonds is small at longer time horizons—for instance, at five years—but increases dramatically as the issuers near default.

RECOVERY RATES BY INDUSTRY

Recovery rates also differ across sectors because of varying values of hard assets and their longevity, revenue-generating capability, regulated environment, and competitive environment. Table 2-9 looks at the recovery rate for various sectors in 2003 and 2002.

Table 2-9 Average Recovery Rates by Industry Category

Price per $100 Par	Issuer-Weighted Mean Recovery Rate		
Industry	2003	2002	1982-2003
Utility-Gas	$48.0	$54.6	$51.5
Oil & Oil Services	NA	$44.1	$44.5
Hospitality	$64.5	$60.0	$42.5
Utility-Electric	$5.3	$39.8	$41.4
Transport-Ocean	$76.8	$31.0	$38.8
Finance & Banking	$18.8	$25.6	$36.3
Industrial	$33.4	$34.3	$35.4
Retail	$57.9	$58.2	$34.4
Transport-Air	$22.6	$24.9	$34.3
Automotive	$39.0	$39.5	$33.4
Healthcare	$52.2	$47.0	$32.7
Consumer Goods	$54.0	$22.8	$32.5
Construction	$22.5	$23.0	$31.9
Technology	$9.4	$36.7	$29.5
Real Estate	NA	$5.0	$28.8
Steel	$31.8	$28.5	$27.4
Telecommunication	$45.9	$21.4	$23.2
Miscellaneous	$69.5	$46.5	$39.5

Source: Moody's report. "Default & Recovery Rates of Corporate Bond Issuers." January 2004.
    Taken from page 14, Exhibit 16.

Worth noting in the preceding figure is the low recovery rate for the telecommunications sector in 2002, and the subsequent rate increase in 2003. The telecom industry went through a fundamental structural change in 2002, following the demise of WorldCom. Recovering debt was difficult until the sector stabilized in 2003, at which point recovery rates shot up again.

Credit Derivatives

With all the credit risk that exists in the market, it is remarkable that anybody still wants to lend money. Credit enhancement techniques, which help reduce the credit risk of an obligation, play a key role in encouraging loans and investments in debt. Some credit enhancement methodologies have existed for centuries, from plain-out refusing to make a loan to asking for guarantees, letters of credit, or other insurance products. However, such mechanisms—let's call them commercial or business oriented—work best during economic upturns. When the economy turns bad, risks normally accumulate and instead of off-setting each other, they start to default at the same time, bringing substantial loan losses to lenders. What does it matter if my obligor has a letter of credit, if the person who issued the letter of credit also went bankrupt?

As an alternative to commercial risk mechanisms, various financial mechanisms have been developed over the past few decades. Such credit risk instruments are normally referred to as **credit derivatives**. (Credit derivatives gain or **derive** their value from an underlying credit instrument, such as a bond or loan.) Instead of looking for guarantees from the obligor to the lender, credit derivatives help to transfer credit risk away from the lender to some other party. The risk is simply passed on to someone else—who of course is paid a fee for the trouble.

The idea of transferring risk to a third party is an old one. Interest rate derivatives, for example, developed in the 1980s, when interest rates started to fluctuate highly, as a result of the U.S. Federal Reserve targeting the money supply instead of interest rates. The resulting high volatility in interest rates made investors seek ways to transfer interest rate risk, and helped develop interest rate derivatives. This explains why the interest risk markets abound in derivative products such as interest rate swaps, caps, floors, forwards, and futures.

Similarly, credit derivatives started to become a necessity in the 1980s and 1990s as individual and corporate bankruptcies began to increase worldwide, starting in the U.S. Credit derivatives were originally used by banks that were involved in the interest rate swaps market and that wanted to hedge against counterparty credit exposures. Over time, credit derivatives grew popular, both as tools for hedging credit risk exposures and as methods of investing in certain types of credit risk.

The use of credit derivatives grew as the number of credit events increased. As an example, Figure 2-12 shows global bond defaults between 1996 and 2004.

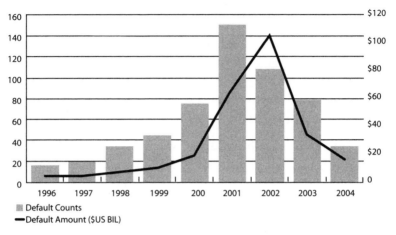

Figure 2-12 Global bond defaults

Source: Moody's Investors Service. "Moody's 2004 Default Review and 2005 Outlook."
    Taken from Figure 1.

Credit derivatives not only helped corporations and financial institutions manage their credit risk, but also enabled a new set of individual retail clients to invest in bonds and stocks previously unaffordable. Through credit derivatives, individual investors can invest indirectly in foreign bonds at a lower price. Derivatives also allow indirect investing in stock, providing a way around regulations prohibiting foreign investors from buying domestic stock. Moreover, derivatives helped entrepreneurial start-ups with no established credit to finance their ventures, offering investors ways to reduce the inherent credit risk involved in start-ups.

Let's use the following working definition for credit risk instruments for the purposes of this book:

Credit risk instruments enable financial institutions and companies to transfer credit risk to a third party and thus reduce their exposure to the risk of an obligor's default.

Credit derivatives help investors isolate credit risk, price it, and transfer it to other investors who are better suited to managing it, or who find the investment opportunity more interesting. As a result of their versatility, credit derivatives can efficiently transfer "tailor-fit" credit risk from one party to another. While transferring a specific type of credit risk, they leave the other types of credit risk with the initial investor. For instance, an investor might like to keep the company-specific risk of an investment in her portfolio, while transferring the market risk of that same investment. Credit derivatives help the investor split out, price, and transfer this particular risk.

In legal terms, credit derivatives are privately negotiated bilateral contracts to transfer credit risk from one party to another. The party that transfers the credit risk to another party is looking for protection against that risk and is willing to pay a fee. The party that takes on the risk, the so-called **protection seller**, is willing to bear the other party's credit risk in exchange for the fee. The contract the two parties enter into defines the credit risk in terms of credit events that will cause the risk-exposed party to experience an economic loss. As we know, credit events include occurrences such as bankruptcy, a failure to pay interest or principal when due, or a restructuring that results in a reduction in interest or principal. If the credit event occurs, the credit derivative contract provides for the settlement of any payment obligation.

In accounting terms, one of the key benefits of credit derivatives for banks is that the bank can transfer the credit risk of a loan through a derivative product, while still keeping the loan on its books.

There are numerous credit instruments in the market. The remainder of this chapter is dedicated to a brief overview of some of the more basic credit risk derivatives. We have chosen the ones that are the most common or the most likely for a new credit professional to encounter. Part III, "Typical Credit Derivatives," of the book then goes into more detail about two specific credit risk instruments: credit default swaps (CDSs) and collateralized debt obligations (CDOs).

Total Return Swap

With a total return swap, an asset owner transfers the total return of a specific asset, such as a bond or trade receivables, to a counterpart in exchange for a fee.

The credit risk mitigation might not be apparent at first sight, so let's go into some greater detail. On the one hand, we have the seller, who holds assets with some credit exposure. These assets are receivables such as a loan, a group of loans, lease payments, or trade receivables. On the other hand, we have the buyer, who wants the economic returns on this asset such as the interest due on the loans or the fees from the lease payments. In principle, the buyer could just purchase the underlying credit—but the buyer does not want to acquire the actual assets. This is where the total return swap enters the picture.

Because the buyer does not actually want to own the assets (perhaps because the upfront cash payment is too large or the investment does not fit the buyer's investment profile), the seller uses a total return swap to pass on the expected returns on the assets. In exchange, the buyer pays the seller a fee (normally set at LIBOR minus an amount for the risk), and if the actual returns turn out to be lower than anticipated, the buyer will have to compensate the seller.

Figure 2-13 illustrates the relationship between the buyer and the seller. As shown in the figure, the total return swap seller can also be seen as a buyer—a buyer of credit protection. The opposite then is true for the total return swap buyer.

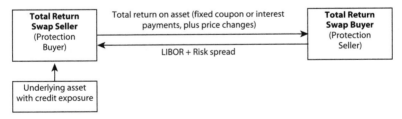

Figure 2-13 Total return swap

The swap benefits both parties. It offers the seller a way to keep a portfolio of assets, while limiting the economic exposure of those assets. If the assets lose value and their returns diminish, the buyer will have to compensate the seller. This is the credit risk mitigating part of the total return swap. A total return swap also frees up the seller's lending possibilities. For instance, picture a bank that wants to grant an additional loan to a valued customer. However, the customer has already reached the bank's credit limit. To avoid losing the client's business, the bank uses a total return swap on the customer's existing loans, and is now free to lend additional funds.

In a total return swap, the buyer enjoys the economic benefits of asset ownership without actually having to hold the assets on a balance sheet or fund the investment up front. Furthermore, should financial regulations prohibit the buyer from investing directly into the reference asset (for instance, if the asset is a loan and the buyer is not a bank), the swap provides a way of "synthetically" investing in the reference asset.

Typical sellers in total return swaps are banks, and typical buyers are hedge funds. The reference asset can be almost any asset, index, or basket of assets, exchanging the total return of an entire portfolio or index. The swap can take place without the knowledge of the initial asset provider, such as the loan taker. The seller is still the lender and maintains the lender-obligor relationship.

Credit Default Swaps

In a credit default swap (CDS), two parties enter into an agreement whereby one party pays the other a periodic fee in exchange for a much larger, but floating, payment should a predefined credit event occur. If the credit event never occurs, the other party does not have to make any payment. The first party, like the seller in the previous total return swap example, is looking for protection against a default. The other party, or protection seller, is available to offer that cover. Figure 2-14 outlines their relationship.

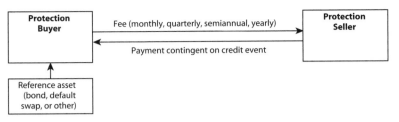

Figure 2-14 Credit default swap

The credit event payment made by the protection seller, who we can also refer to as the risk buyer, usually makes up for the economic loss on the underlying credit, suffered by the protection buyer, otherwise known as the risk hedger. The credit event that triggers the payment from the protection seller could be a material default, bankruptcy, or debt restructuring for the reference asset.

Although similar at first glance, total return swaps and credit default swaps differ in the type of protection they offer. CDSs provide protection against specific credit events that have to be named in the contract. Total return swaps by contrast protect against loss of value regardless of the reason (a default, growing credit spreads, and so on).

CDSs can be gathered and traded as a group, normally referred to as a **basket credit default swap**. In many ways, a basket CDS is similar to a single CDS. However, the default profile and payments schedule differ. With a first-to-default (FTD) swap, a credit event is said to occur the first time *any* of the underlying issuers defaults. Similarly, there are second-to-default, third-to-default, and so on basket CDSs. A slight modification to this type of CDS basket is First-to-Loss Protection (FLP), which is only activated after a predefined loss amount has been reached.

Credit Linked Notes

Strictly speaking, credit linked notes (CLNs) are not pure credit derivatives. A CLN is a combination of a standard debt note such as a bond, and a credit derivative such as a credit default swap. In industry terms, CLNs are financial securities that are issued with an embedded credit derivative. The coupon or price of the security is then linked to the performance of a reference debt. The yield that the investor receives on the note is set higher than normal, because the investor takes on exposure for a specified credit event.

Let's use the example given in Figure 2-15 to clarify how a CLN works. The Note Issuer issues bonds that have a larger-than-normal yield because they are tied to the performance of an underlying asset, bond ABC. The note issuer transfers the credit exposure of bond ABC by issuing a note that is linked to the performance of a credit default swap that has ABC as the underlying reference entity. The note issuer has to pay a higher-than-normal interest rate to attract investors. In return, the note issuer receives protection from the protection seller if bond ABC has a predetermined credit event. In that case, the note matures and the protection seller receives its principal back minus the predetermined credit event payment.

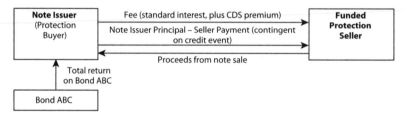

Figure 2-15 Credit linked note with embedded credit default swap

Source: Adapted from George Chacko, Eli Strick, and Constantinos A. Vingas. "Credit Risk Instruments." Harvard Business School Note No 201-119. Boston: Harvard Business School Publishing, 2001.

CLNs often involve the use of special purpose vehicles (SPVs). Also known as special purpose companies (SPCs) or special purpose entities (SPEs), these are separate legal entities created for specific transactions, and typically are incorporated in offshore tax havens such as the Cayman Islands. Through the SPV, the assets are securitized in that they will not be affected should the originator go bankrupt or have to default on its debt. In fact, it is the SPV that issues the CLN for the investors to buy. To do this, the SPV enters into a default swap with the originator (in the preceding case, it is the note issuer), taking on the credit exposure of the underlying asset. If the underlying asset defaults, the SPV pays the originator for the losses. In exchange for this coverage, the originator pays the SPV a fee, which the SPV passes on to the investors under the terms of the CLN that it has issued. The fee is set so that it will provide a higher yield than on a comparable note with no credit risk component. The SPV then continues to pay the fee, in the form of a coupon, during the life of the note. When the note expires, the investors receive their principal payment back, unless the underlying creditor has defaulted or declared bankruptcy. In that case, the investors receive anything between nothing and the amount equal to the recovery rate for the bond.

An SPV can issue debt based on several different credit swaps. In this way, CLNs allow banks to transfer their credit exposure to a range of credits through the use of one SPV.

From an investment point of view, CLNs provide the same benefits as other credit derivatives, enabling "synthetic" investment in assets rather than requiring their direct purchase. The reasons for issuing CLNs are similar to those for issuing other credit derivatives, such as splitting off risk that is unessential to core operations, or managing regulatory capital. However, through their liaison with the traditional debt note, CLNs are more flexible for the issuer, because they can be tailored to offer investors spreads and maturities that might be difficult to find elsewhere in the bond market.

Credit Spread Option

Credit spread options (CSOs) are hedging and investment instruments that protect against changes in credit spreads. A CSO can be based on changes in credit spread between two different credit instruments, or between a credit instrument and a risk-free benchmark, such as LIBOR or U.S. Treasury Bonds.

CSOs give the protection buyer the right to sell (put) or buy (call) a reference credit at a specified spread at a certain date. In exchange, the protection buyer has to pay a premium fee. The payoff is then determined by where the actual spot spread is at the maturity date (over or under the spread of the reference credit). A call-CSO pays out if the underlying spread is over the strike spread (the opposite is true for a put-CSO). Investors who believe that the spread will tighten might therefore opt for a call-CSO. Figure 2-16 shows a typical credit spread option.

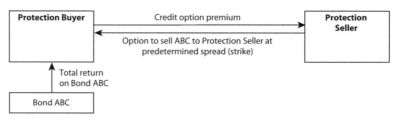

Figure 2-16 Credit spread option (Put)

Note: The figure shows a put option. A call option would give the protection buyer the right to purchase ABC at a predetermined credit spread.

Source: Adapted from George Chacko, Eli Strick, and Constantinos A. Vingas. "Credit Risk Instruments." Harvard Business School Note No 201-119. Boston: Harvard Business School Publishing, 2001.

Portfolio and Collateralized Credit Products

In addition to individual total return swaps, credit default swaps, and credit linked notes, many credit derivatives are sold bunched together as portfolio products. The benefit of a portfolio product is that investors invest not in individual credit risk, which they may be unable to value correctly, but in a combined portfolio where the individual risk matters less. Portfolio products are backed by portfolios of assets that may include a combination of bonds and loans, or more advanced financial instruments such as securitized receivables or asset-backed securities.

Portfolio products can also be taken a step further and securitized using different types of collateral.[8] Collateralized products are thus backed by various reference assets such as loans, bonds, mortgages, or just general debt. The name of the instrument reveals which asset has been used: collateralized loan obligations (CLOs), collateralized bond obligations (CBOs), collateralized mortgage obligations (CMOs), or collateralized debt obligations (CDOs).

The benefit of both the plain portfolio product and the more advanced collateralized obligations is that investors don't have to invest in individual credit risk. Instead, they can choose to invest in select slices of the portfolio called **tranches**. The tranches differ in terms of seniority and hedge structure, allowing risk to be distributed more efficiently to investors with different risk preferences.

Collateralized debt also allows credit holders to sell off credit in tranches rather than find investors who accept the full risk. CDOs have become a common tool for financial firms needing to dispose of bad loans (loans with high likelihood of default and/or low recovery rates). Japanese banks used CDOs to clear up their loan books in the 1990s after an economic downturn, as did Sweden's Nordbanken in the mid-1990s and Germany's Dresdner Bank in 2003.

Credit Derivatives Market

Trading in credit derivatives began in the early 1990s in New York and London. By 1996, the global market size was estimated roughly between $100 billion and $200 billion. By 2003, it had grown to $3.5 trillion. Figure 2-17 shows an estimate of the credit derivatives market done by the British Bankers' Association (in USD billion notional value).

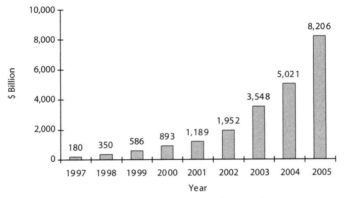

Figure 2-17 Global credit derivatives market, excluding asset swaps (1997-2003, with estimates for 2004-2006)

Source: British Bankers' Association. Credit Derivatives Report 2003/2004. Taken from page 5.

Estimating the size of the market is difficult, because credit derivatives are not traded on public exchanges but on private negotiation basis in the so-called over-the-counter (OTC) market. The actual market might therefore very well be larger, because sellers and buyers have a natural inclination *not* to reveal their trading information. Some recent index products—notably iTraxx, which groups individual derivatives into baskets and portfolios—have simplified trading by allowing for more liquidity and transparency. Still, the OTC dominance makes it more difficult for sellers and buyers to find each other than if the instruments were exchange traded. This imbalance also creates a situation conducive to arbitrage in the market.

Despite the lack of exchange trading, the credit derivatives market has continued to grow. Whereas other financial markets have suffered from the downturn of the global economy since the turn of the new century, the credit derivatives market has continued to show a strong growth rate. As seen in the Figure 2-17, the credit derivatives market is expected to reach more than $8 trillion by 2006, about 45 times the size of the market in 1997.

Let us take a closer look at the market for credit derivatives, breaking it down by regional markets, market participants, product usage, and underlying asset.

Regional Markets

Figure 2-18 breaks down the global credit derivatives market by geography.

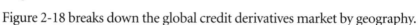

Figure 2-18 **Breakdown of geographical credit derivatives market (2003, 2004, estimated 2006)**

Source: British Bankers' Association. Credit Derivatives Report 2003/2004. Taken from page 7.

As Figure 2-18 shows, London and New York dominate the market with a market share of more than 40 percent each. As we have seen in earlier figures, the credit derivatives market has grown explosively since 1996. Although the market shares for London and New York are decreasing between 2003 and 2006 (estimated), their gross market volumes are increasing.

Market Participants

The participating actors in the market for credit derivatives can be divided into two groups: buyers of credit protection and sellers of credit protection. As the British Bankers' Association (BBA) showed in a recent survey,[9] the same types of firms can be seen on both sides: banks, securities houses, hedge funds, and insurance companies.

Starting with the buy-side of the market, Figure 2-19 shows buyers of credit protection market share by participants.

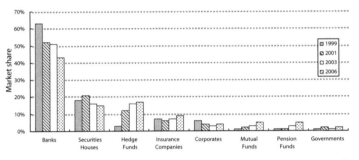

Figure 2-19 Buyers of credit protection (1999, 2001, 2003, estimated 2006)

Source: British Bankers' Association. Credit Derivatives Report 2003/2004. Taken from page 17.

Although their dominance is decreasing, banks are still the primary buyer of credit protection. Figure 2-19 also shows that hedge funds have increased their activity considerably over the past years. By 2006, the BBA estimates that hedge funds and securities houses would be the second and third largest credit protection buyers.

Figure 2-20 then shows the sellers of credit protection market and their market shares.

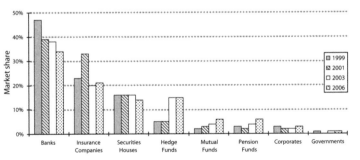

Figure 2-20 Sellers of credit protection (1999, 2001, 2003, estimated 2006)

Source: British Bankers' Association. Credit Derivatives Report 2003/2004. Taken from page 18.

Just as on the buy-side, banks are ranked first, although their dominance is decreasing. In 2003, banks accounted for 38 percent of all sell-side activities.

On both sides of the market, Figures 2-19 and 2-20 show how smaller actors are growing in size. Clearly, the credit derivatives market is growing in attraction, inviting more and more various types of participants. As more participants enter the market, liquidity in trading increases and more products are made available, which in turn is likely to attract even more participants, thus continuing to grow the market.

Product Usage

Figure 2-21 takes the credit derivatives market and breaks it down by type of product.

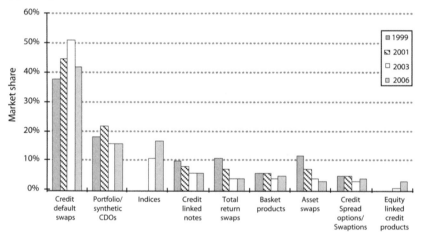

Figure 2-21 Credit derivative products (1999, 2001, 2003, estimated 2006)

Note: The figure breaks out asset swaps as a type of credit derivative. Technically, an asset swap is not a credit derivative because the swap is not affected by any credit events.

Source: British Bankers' Association. Credit Derivatives Report 2003/2004. Taken from page 21.

As Figure 2-21 shows, credit default swaps (CDSs) dominate the market. The BBA report on which this data is drawn also explains that CDSs commonly have a five-year maturity and a notional amount between $5 million and $20 million. Coming in a clear second are portfolio-related credit derivatives such as collateralized loan obligations

(CLOs) and synthetic collateralized debt obligations (CDOs). Worth noting is that in 2003, credit indices were introduced. Important to the development of the market, especially its liquidity, transparency, and product range, this category consists of full index trades and tranched index trades, mostly issued by the index iBoxx. Indexes accounted for 11 percent of the market in 2003, with an expected growth to 17 percent in 2006.

Underlying Reference Assets

Credit derivatives, as we know, trade the credit risk of an underlying reference asset. Figure 2-22 breaks down the credit derivatives market by categories of underlying reference assets.

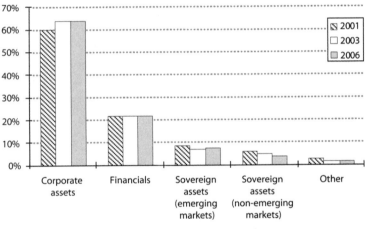

**Figure 2-22 Category of underlying reference assets
(2001, 2003, estimated 2006)**

Source: British Bankers' Association. Credit Derivatives Report 2003/2004. Taken from page 23.

As Figure 2-22 shows, most credit derivatives are written on corporate assets. This category consistently accounts for more than 60 percent.

We can also look at the quality of the underlying reference asset, as indicated by its credit rating. Figure 2-23 looks at the credit rating of underlying reference assets in 2003.

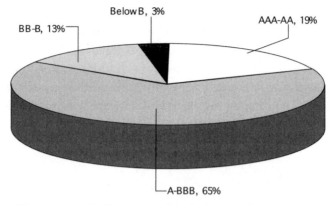

Figure 2-23 Credit rating of underlying reference assets

Source: British Bankers' Association. Credit Derivatives Report 2003/2004. Taken from page 23.

The majority of underlying reference assets are rated A-BBB, which accounts for 65 percent. Following A-BBB, the top-rated category of AAA-AA comes in second at 19 percent. Together, these top-ranked underlying assets, normally categorized as investment grade, account for 84 percent of the credit derivatives market. Intuitively this makes sense; we'd expect the credit derivatives to trade on medium- to high-quality reference assets.

Endnotes

[1] This section draws on the reading note by George Chacko, Peter Hecht, Vincent Dessain, and Monika Stachowiak, "Note on Bond Valuation and Returns," Harvard Business School Note No. 205–008 (Boston: Harvard Business School Publishing, 2004).

[2] LIBOR (London Inter Bank Offered Rate) is the interest paid for dollars and euros at international markets in interbank borrowings. The LIBOR rate is fixed daily by the British Bankers' Association (BBA). It is similar to the U.S. Federal Reserve rate, in that it is used as a reference rate for other short-term interest rates.

[3] Derivatives Study Center at the Financial Policy forum, www.financialpolicy.org/dsc%20sovdebt.pdf, accessed 19 December 2004.

[4] Exposure levels and similar measurements are often developed jointly by national central banks through the cooperative organization, the Bank for International Settlements (BIS).

5   For those familiar with calculating value-at-risk for market risk, the potential future exposure of credit exposure is calculated in similar ways, using market volatility and portfolio effects for all obligations with a counterparty.

6   Yield is a common measure of how much income an investment generates over time, put in relation to the initial investment. It applies both to financial and non-financial situations. In finance, yield measures how much an investment in a security brings; in farming, for instance, yield would be how much crop a hectare of land would bring.

7   Basis points represent one hundredth of 1 percent, or 0.01 percent.

8   Collateral is an asset held to secure an obligation. For instance, when taking out a loan to buy a house, the bank normally asks you to put the house itself as collateral. Should you default on the loan, the bank can then acquire the collateral and liquidate it.

9   British Bankers' Association, Credit Derivatives Report, 2003/2004.

Part II

CREDIT RISK MODELING

Chapter 3   Modeling Credit Risk: 63
Structural Approach

Chapter 4   Modeling Credit Risk: 119
Alternative Approaches

3

MODELING CREDIT RISK: STRUCTURAL APPROACH

What Do Credit Risk Models Do?

In the first part of this book, we defined credit risk and discussed how credit derivatives can help transfer credit risk from one party to another. When a party agrees to take on credit risk, she naturally wants to be compensated for the additional risk. Both parties are therefore interested in arriving at a fair price for the credit risk—or more specifically, for the credit derivative used to transfer the risk. We already introduced the idea that traders normally use the credit spread as a price quotation mechanism for credit risk. You might recall that credit spread is the difference in yield between identical Treasury Bonds and nonTreasury Bonds, and that it incorporates both the default probability and recovery rate concepts. As we will show later in this chapter, credit risk models can help us estimate a default probability, and if we then combine that value with some market data, it is feasible to arrive at a value for the credit spread.

In addition to using credit spread, traders can also base their prices on external credit ratings or a proprietary valuation model of the credit in question. Regardless of the measurement used—credit spread, credit rating, credit score—there needs to be a theoretical construct, or model, underlying the measurement. This part of the book focuses on exactly that: the credit models that help participants evaluate and price credit spread.

The Structure of a Credit Risk Model

The role of any credit model is easy to describe: It takes as input the conditions of the general economy and those of the specific firm in question, and generates as output a credit measurement such as credit spread, credit score, or credit rating. Figure 3-1 outlines the credit model's role in the process.

Figure 3-1 The basics of a credit model

Worth noting is that the model should work given inputs that are observable in the market. Models often include variables that are hard or impossible to actually determine or assign a value to. For instance, suppose that you want to rate the credit of a company and that the model you use needs to take into account the status of the firm's individual projects—which is information that the firm naturally does not release to an outsider. A good credit model should allow for approximations of these values, by implying them for instance from other observable parameters (which we will discuss in more detail later, for instance when we describe implied volatility) if the values are not directly recognizable in the real world.

After it is fed with the required variables, the model should then produce a credit measurement, preferably one that lends itself to quick pricing of the credit risk at hand. Some models turn out general measurements such as the credit ratings used by rating agencies or just a plain numerical score for easy comparison with other credit risk. However, most credit risk models aim at giving a value for credit spread. As we know, credit spread is nothing more than an interpretation of the price, and it should logically be a function of the default probability for the debt and the recovery rate in case of default.

In this part of the book, we will primarily use credit risk models to arrive at a value for credit derivatives and other credit-sensitive instruments. Credit models are naturally also used to support the credit analysis of a counterparty, such as a borrower or customer, and to establish the credit risk limits of that counterparty, but we will not address such uses here.

Classes of Risk Models: Structural, Empirical, and Reduced Form

Credit risk models are usually divided into three main classes: structural, empirical, and reduced form models. **Structural models** all share the common approach of replicating the firm and its economic structure. The basic idea is that a company defaults on its debt if the value of that company's assets falls below a certain default value. As the company's stock equity decreases, the model predicts that default is more likely. Following this logic, it is possible to predict a company's likelihood to default, provided that the model is loaded with the necessary inputs.

Empirical models approach the situation differently: They assume that it is too difficult to model the company and its environment accurately. Instead, they look at companies that have defaulted, evaluating their financial data to arrive at a specific score. The score given to defaulted companies is then compared to that of nondefaulted firms—the nondefaulted firms with scores close to those of the defaulted ones can then be assumed to be less creditworthy than other firms.

Finally, **reduced form models** try neither to create a model nor arrive at a score. Rather than look inside the firm, these models attempt to model the likelihood of default by assuming that default simply is tied to an external signal such as a statistical or econometric value. This value becomes the deciding factor of default, rather than a model of the firm or a score attributed to it. As we'll show later, these models build on the assumption that default occurs as a random event.

This chapter discusses in detail the structural approach to credit risk models, especially the so-called Merton model; the next chapter looks at empirical and reduced form models.

Structural Credit Risk Models

The structural approach to credit risk models says that a firm defaults when the market value of its assets is less than the obligations or debt it has to pay. (Structural models are therefore sometimes also referred to as **asset value models**.) These models look at a company's balance sheet and its capital structure to assess its creditworthiness. However, one of the inherent problems with this approach is that the value of a company's assets is hard to observe. The annual report only provides an adjusted accounting version of the company's real assets. However, the market value of a company's stock equity is normally observable, as is its debt. It has been shown that default can be modeled as an option on a company's debt— that means we can use option pricing theory to infer the market value of the firm's assets.

This approach of linking option pricing theory with the assessment of risky debt was pioneered by Black and Scholes (1973) and Merton (1970, 1974) in three seminal papers on capital structures and option pricing.[1] It is often referred to as the **Merton model**, after Robert C. Merton. Strictly speaking, Merton's model is but one implementation of the approach, but because it was the first structural model, and still is one of the most commonly used, we will spend a considerable part of this chapter discussing it.

Before attacking the Merton model, however, we need to look more carefully at the balance sheet, which is the fundamental building block of any structural model. We will then also review option pricing theory in order to prepare for our discussion on the Merton model.

The Balance Sheet: The Building Block of the Structural Approach

The structural approach states that the fundamental source of uncertainty when it comes to a company's credit risk is its market value. The balance sheet of the company is therefore a natural starting point when we want to assess market value.

As a standard corporate financial statement, the balance sheet reports the company's **assets, liabilities** (or debt), and **equity** (or stock) at a specific point in time. You could say that the company's assets are divided into two groups—or tranches—for two different types of stakeholders: On the one hand, the company's creditors and on the other, its owners or shareholders. A fundamental equation that holds true for all balance sheets is that assets equal liabilities plus shareholder equity. They balance each other out; hence, the name and the reason why balance sheets are often presented as a two-part graphic, with assets listed on the left side, and debt and equity on the right side. Table 3-1 illustrates.

Table 3-1 A typical balance sheet

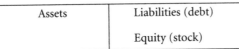

Assets	Liabilities (debt)
	Equity (stock)

Typical assets include cash, accounts receivable, inventory, machinery, buildings, and land. Intangible assets such as brand names or patents can also be included. On the right hand side of the balance sheet, the liabilities are then the financial obligations that the company owes to outside parties such as customers, banks, and other lenders. Corporate bonds, which the company issues to raise money from outside lenders, are a typical example of a firm's liabilities. Finally, the difference between the assets and the liabilities corresponds to the company's net worth, or its shareholders' equity, which is the stock that the company's owners hold.

The basic idea behind the structural approach is that a firm will go into default when its assets have a lower value than its outstanding debt and equity. This shouldn't strike anyone as an unnatural assumption: When you owe people more money than you have or that you would have if you sold off what you own, you are bankrupt.

Let's exemplify with a simplified balance sheet. Note that we are using an economic balance sheet, which shows market values, and not an accounting balance sheet, which reports legally mandated values. Table 3-2 shows company Acme, Inc.'s balance sheet at three different points in time, and how its debt becomes riskier and riskier.

Table 3-2 Example of risky debt in a balance sheet (in $ million)

A. No Default

Asset	100	Debt	70
		Equity	30
	100		100

B. Approaching Default

Asset	70	Debt	70
		Equity	0
	70		70

C. Default

Asset	60	Debt	70
		Equity	0
	60		70

Panel A in Table 3-2 displays Acme, Inc. at its healthiest: It has $100 million in assets, with $70 million in outstanding liabilities. If it sold off all its assets and thus turned them into liquid cash, it could easily pay off its debt and still have $30 million in equity for its shareholders to share.

In panel B, however, the situation looks bleaker for Acme. The value of its assets has dropped to $70 million. There are countless reasons for such a drop in asset value. Perhaps the company is in real estate and some of its buildings recently burned down. Perhaps the firm owns music recordings that have lost in value since its customers started downloading songs from a competitor. Regardless of why it happened, the change in asset value automatically affects the equity value. As long as there is equity to take from, all fluctuations in asset value—both gains and losses—accrue to the equity holders. Put differently, as long as the asset value is above the debt value, changes in the asset value are perfectly matched by changes in equity value. Expressed using industry jargon: Equity has to drop to zero before debt is hit. Thus, equity holders are the cushion that softens the blow for debt holders from a drop in asset value. Because equity is hit before debt when asset values start to fall, investors naturally see equity as a much riskier investment than debt, which explains the old investment rule-of-thumb that stock is riskier than bonds.

Things eventually worsen for Acme, which ultimately defaults on its debt and declares bankruptcy. Panel C shows why. Because the company's asset value has dropped to $60 million, and there is no more equity to take from, its liabilities are hit. In other words, Acme can no longer pay back its creditors or lenders. Because a company that defaults on one loan or bond typically has to default on all, Acme goes into full bankruptcy.

Looking at the development over time, we see that the first drop in asset value between panels A and B is completely absorbed by the equity holders. However, after all equity has been wiped out, any subsequent drops in asset value affect the debt portion of the balance sheet. This is what happens between panels B and C. Because there is no more stock to absorb the value drop, the liabilities are affected—and as we know, a company that cannot meet its liabilities goes into default.

Limitations and Types of Structural Models

The preceding Acme example is very simplified. Both assets and liabilities can be broken into thousands of subcategories, making their true value very hard to observe in the real world. Again, remember that this is an economic model, and not an accounting-based model. The balance sheet that is printed in a company's annual report is an accounting statement, and as such it only gives a very polished snapshot of the company's financial situation. To fully calculate the value of the assets, liabilities, and equity, you would have to know the value of each piece, which is virtually impossible. Estimates would have to be used instead. Of the three parts, equity would be the easiest to estimate because it is generally traded. Liabilities are at times also traded, in the form of bonds. However, assets are never traded. This explains one of the main drawbacks of the structural approach to credit risk modeling; it is simply very difficult to implement in the real world. The alternative approaches to credit risk modeling that we'll cover in the next chapter attempt to eliminate this disadvantage.

The various structural models that exist—such as the Merton, Black and Cox, or Longstaff and Schwartz models—are similar in that they use the firm's structural variables such as asset and debt values as the basis for their modeling—hence the name *structural* approach. However, they differ in the assumptions they make for their models. Merton's model lays the groundwork by saying that a firm defaults if its assets fall below its outstanding debt at the time of servicing or refinancing the debt. The Black and Cox model then builds on Merton but states that default occurs when a firm's asset value falls below a certain threshold value, which does not have to equal the debt value, and that default can occur at any time, not just at the expiration of the debt, which is one of Merton's assumptions. Other models have further extended the original Merton model, by loosening assumptions or adding new ones. This chapter focuses on Merton's model, but it also covers two extensions of that model—Black and Cox, and Longstaff and Schwartz—both of which are still within the structural framework of credit risk modeling.

In the end, all models come with their own set of simplifying assumptions, and your choice of model is based on which assumptions best fit your need, the type of instrument you are pricing, or the situation in which you find yourself. All assumptions simplify the real world and take you away, in a manner of speaking, from reality.

The Relationship Between Option Pricing and the Structural Model

The balance sheet is one of the two pillars of the structural approach. The other fundamental concept that forms the basis for the approach is that corporate liabilities can be seen as contingent claims on the assets of a firm. Given this perspective, debt holders have in fact an option on the company's assets. A creditor that holds a bond issued by a company can then be said to have the right, but not the obligation, to receive assets as payments for the debt the company owes him. The words "having the right, but not the obligation" are key, because they are the very definition of an option—and most clearly show the link between the structural models of credit risk and option pricing. It is this connection that explains why default can be modeled as an option.

This means that we can use option pricing theory to infer the market value of the firm's assets. Specifically, we can take advantage of the fact that the structural approach and option pricing theories both model changes in reference assets. For option pricing, the reference asset corresponds to the underlying security, and for the structural models, it equals the firm's asset value. In addition, we can match the models by their so-called **breaking points**. In structural models, the breaking point for default occurs when the liabilities equal the assets and there is no more equity. In option terms, this breaking point corresponds to the strike price of an option. The structural model measures the probability of default by calculating the probability that the asset value will drop below the debt value—using option-pricing techniques.

Because all structural models rely on this relationship with option pricing for pricing risky debt, we spend some time reviewing options before presenting the Merton model as the classic example of a structural model.

Review of Options

Options are contracts that give their holder the right, but not the obligation, to either buy or sell a specific underlying security for a specified price on or before a specific date. In theory, options can be written on almost any type of underlying security. Equity is the most common, but there are also several types of non-equity options based on securities such as bonds, foreign currency, financial indices, or physical goods like gold or coffee.

There are two fundamental types of options: **call options** and **put options**. Call options give you the right to purchase the underlying security at a certain price. Conversely, put options give you the right to sell the underlying security—which you presumably own—at a certain price.

In addition to clarifying the type of option, the contract that defines the option also specifies the price at which the underlying security will be either bought or sold, known as the **strike price**. The future date that marks the end of the contract is known as the **maturity date** or **exercise date**. Further option terminology specifies whether the option can be exercised only at the maturity date or before. **European options** can only be exercised at the maturity date, whereas an option that can be exercised at any time prior to that date is called an **American option**.

A Simple Example of Call and Put Options

Let's illustrate the workings of options with a simple example. Say you are interested in owning stock in Acme, Inc. Currently, Acme's shares trade at $100, which you think is low. You believe the stock should be valued more highly and that its price soon will rise. If you bought now and sold later, you would therefore make money. However, you are not completely sure, so rather than buy the stock outright, you buy an option from someone who does own Acme stock. The option contract gives you the right to buy the stock at $100, no matter what the actual stock price is, before a certain end date specified in the contract. Of course, you have to pay an upfront fee to the person who owns the stocks and who might have to part with them. Note that you don't own the underlying stock just because you purchased an option. The option derives its value from the stock, but it is not the stock itself. The party who sold you the option contract still holds the stock; what you have is a promise to own the stock later in time, should the share price rise above the level you chose. Your contract also specifies a maturity date, a time after which the option no longer is valid.

Trading in options in order to speculate on a change in value of the underlying security is one of the most basic uses of options. For instance, the person who sold you the option on Acme's stock is probably speculating that the stock price will *not* rise above $100. If the price is below $100 by the end of your contract, the seller can then simply pocket the upfront fee. You, on the other hand, speculate that it will rise. If at maturity (for a European style option), the stock price is above $100, you exercise your right to buy the stock at $100, immediately sell the stock, and pocket the difference.

Because a put option is the opposite of a call option, the put option becomes valuable for its holder if the price of the underlying security falls. For example, assume you own 100 Acme shares and that you buy an Acme 100 put option. This gives you the right to sell your 100 shares at a strike price of $100 on or before the expiration date. Say that the Acme shares drop to $80 during the option term. You can then realize a profit of $20 per share by exercising the option because it guarantees you a price of $100. Just as a call option allows you to speculate on rising stock prices, a put option lets you speculate on falling stock prices.[2]

Payoffs for Holding Options

As we just exemplified, the payoff pattern for call and put options are each other's opposites. Using our Acme example as a base, we can illustrate in a graph what the payoffs for a call and a put, respectively, would be. Figure 3-2 shows a typical payoff pattern for holding a call option, also known as **being long** the call option.

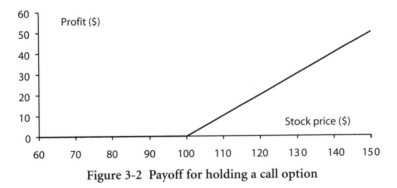

Figure 3-2 Payoff for holding a call option

Based on our Acme example, the call option does not start to pay off unless the stock price goes above the strike price of $100. After that, for every $10 that the stock price increases, the value of the option also increases by $10. In other words, the slope of the line is 1.

The reverse payoff relationship is then true for a put option, as shown in Figure 3-3. The option has a positive payoff as long as the stock price is *below* $100. However, if the stock price reaches $100 or more, the option becomes valueless to the holder, who therefore chooses not to exercise it.

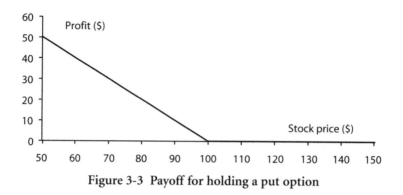

Figure 3-3 Payoff for holding a put option

Payoffs for Selling Options

The payoff schemes in the preceding section are for when you buy options. In trader jargon, buying options is known as holding or **going long** the options. Holding a call option gives you the right to buy the underlying security; holding a put option gives you the right to sell the underlying security.

Now, if instead you write or sell the option, this is known as **shorting the option**. In the case of selling a call option, you are giving someone else the right to buy the underlying security, which you presumably own. Shorting a put option then means giving someone else the right to sell you the underlying security.

As we will demonstrate, the payoffs for shorting call and put options are the same as for holding options, except that mathematically the payoffs for shorting options are multiplied by negative one (−1). Let's assume for example that you go short a call option with the same characteristics as the call option in Figure 3-2. From the holder's perspective, we already know that the option is only worth something if the underlying security rises above $100 in value. Now, for the person who sold the call option, the option has zero value until the underlying security hits $100—past that point, the payoff becomes negative. This makes intuitive sense: The holder can exercise the option, forcing the seller to pay out the difference in value. For example, the payoff for a short call is *negative* 10 if the stock price is 110, whereas the payoff to the holder of the option is *plus* 10. Figure 3-4 shows what the payoff looks like when you short a call option on Acme stock.

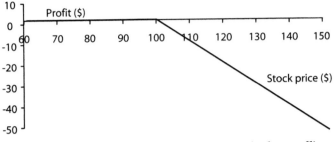

Figure 3-4 Payoff for selling a call option (a short call)

The same multiplied-by-minus-one approach holds true when comparing going long or shorting a put option. For the holder, the put option has a value when the underlying stock is worth less than $100. For the seller, that same put option has a negative value up until the same level. Figure 3-5 shows the payoff for shorting a put option on the same stock that we held in Figure 3-3.

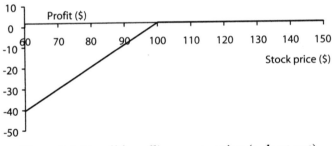

Figure 3-5 Payoff for selling a put option (a short put)

Given these negative payoff schedules, it might appear as if no one would ever want to be the seller of options. Let's not forget, though, that the seller retains a fee for taking on the risk of potentially having to pay out a profit to the option holder.

The Merton Model

Now that we have reviewed option theory, we are ready to look closer at Merton's model of credit risk. Robert C. Merton developed what became the first structural credit risk model based on his own option-pricing work and that of Fischer Black and Myron S. Scholes.

The Intuition Behind the Merton Model: Debt and Equity as Payoffs of Asset Value

We can use our knowledge of payoff schedules to inform our deeper understanding of the Merton model. In fact, we can compare the payoffs of options to the payoff of risky debt such as the debt illustrated in Table 3-2. As a starting point, we'll return to the firm Acme, Inc., but this time, we'll assume that it starts out with $200 million in assets, $70 million in debt, and $130 million in equity—a rather healthy company, in other words. As time goes by, however, the situation deteriorates; the company's asset values decrease progressively, as shown in the panels A through F in Table 3-3.

Table 3-3 Risky debt

A				B				C			
Asset	200	Debt	70	Asset	150	Debt	70	Asset	100	Debt	70
		Equity	130			Equity	80			Equity	30
	200		200		150		150		100		100

D				E				F			
Asset	70	Debt	70	Asset	50	Debt	70	Asset	0	Debt	0
		Equity	0			Equity	0			Equity	0
	70		70		50		70		0		0

Panel A in Table 3-3 shows the starting situation. The asset value then starts dropping. In panel B, it has dropped to $150 million, taking $50 million from the equity of the company. The trend continues in panel C with another $50 million drop. Finally, in panel D, the company no longer has any equity, but only assets and debt, both valued at $70 million. The company is now on the brink of defaulting on its debt—something that then happens in panel E where the asset value has dropped to $50 million, and now is lower than the debt value of $70 million. To complete the picture, panel F shows the bankrupted company with no assets, debt, or equity left.

As the panels of the figure show, the debt and equity values—or payoffs—are a direct function of the asset value. This relationship can be depicted in a graph, just as the payoffs for call and put options were depicted earlier. Figure 3-6 starts by showing the payoff of equity as a function of the asset value.

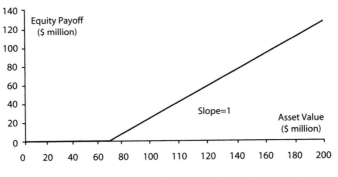

Figure 3-6 Equity payoff as a function of asset value

The preceding graph illustrates what the panels in Table 3-3 have already shown: Equity changes in value as the assets change in value, and it does so by the same amount. Hence, the slope of the line is 1. As we can see more clearly now, equity decreases in value as asset value decreases—until equity loses all value. In this example, given the numbers we have used, this occurs at an asset value of $70 million.

The debt part of the balance sheet can also be drawn as a function of the asset value, as in Figure 3-7.

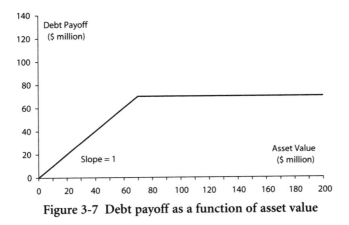

Figure 3-7 Debt payoff as a function of asset value

The figure shows that debt is consistently valued at $70 million until the asset value goes below $70 million. At that point, the debt value will match the decline in asset value one to one, as illustrated by the slope of one in the graph.

Armed with the two figures of equity and debt payoffs, let's interpret the graphs given what we have just learned about option payoffs.

Equity Interpretation

Comparing the payoff of equity (refer to Figure 3-6) to that of a call option (refer to Figure 3-2), we see that the payoffs are identical. The difference is that the call option is written on a firm's stock price and the equity payoff is written against the firm's full asset value, not just against its stock. The comparison illustrates the fundamental building concept of the Merton model that we already mentioned: Equity is nothing other than a call option on the assets of a firm. According to this concept, you have the right, but not the obligation, to sell the stock of the company; exercising this right allows you to cash out on your option. Because option models set out to price an option, and because we now view equity as a call option on assets, we can use option-pricing models to find the value of equity. After we have the value of the equity, we can then simply calculate debt value as the difference between assets and equity. This, in all its simplicity, is the link between option pricing and credit risk modeling.

It should be noted that in this view of the world, we assume that the firm belongs to the people to whom it owes money: its creditors or debt holders. Therefore, it follows that when the asset value is in excess of the debt value—or put differently, when the firm is worth more than what it owes the debt holders—the equity holders will end up calling the firm away from the debt holders. Let's exemplify: Say that the firm is worth $150 million and its debt is at $70 million. The call option that the equity holders have on the company is then valued at $80 million. (In options jargon, we would say that the option is **in-the-money** because it is worth money to its holder. If it held no value, it would be **out-of-the-money**.) The equity holders exercise their call option by paying the debt holders $70 million—an amount that can be compared to the strike price for an equity option—and it would make the debt holders the new owners of the firm, a firm that is now valued at $150 million. On a net basis, the equity holders would receive a payoff of $80 million, the value we used for equity in panel B of Table 3-3.

Let's now turn to the debt part of the balance sheet, and compare its pay-off to our option payoffs, just as we compared the equity payoff to holding a call option. The comparison here is a bit more difficult, however, because there is no single options diagram that corresponds perfectly to the debt payoff. What we have to do is replicate the debt payoff with a combination of payoffs from options and also from other securities.

To construct the debt payoff, let's introduce one more security: a zero-coupon Treasury Bond with a face value of F dollars. Put differently, it is a bond issued by the U.S. Treasury that pays no monthly interest or coupons, and that upon maturity returns the F dollars that the bond owner initially paid. It should also be noted that there are no interme-diate interest payments. The payoff for such a Treasury Bond, plotted against the asset value of the company, is given by Figure 3-8.

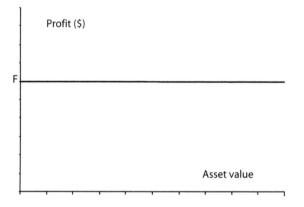

Figure 3-8 Payoff of a zero-coupon Treasury Bond

As the line shows, no matter how the asset value changes, the bond holder only receives the principal value of the bond when the bond matures (illustrated in the figure with F). Because the asset value of a firm has no effect on a government bond, the line is flat; the two are simply not connected. However, we want to include the bond instru-ment in our argument. We'll now show why. By combining the payoff of a Treasury Bond with the payoff of a short put (refer to Figure 3-5), we actually arrive at the payoff of risky debt, as shown previously in Figure 3-7. This combination of a Treasury Bond and a short put can be described graphically as in Figure 3-9.

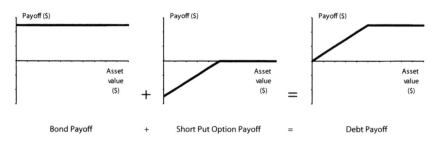

Bond Payoff   +   Short Put Option Payoff   =   Debt Payoff

Figure 3-9 Constructing the payoff of debt by combining the payoffs of a Treasury Bond and a put option

Just as we replicated the equity payoff with a call option on stock, we have now replicated the debt payoff by combining the payoffs of a Treasury Bond and a short put option on the company's assets. The intuition behind this last comparison is that investing in risky debt is the same as buying a Treasury Bond and writing a put option on the company assets. Of course, the natural question then is to whom do you write this put option? To whom is it that you are giving (because you are shorting) the right to sell (because it is a put option) the company assets? The answer, given our approach to explaining the Merton model, is that you write the put option to the equity holders of the firm. If the company does poorly, the equity holders give the firm to you, the debt holder, allowing you to collect their payoff out of whatever is left in the firm. This rhymes with Table 3-3, in which the equity portion appears as the first part of the balance sheet affected when assets fall. When there is no more equity, the company defaults—and the debt holders are paid with whatever is left of the firm.

To exemplify, let's think of two scenarios: In one scenario, the firm does well and in the other, the firm does poorly. When the firm does well, the equity holders own the firm. They have enough resources to pay off the debt holders, using whatever assets are in the firm. They can then keep the remainder of the firm, which is the residual equity value. This is exactly what the balance sheets in Table 3-3 show us. When the firm is worth $200 million, the equity holders pay off the debt holders with $70 million, and keep the remaining $130 million for themselves. However, when the firm is not doing so well, the assets of the firm are less than the amount owed on the debt. The equity holders thus have to default, declare the company bankrupt, and put the firm to the debt holders. The debt holders now own the assets and their payoffs come from whatever remaining assets there are in the firm.

Let's use a numerical example to explain further. We return to panel E of Table 3-3, where the firm is worth only $50 million, but has outstanding liabilities of $70 million. At this point, the equity is worth -$20 million. As owners of the company, the equity holders would normally have to pay $20 million out of their own personal funds to pay off the debt holders. However, because they have a put option with a strike price of $70 million dollars, they have an alternative. What they do is exercise the put option, with a strike price of $70 million. In essence, the put is worth $20 million to them (the strike price minus the value of the remaining assets). This is the additional $20 million they need to pay off the debt holders. The debt holders, in turn, have their debt of $70 million paid off in full: $50 million comes in the form of assets in the company and $20 million comes from the equity holders.

Of course, let's not forget who wrote the initial put option to the equity holders, giving the equity holders the needed $20 million. It was the debt holders themselves! This means that, net-for-net, they only receive $50 million, which is the debt payoff for that asset level as shown earlier in Figure 3-7.

MORE ON THE EQUITY INTERPRETATION

To complete our argument, let us return to the subject of equity payoffs. Remember that the Merton model assumes the firm belongs to the people to whom it owes money—its debt holders. Recall also that the equity holders have a call option on the firm's assets. Given our previous line of reasoning, we should now realize that the call option was actually sold to the equity holders by the debt holders.

With this new piece of information, let's consider the net payoff for the debt holders. They own the firm, which in other words means that they are long the assets of the firm. The payoff that comes from owning a firm is shown in Figure 3-10.

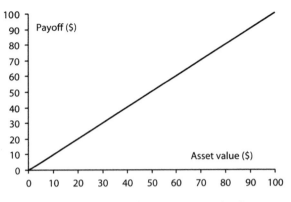

Figure 3-10 Payoff from owning the firm

The debt holders are also short a call option on the assets of the firm. Let's combine what it means for the creditors to be long the assets and short a call option on the same assets. We do this in Figure 3-11.

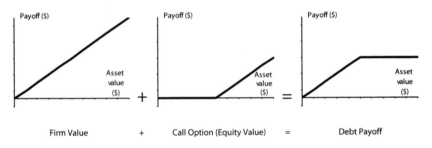

Firm Value + Call Option (Equity Value) = Debt Payoff

Figure 3-11 Constructing the payoff of equity by combining the payoffs of owning a firm with a call option

As the figure illustrates, the resulting payoff is the same payoff of risky debt we saw earlier in Figure 3-9! This means that no matter whether we choose the equity interpretation (of viewing equity as being long a call option) or the debt interpretation (of viewing debt as being short a put option and holding a Treasury Bond), we still arrive at the same economic conclusions for risky debt.

LINKING OPTION PRICING AND THE MERTON MODEL

In the preceding examples, we used option pricing arguments to explain the economics behind valuing risky debt. Table 3-4 summarizes the link between the Merton model and option pricing concepts.

Table 3-4 Link between the Merton model and equity option pricing

Equity Option	Merton Model
Stock price (S)	Asset value (A)
Strike price (K)	Debt value (D)

A regular equity option is written on the stock price of a company; it gives you the right to buy the firm's stock. Table 3-4 shows how the Merton model allows us to see the option as being written on the company's asset value. The strike price of a regular equity option is the level at which the option comes in-the-money for the holder. It is the breaking point between making a profit or not. As we have shown, starting with Table 3-3, the same type of breaking point occurs when the asset value of the company equals the debt value. In other words, in the Merton model, the debt value becomes the strike or exercise price.

Applying the Merton Model in a Black-Scholes Economy

The link between the Merton model and option pricing holds true no matter which option pricing model you choose to apply. This connection between option theory and credit risk is the essence of the Merton model. Thus, the Merton model eventually allows us to value risky debt—more specifically, to put a number on that value in the form of a credit spread. The Merton model lets us compute the discount of risky debt relative to its value, or conversely, its credit spread.

To actually apply the Merton model to the real world, we need to pick an option pricing model. Formulas for pricing options exist in abundance; virtually every bank and financial institution has its own variation. The difference between them comes from varying assumptions in the option pricing model itself. Traders choose the model that most closely resembles their own assumptions about the economy or that best fits the pricing task at hand. In this book, we will pick one of the fundamental option pricing models and the first ever created: the Black-Scholes model.

In the world according to Black-Scholes, the price of an equity option is entirely a function of five variables: the price of the underlying stock, the strike price of the option, the prevailing interest rate, the volatility of the stock price (also known as the asset volatility), and the option's time to maturity. For instance, the value of a put option, f, can be defined in the Black-Scholes model as the following five parameter formula:

$$\text{Put option for stock f: } (A, X, r, \sigma_A, \tau) \qquad [1]$$

where

- A = Asset price[3]
- X = Strike price
- r = Interest rate
- σ_A = Volatility of stock price (asset price volatility)
- τ = Time to maturity for put option

Next, if we apply Merton's model to a Black-Scholes economy, we can derive a formula for the value of zero-coupon risky debt, B, with a principal value of F. The formula can be shown as

$$B = PV(F) - f \qquad [2]$$

where

- $PV(F)$ = Present value of the bond
- f = Put option for stock according to Black-Scholes, as shown in equation 1

THE BLACK-SCHOLES FORMULA FOR A CALL OPTION

The Black-Scholes formula for a call option—which as we know corresponds in the Merton model to a call option on equity—is presented next. Actually deriving the formula is done in several other papers and is beyond the scope of this book, so let us just state it as

$$c = S_0 N(d_1) - Ke^{-rT} N(d_2) \qquad [3]$$

where the factors d_1 and d_2 are given by

$$d_1 = \frac{\ln(S_0 / K) + (r + 0.5\sigma^2)T}{\sigma_A \sqrt{T}} \qquad [4]$$

$$d_2 = d_1 - \sigma_A \sqrt{T} = \frac{\ln(S_0 / K) + (r - 0.5\sigma^2)T}{\sigma \sqrt{T}} \qquad [5]$$

And where

- c = Premium of call option
- S_0 = Stock price at time 0
- K = Strike price
- r = Risk-free interest rate
- T = Maturity time
- $N(.)$ = Cumulative probability distribution function for a standard normal distribution
- σ = Volatility of stock price (asset price volatility)

Because the options in the Merton model are written on the assets of the firm rather than the stock, we need to replace the parameters in the Black-Scholes formula like this:

$$c = E_0, S_0 = A_0, K = D \qquad [6]$$

where

- E_0 = Equity value at time 0
- A_0 = Asset value at time 0
- D = Principal amount of debt

Therefore, the equity value today is given by

$$E_0 = A_0 N(d_1) - De^{-rT} N(d_2) \qquad [7]$$

where the factors d_1 and d_2 are given by

$$d_1 = \frac{\ln(A_0/D) + (r + 0.5\sigma_A^2)T}{\sigma_A \sqrt{T}} \qquad [8]$$

$$d_2 = d_1 - \sigma_A \sqrt{T} = \frac{\ln(A_0/D) + (r - 0.5\sigma_A^2)T}{\sigma_A \sqrt{T}} \qquad [9]$$

And where

- E_0 = Equity value at time 0
- A_0 = Asset value at time 0
- D = Principal amount of debt
- σ_A = Volatility of stock price (asset price volatility)

Just as deriving the call option formula according to Black-Scholes is beyond the scope of this book, so is deriving the put option formula. This has also been done in numerous other publications. Here, it suffices to say that the formula, after adjusting it for use in the Merton model according to equation 6, can be written as

$$p = De^{-rT}N(-d_2) - A_0N(-d_1) \qquad [10]$$

where the factors d_1 and d_2 are given by the same formulas as before:

$$d_1 = \frac{\ln(A_0/D) + (r + 0.5\sigma_A^2)T}{\sigma_A\sqrt{T}} \qquad [11]$$

$$d_2 = d_1 - \sigma_A\sqrt{T} = \frac{\ln(A_0/D) + (r - 0.5\sigma_A^2)T}{\sigma_A\sqrt{T}} \qquad [12]$$

where

- E_0 = Equity value at time 0
- A_0 = Asset value at time 0
- D = Principal amount of debt
- σ_A = Volatility of stock price (asset price volatility)

ASSUMPTIONS UNDERLYING THE BLACK-SCHOLES/MERTON APPROACH

For the sake of completeness and clarity, let's state the assumptions for the Black-Scholes model. Fundamentally, the model gives a replication-based result that does not require knowledge of the stock's expected return. However, the price of the option does depend on the volatility of the stock price, also referred to as the **asset price volatility**. In fact, the Black-Scholes model assumes that the volatility of the underlying stock price remains constant over the period of analysis. It further assumes that the option can be exercised only at expiration (it therefore applies only to European options), and it supposes that no dividends are paid. In addition, the model assumes

- The existence of a complete, efficient, and frictionless market, without transaction costs for buying or selling the option or the underlying stock.

- All options and securities are perfectly divisible (if you want to sell 1/100th of an option, you can).

- There are no riskless arbitrage opportunities.

- All market participants can lend and borrow money at the same risk-free interest rate.

- This risk-free rate is known to all and constant during the life of the option.

- Security trading is continuous.

- The share price evolves over time following a random walk[4] or a lognormal distribution.

Concerning the last item in the list, a lognormal distribution is used in mathematics and statistics as the probability distribution of any random variable whose logarithm is normally distributed.[5] For example, if the random variable y is described as $y = e^x$, the shape of its lognormal distribution is shown in Figure 3-12.

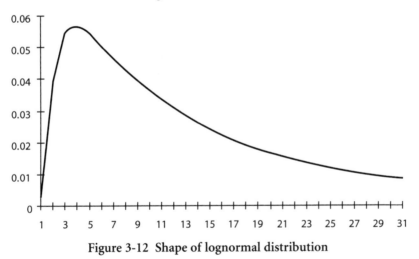

Figure 3-12 Shape of lognormal distribution

Applying the Merton Model: Example

We've defined the Merton model, we've shown how to use it for both equity and debt calculations, and we've also shown how to apply it in principle to a Black-Scholes economy. Let's now try it out by using the Merton model on a company. With the Black-Scholes model as our chosen option pricing model, we will use the Merton model to calculate the value of a company's risky debt, and from that arrive at the credit spread. When calculating the debt value, we will use both the equity and dept approaches covered previously. You will recall that regardless of the approach, we should still arrive at the same credit risk valuation.

Let's suppose there is a privately held company, ABC Corp., which is about to go public and start selling equity shares to the general public. Because it is still a private company with no traded equity, its debt and equity are impossible to observe. We do know, however, for the sake of this example, the value of its assets. Because the assets are made up of a portfolio of various equity type securities that are publicly traded, their value is easy to observe. We can therefore estimate the value of these assets to be $100 million.

Let's further imagine that we are the investment bank that is preparing to take this company public. Our job is to set a fair value for its shares. To do this, we split the assets into two parts, or tranches. One tranche is a zero-coupon bond with a four-year maturity and a face value of $70 million. The other tranche corresponds to what is left—that is, the equity. Our job as bankers is then to value the company's debt and equity—a perfect situation in which to apply the Merton model.

Table 3-5 summarizes what we know about the company so far. It is not much; in fact, we only know the asset value. To be able to use the Merton model, we make a few more assumptions, namely that the average asset price volatility is 20 percent (which we have calculated based on the traded securities in the asset portfolio) and that the risk-free interest rate is 5 percent.

Table 3-5 Balance sheet of ABC Corp. ($ million)

Asset	100	Debt	?
		Equity	?
	100		100

Our ultimate goal is to calculate the value of the debt. We can do so either directly or by first calculating the equity value. We'll go through both approaches here, starting with the equity value method.

As we know, we view equity as a call option on a portfolio of assets, and we value it using the Black-Scholes formula for a call option. The debt is simply going to be what is left after the equity value we calculate has been taken from the assets.

Using what we know about the company from earlier, we plug these numbers into equations 7, 8, and 9. This gives us the following equations for variables d_1 and d_2:

$$d_1 = \frac{\ln(A_0/D)+(r+0.5\sigma_A^2)T}{\sigma_A\sqrt{T}} = \frac{\ln(100/70)+(0.05+0.5\times0.2^2)\times4}{0.20\times\sqrt{4}} = 1.592 \quad [13]$$

$$d_2 = d_1 - \sigma_A\sqrt{T} = 1.592 - 0.20\times\sqrt{4} = 1.192 \quad [14]$$

We then use a normal distribution to find the values of $N(d_1)$ and $N(d_2)$.

$$N(d_1) = N(1.592) = 0.944 \quad [15]$$

$$N(d_2) = N(1.192) = 0.883 \quad [16]$$

With these two numbers, we can then make use of the baseline call option equation.

$$E_0 = A_0 N(d_1) - De^{-rT} N(d_2) = \quad [17]$$

$$100 \times 0.944 - 70 \times e^{-0.05 \times 4} \times 0.883 = 43.79$$

We obtain that the estimated equity value or market value of ABC Corp today is $43.79 million. Because we know that the assets are worth $100 million, the debt must be worth the difference, or $56.21 million.

CALCULATING THE DEBT VALUE DIRECTLY

Instead of arriving at the debt value via a calculation of the equity value, we can also directly calculate the value of the liabilities, which we now know can be computed as the value of a Treasury Bond minus a put option, or

$$\text{Debt} = \text{Treasury Value} - \text{Put Option Value} \quad [18]$$

This value of debt, D_0, can be written more formally as

$$D_0 = De^{-rT} - [De^{-rT}N(-d_2) - A_0N(-d_1)] \quad [19]$$

where the first part (De^{-rT}) is the value of the Treasury and the second part is the put option we recognize from equation 10.

We can now use this formula to verify the result of our previous equity-based calculation. Again, the time to maturity for the bond is 4 years, the volatility of the firm's assets is 20 percent, and the risk-free interest rate is 5 percent per year. We then also need the values for $N(-d_1)$ and $N(-d_2)$. We already know the values for d1 and d2 to be 1.592 and 1.192, respectively. Using the normal distribution to find values for $N(-d1)$ and $N(-d2)$ gives us

$$N(-d_1) = N(-1.592) = 0.056 \qquad [20]$$

$$N(-d_2) = N(-1.192) = 0.117 \qquad [21]$$

We plug all these values into equation 19, which gives us the market value of the debt, D_0 as

$$D_0 = 70e^{-0.05*4} - [70e^{-0.05*4} - *0.117 - 100 * 0.056] = 56.21 \qquad [22]$$

We obtain that the market value of the debt is $56.21 million—just as in our previous calculations. We have now thus come up with the same value for the debt using both the call option approach (equity based) and the put option approach (debt based).

ARRIVING AT THE CREDIT SPREAD

Of course, the goal of the preceding exercise is not to calculate the debt value. We need the debt value as a base from which to calculate the credit spread, which you will recall is a measurement not only of price, but also of the company's default risk. Let us therefore calculate the credit spread for this particular debt, which we have established to be $56.21 million.

We know from earlier chapters that the credit spread is the difference between a bond's yield and the yield of a risk-free government bond such as a U.S. Treasury Bond. We demonstrated this with a simple calculation example in Chapter 2, "About Credit Risk." Recall also that to calculate the yield to maturity, you take the face value of the debt (which is what it is worth at expiration to its holder) and use a discount value to arrive at today's market value. That discount value is the yield to maturity. If we apply this to our current ABC Corp. example, we have a face value of $70 million, a newly computed market debt value of $56.21 million and a time to maturity of 4 years. However, we do not know the yield to maturity, y. This gives us the following equation:

$$56.21 = 70 \text{ x e}^{-4y} \tag{23}$$

Solving for y gives us

$$0.054850141 = 5.49\% \tag{24}$$

To arrive at the credit spread, we then take the yield we just calculated and subtract the corresponding Treasury rate. We have assumed throughout this example that the risk-free rate is 5 percent, so let us use that value. This gives us a credit spread of

$$5.49\% - 5\% = 0.49\% \tag{25}$$

In a Black-Scholes economy in which ABC Corp. plans to go public, the credit spread for this particular debt is therefore 0.49 percent or 49 basis points.

Applying the Merton Model: Another Example

Because the Merton model is a core part of our discussions on credit risk modeling, let's use another example to further our understanding of how to use the model to arrive at a credit rating or score. Again, we will use the Black-Scholes model as our option pricing model.

In the previous example, we assumed you could observe the volatility of assets. Realistically, this is not possible. This time, let's start with a more true-to-life example. The more complete balance sheet of another company, XYZ Ltd., is shown in Table 3-6.

Table 3-6 Balance sheet of XYZ Ltd. ($ million)

Asset	100	Debt	40
		Equity	60
	100		100

This time, the balance sheet shows that both the debt and the equity are fully traded in the open markets. This allows us to assign them market values, and in turn come up with the asset value. As the figure shows, the debt has a market value of $40 million and the equity has a market value of $60 million, giving us assets of $100 million. It should also be noted that the debt has a face value of $50 million, the outstanding debt has a 5-year time to maturity, and the current interest rate is 3 percent.

Now, the Chief Financial Officer of XYZ Ltd. is considering recapitalizing the balance sheet; in other words, she wants to eliminate some of the debt. She specifically considers issuing $20 million of equity so that the firm can repurchase $20 million of debt. However, the CFO is not sure how that would impact the company's credit spread if XYZ Ltd. lowered its debt to $20 million and raised its equity to $80 million. Put more accurately, what will be the firm's marginal credit spread, or the credit spread on the next dollar of issuance, *after* the recapitalization? Again, we find ourselves with a great situation in which to apply the Merton model.

As in the previous example, our goal is to calculate the credit spread. However, this time we assume that the firm is a technology company whose assets are not traded. That means we cannot observe the company's asset volatility directly. (In the previous example, we simplified the situation by saying that the assets were a portfolio of traded securities.) Because asset volatility is required in the formulas we will use, we have to assess it somehow for this particular company. One method is to imply it from what we *can* observe.

As it turns out, **implied volatility** is a recurring concept in both option pricing and credit risk modeling because you generally cannot observe asset volatility in most credit model applications. When dealing with finance problems, you often find that the theoretical models you use call for one or more parameters that you cannot observe, let alone quantify, in the real world. The solution is to use other data such as the prices of traded securities to calibrate the model that you are using. This is done by matching the actual prices to your model. In other words, you find the values of the unknown or unobservable parameters such that the model prices match the observed prices exactly. You then use these implied values for the unobservable parameters to solve the problem at hand.

For example, the Black-Scholes model of pricing options calls for a volatility value that is very hard to observe in real life. However, given that numerous options are traded, their price is known. When you try to price a new option, you can therefore take the price for a similar option, and "back out" a volatility value using the Black-Scholes formula. You can then apply this volatility value to your new option. In this way, you can use your value for implied volatility to price new options on similar or identical securities that are not yet traded.[6]

Let's now compute the implied asset volatility of XYC Ltd, the technology company we introduced earlier. We are going to calibrate the Merton model such that it prices the debt to its known market price, which is $40 million. We plug known parameters for face value, interest rate, and time to maturity into equation 19—the equation for calculating debt. In this equation, the only unknown is the volatility, σ. We plug in all the other numbers we have.

$$40 = 50e^{-0.03*5} - [50e^{-0.03*5}N(-d_2) - 100N(-d_1)] \qquad [26]$$

where the formulas for d_1 and d_2 are

$$d_1 = \frac{\ln(100/50) + (0.03 + 0.5\sigma_A^2)5}{\sigma_A\sqrt{5}} \qquad [27]$$

$$d_2 = d_1 - \sigma_A\sqrt{5} = \frac{\ln(100/50) + (0.03 - 0.5\sigma_A^2)5}{\sigma_A\sqrt{5}} \qquad [28]$$

Using a spreadsheet program, we solve for σ_A, which ends up being 0.334. The asset volatility value we needed is, in other words, 33.4 percent.

Now that the firm has a value for asset volatility, it can set out to calculate the credit spread after recapitalization. We return to equation 19, which asks us for the values of d_1 and d_2. We calculate these to be

$$d_1 = \frac{\ln(100/30) + (0.03 + 0.5*0.334^2)5}{0.334\sqrt{5}} = 2.186 \qquad [29]$$

$$d_2 = d_1 - 0.334\sqrt{5} = \frac{\ln(100/30) + (0.03 - 0.5*0.334^2)5}{0.334\sqrt{5}} = 1.439 \qquad [30]$$

Plugging all values into equation 19, we end up with the following debt calculation:

$$D_0 = 20e^{-0.03*5} - [20e^{-0.03*5}N(-1.439) - 100N(-2.186)] \qquad [31]$$

In other words, the debt value after recapitalization is $25.32 million.

We now need to convert this debt value into a credit spread, just as we did in the previous example. We start by figuring out the yield to maturity, y. The face value after recapitalization is $30 million, because the firm just paid off $20 million of the $50 million debt. We just calculated today's market value to be $25.32 million, and the time to maturity is 5 years. This gives us the following equation:

$$25.32 = 30 * e^{-5y}$$ [32]

Solving for y, yield to maturity, gives us

$$y = 3.39\%$$ [33]

Subtracting the corresponding Treasury rate gives us the credit spread. Our assumed risk-free rate is 3 percent, which then gives us a credit spread of

$$3.39\% - 3\% = 0.39\%$$ [34]

The credit spread for this particular debt, in a Black-Scholes economy, is therefore 0.39 percent or 39 basis points.

As a reference, the original yield to maturity before capitalization can be computed (using the same approach we just used) to be 4.46 percent, meaning a 146 basis points spread. The recapitalization would therefore diminish the company's credit spread by 105 basis points.

Using Risk-Neutral Probability to Calculate Default Probability

The various concepts we have used so far such as credit spread, discount from face value, and so on, all describe the same thing: the likelihood that a firm will default. The higher the credit spread, the more likely the firm will default. The higher the discount of a bond's value to its face value, the more likely the firm will default.

You might find yourself wanting to find the actual probability of default, rather than these proxies or substitutes. However, to compute default probability requires models and data beyond the scope of this book. (There is plenty of literature on how to do this, to which the interested reader can turn.) For the purposes of this book, however, we can still compute a quantity that gives an indication of a probability of default if we use the assumption of so-called **risk-neutral default probability**. The risk-neutral probability of default describes the likelihood that a firm would default if that firm was active in a risk-neutral economy, or put differently, an economy where investors did not command a premium for bearing default risk.[7]

Based on the risk-neutral assumption, we can use as an approximation of default probability a value we in fact have already seen. In the previous formulas, we consistently used a variable referred to as $N(d_2)$. It can be shown that $1 - N(d_2)$ is the probability that the firm is bankrupt at the expiration of the zero-coupon bond contract. Although this is not the actual probability of default, it still gives us some indication of a debt's likelihood to default. In the previous example, we saw for instance that the credit spread of the firm dropped from 146 basis points to 39 basis points after it recapitalized. We can now state this in terms of the risk-neutral probability of default, using the $1 - N(d_2)$ formula. The credit spread of 39 basis points then corresponds to about 7.5 percent default probability. The probability of default prior to recapitalization was 22.5 percent. The recapitalization clearly helped the firm improve its credit standing.

Sensitivity Analysis of the Merton Model

Throughout this chapter, we have used the Merton model to calculate credit spreads in various examples. We have just now also introduced a simple way to calculate a value for default probability, using the so-called risk-neutral assumption. Let's take these two concepts—credit spread and default probability—and see how they react to changes in the values of the Merton model. More generally, we will look at how sensitive the model is to changes in its parameters; hence, we call this our sensitivity analysis of the Merton model. This exercise helps us explore how the concepts of credit spread and default probability are related to the parameters in the model, which in turn helps us to better understand the determinants and outputs of the Merton model. This is also an exercise that traders do regularly: They take an existing company or debt and look at how changes to, for instance, the risk-free rate would change the credit spread or default probability. Combined with the trader's view on how the interest rate will develop over time, this can then be used to forecast credit spread and default probabilities.

For our sensitivity analysis, we will use a company whose outstanding debt has the characteristics that are described in Table 3-7.

Table 3-7 Baseline data for the sensitivity analysis

Asset value	$100 million
Principal value	$40 million
Risk-free rate	5%
Volatility	40%
Time to maturity	Variable parameter from 1 to 20 years

This is the benchmark against which we now will study how changes to the parameters affect the credit spread and default probability. For instance, if all other variables remain the same, how will the default probability change if the asset volatility rises from 40 percent to 60 percent—or if it drops to 20 percent? With the same changes, what happens to the credit spread? To find out, we will separately test the sensitivity of the model to changes in the following:

- Asset volatility
- Interest rate (defined as the prevailing risk-free interest rate)
- Asset value
- Principal value of debt

As a starting point, let us chart the default probability and credit spread for the company debt against maturity times. The graph for default probability is shown in Figure 3-13.

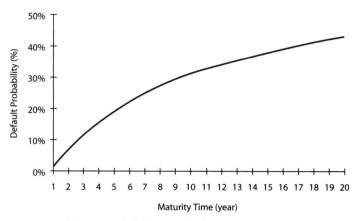

Figure 3-13 Risk-neutral default probability against maturity time for a sample debt

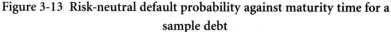

Figure 3-13 gives us a graphical illustration of something we know intuitively: the longer the debt is outstanding, the more likely the company is to default on it. Another way to phrase it would be to say that as time increases, the asset value simply has more time to drop below the principal value of the debt, which as we know is the structural model's definition of default. Longer maturity times simply increase uncertainty.

We can also create a similar baseline graph where we plot the credit spread against maturity time, as shown in Figure 3-14.

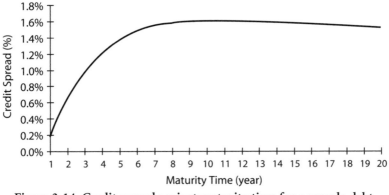

Figure 3-14 Credit spread against maturity time for a sample debt

As expected, the credit spread initially increases as the maturity time increases. The longer the debt is outstanding, the higher the compensation that an investor will seek for investing in that particular debt. However, this does not hold true for all maturities. As the figure shows, the credit spread actually starts to decrease at a certain point when maturities start to become long. This is puzzling, because it appears as if investors want *less* compensation as the risk inherent in longer maturities increases. Before we launch into our sensitivity analysis, let's take some time to explain this apparent anomaly, which is present no matter how we change the underlying variables.

So, why does the credit spread start to decline as maturities become longer and the default probability increases? Are investors really looking for *less* compensation to take on *more* risk? Actually, they are not. The explanation lies in the inherent nature of options; there is always an optimal time at which a call option holder can exercise a given option. The reasoning behind this is somewhat complicated, but goes as follows: First, let's remind ourselves that a call option increases in value as time to maturity increases. We know this intuitively because an option with a longer time to maturity than an otherwise identical option must have at least the same value—and then a little more. The option holder wants to be compensated for the extra time he holds the option. This is generally not true with a put option. A put can increase *or* decrease in value as time to maturity increases. The driving factor here is whether the put is a European-style option, which can be exercised only at its expiration date, or an American-style option, which can be exercised at any point up to its expiration date. As other books have covered and other authors shown in numerous examples, there is an optimal time to exercise the American put option *before* it matures. We will not repeat those examples here, but simply state that the value of an American put option peaks at that optimal time, which occurs, again, before the option's expiration. In the case of a European put, however, the investor cannot exercise at that optimal time unless the optimal time accidentally occurs at the same time as the expiration date. Therefore, if you change the maturity of the European put to be sooner or later than that optimal time, the value of the put decreases. This is what happens in Figure 3-14. The peak in the curve marks the expected optimal time to exercise an American put option. On either side of this peak, optimizing is suboptimal because the investor does not receive the full potential value of the option. Exercising on either side of the peak decreases the value of the put, and consequently increases the value of the risky debt itself, thus decreasing the credit spread. This is the logic behind what appears at first glance to be an anomaly. It is important to realize, however, that this behavior is simply a consequence of the optimal exercise time of options, and that it has nothing to do with the probability of default. As we saw in Figure 3-13 on default probability, the riskiness of the bond increases with time to maturity, despite the fact that the value of a put option decreases for the investor, given her lack of control over the optimal exercise point.

After that explanation of an apparent credit spread irregularity, we are ready to start our sensitivity analysis of the Merton model in a Black-Scholes economy.

Figure 3-15 shows how the default probability for various maturities reacts as the asset volatility (σ_A in the formulas we have defined earlier) changes. The three volatilities that the figure compares are 20 percent, 40 percent, and 60 percent. For example, if the asset volatility of the firm is at 60 percent, a point on the 60 percent volatility line is the default probability for that particular maturity.

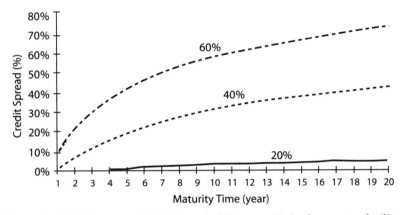

Figure 3-15 Risk-neutral default probability sensitivity by asset volatility

Figure 3-16 then shows how the credit spread for various maturity times reacts to the same changes in asset volatility.

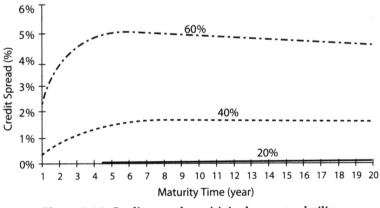

Figure 3-16 Credit spread sensitivity by asset volatility

Figure 3-15 shows how the default probability increases as the volatility in asset value increases. As asset volatility increases, meaning that the value of the company fluctuates more and more over time, the likelihood that the asset value will fall below the debt value at maturity increases. Simply put, with higher volatility, there is a greater chance for the asset value to reach zero, and for the company to lose all value.

The same thing occurs with credit spread. In Figure 3-16, we can see that the default probability increases as the volatility increases. Investors consequently require higher compensation—a higher credit spread—to accept the higher risk. (Note again how the credit spread peaks and then starts to decline for longer maturities as a consequence of the optimal exercise time of options we discussed earlier.) Another way to think about the credit spread is in terms of the Black-Scholes framework. In that framework, the value of both call and put options increases as volatility increases. If we return to seeing risky debt as a Treasury Bond minus a put option, we observe that the put value increases when volatility increases. The Treasury minus the put decreases therefore in value. As the debt decreases in value, its credit spread increases. Note also that the debt value is not the debt's principal amount but its market value. This tells us that the lower the market value of the debt, the higher the yield resulting in a higher credit spread.

SENSITIVITY TO INTEREST RATE

Adjusting volatility back to its benchmark 40 percent level, we can now see how the Merton model reacts to changes in the levels of the risk-free interest rate. Figure 3-17 shows how the default probability reacts to interest rate levels of 1.0 percent, 5.0 percent, and 10 percent.

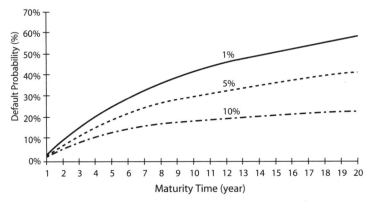

Figure 3-17 Risk-neutral default probability sensitivity by interest rate

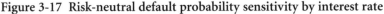

Figure 3-18 then shows credit spread sensitivity for the same different interest rates.

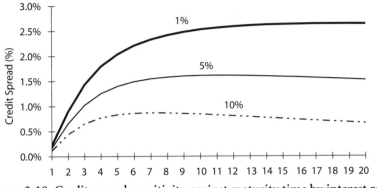

Figure 3-18 Credit spread sensitivity against maturity time by interest rate

Figure 3-17 shows that the higher the interest rate, the lower the probability of default. The expected return on assets is composed of two pieces: the risk-free rate plus a risk premium.[8] Therefore, as the risk-free rate increases, the expected return on the asset increases—and if the expected return on assets increases, the probability that the assets value will be below the principal debt value on maturity declines; hence, the lower default probability for higher interest rates.

This behavior is also reflected in the credit spread in Figure 3-18. The higher the interest rate, the lower the credit spread demanded by the investor. This is because the investor bears a lower probability of default. This too can be explained in option terms: As the interest rate increases, the value of the put option decreases. A put when exercised gives you cash, so as interest rates increase, an unexercised put declines in value because you are not exercising the put and reinvesting the cash at higher interest rates. In other words, the opportunity cost of not having the cash available makes the put option decline in value. This decrease results in an increase in the value of risky debt, and thereby decreases credit spreads.

As described earlier, the credit spread peaks at a certain point, and then starts to decline for higher maturities. The reason is the same as described earlier: The peak simply reflects the optimal time to exercise the corresponding American put option.

Figure 3-19 shows default probability sensitivity by asset value. We keep all the values of our baseline case from Figure 3-13, except for the asset value, which in this figure can be either $60 million, $100 million, or $140 million.

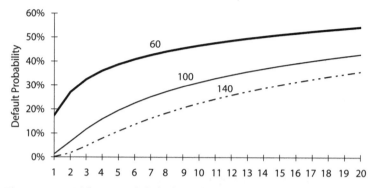

Figure 3-19 Risk-neutral default probability sensitivity by asset value

Figure 3-20 shows how the credit spread reacts to the same changes in asset value.

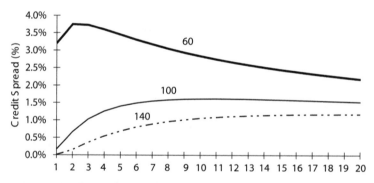

Figure 3-20 Credit spread sensitivity against maturity time by asset value

As the asset values increases, the probability of default decreases—that is, as the asset value increases, the chances of the asset being below the principal amount of debt (a constant) at any time in the future is by definition lower. The probability of default is therefore lower.

As to the credit spread, using option terms, the value of a put strictly decreases as asset value increases. As the value of the put decreases, the value of risky debt increases, and its credit spread in turn decreases.

Figure 3-21 shows default probability sensitivity against maturity time by debt value. We keep our baseline case steady, with the exception of debt value, which here can be either $20 million, $40 million, or $60 million.

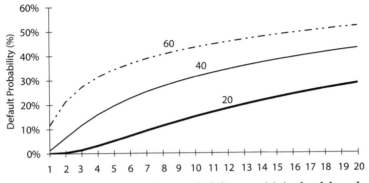

Figure 3-21 Risk-neutral default probability sensitivity by debt value

Figure 3-22 shows how the credit spread reacts to the same changes in debt value.

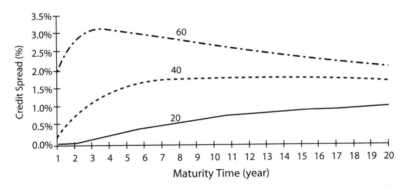

Figure 3-22 Credit spread sensitivity against maturity time by debt value

We observe in Figure 3-21 that as the principal amount of debt increases in a firm, the probability of default increases. As the debt value increases, the firm's debt-ratio increases because we keep the asset value fixed. As the firm's debt ratio (or debt leverage) increases, the chances of its assets falling below the required repayment of the debt increases. In other words, the probability of default increases.

As to the credit spread, Figure 3-22 shows that the higher the debt value, the higher the credit spread. The explanation is the same as that used for the default probability illustrated in Figure 3-21. We can also explain the relationship using option terms: The principal debt amount corresponds to the strike price of the put option. In general, as the strike price of a put increases, its value increases. As the value of the put increases, the value of the risky debt decreases, thereby resulting in a higher credit spread.

Extending the Merton Model

As we established earlier, the structural approach to credit risk modeling began in the 1970s with the work of Robert Merton, who applied the option pricing theory developed by Black and Scholes to the modeling of a firm's liabilities. You may remember from the beginning of the chapter that the structural approach uses the firm's fundamental structural variables, mainly its assets and liabilities, to work out the default time. A fundamental assumption in Merton's application of the approach is that default can only occur if the value of the assets is below the value of the debt at the time that the debt expires. If asset values are below debt values, but the debt is not due for servicing, default does not occur. Merton's assumption of default timing is but one of many assumptions that underpins the model.

When creating economic models, there is always a trade-off between realistic assumptions and ease-of-use in applying the model. Previously, we covered some of the assumptions behind the Black-Scholes model. These assumptions simplified the model to the point where it became easy to use. However, other researchers have taken Merton's model and modified it in ways that address some of his assumptions. In other words, they extended his model by introducing some of the complexity that the initial assumptions removed.

The first such extension came in 1976 from Fischer Black and J.C. Cox.[9] Still working within the structural framework to credit risk modeling, Black and Cox's approach differs from Merton's in two aspects. First, it allows for defaults to occur as soon as the firm's asset value falls below a certain threshold, which does not necessarily have to be the debt value. Second, default can occur at any time and not just at expiration or maturity. In contrast, Merton assumes the whole debt consists of just one bond issue, and that default happens when that bond issue matures. The intuition behind this is that a firm can really only go into default if it misses a payment on its debt. Because there are no interest payments in the Merton model (another of its assumptions), there is really only one payment, which happens at maturity when the full principal value is paid back. If the company misses this payment, it defaults. However, in the real world, bond indentures[10] often contain so-called **safety covenants** or clauses. These covenants allow bond holders to push a firm into bankruptcy under certain special situations, even if the firm has not explicitly defaulted on a payment. A covenant could, for example, require a company to maintain a certain minimum working capital ratio or to place a ceiling on its long-term debt-to-equity ratio. If the firm breaches one of these covenants, bond holders are immediately due the entire principal amount of the debt, even if the firm has not explicitly defaulted on a payment. The activation of such a safety covenant normally has spill-over effects on the company's other debt obligations. It most likely affects *all* the firm's bond issues because a fundamental part of bond indentures are **cross-default provisions**. These state that if one bond issue from the company defaults, all bond issues default. This pushes the company in effect over the brink of bankruptcy.

Black and Cox's extension to the Merton model addresses this possibility, and attempts to capture the fact that a firm can default at any time due to violation of a safety covenant, not just at the maturity time of the debt.

The Black and Cox Extension: The Barrier Function

At times referred to as a First Passage model, the Black and Cox model has an explicit function known as a **barrier function**. If the value of the firm drops below this barrier at any point prior to the maturity of the debt, the firm is considered to have violated one of the safety covenants, and the firm immediately goes into default. (The barrier function replaces, in other words, the role of the debt value in the original Merton model.)

A standard barrier function could be depicted as

$$A_t = \begin{cases} A^*(t) \, for \, t < T \\ D, \quad for \, t = T \end{cases}$$ [35]

where

- A_t = Asset value
- A^* = The predefined barrier function
- T = Maturity
- D = Principal value

The function states that if the firm's asset value, A, either hits or drops below the barrier value, A^*, prior to maturity, the firm is in default. A^* is the barrier function, or in other words the safety covenant, which says that even though the firm has not explicitly defaulted on a payment, the bond holders can still push the firm into bankruptcy when the value of the firm hits A^*. If the firm value never dips below the barrier value prior to maturity, T, the usual condition in the Merton model applies: The asset value has to be greater than the principal value of the debt.

In fact, the Merton model can be viewed as a special case of Black and Cox, where the barrier function is zero up until the maturity of the debt, at which point the barrier function takes on a value equal to the debt's principal amount. The A^* of T is simply zero. Equation 36 shows the barrier function when it has been modified to work in the Merton model.

$$A_t = \begin{cases} 0, for \, t < T \\ D, for \, t = T \end{cases}$$ [36]

Applying Black and Cox's Extension

To further our understanding of the Black and Cox extension to the Merton model, suppose that we set the barrier function to be a constant, K.[11] This gives us the barrier function

$$A_t = \begin{cases} K, for \, t < T \\ D, for \, t = T \end{cases}$$ [37]

In this case, the formula for the probability of default of risky debt can be shown to be

$$P = N(h_1) + \exp\{2(r - \frac{\sigma_A^2}{2})\ln(\frac{K}{A})\frac{1}{\sigma_A^2}\}N(h_2) \qquad [38]$$

where the factors h_1 and h_2 are given by

$$h_1 = \frac{\ln(\frac{K}{e^{r(T)}A_t}) + \frac{\sigma_A^2}{2} \times T}{\sigma_A\sqrt{T}} \qquad [39]$$

$$h_2 = h_1 - \sigma_A\sqrt{T} \qquad [40]$$

and where

- $N(.)$ = Normal distribution function
- K = Default barrier
- A = Asset value
- σ_A = Volatility of asset
- r = Risk-free interest rate

We can now derive the price of a zero-coupon bond that pays off $1 at maturity as equal to

$$e^{-rT}(1 - P) \qquad [41]$$

An Example of Applying Black and Cox's Extension

Remember that the Black and Cox model relaxes two of Merton's assumptions by allowing early default timing and by using a threshold as a signal of default instead of the debt value. Let's now use a numerical example to show how these two extensions affect an actual credit spread. To do so, we will return to the ABC Corporation example we used earlier in the section, "Applying the Merton Model: Example," to calculate a spread using the Merton model. We'll use the same data, repeated in Table 3-8, to calculate a credit spread using the Black and Cox model.

Table 3-8 ABC Corp. financial data

Asset value	$100 million
Principal value	$70 million
Risk-free rate	5%
Volatility	20%
Time to maturity	4 years

For this exercise, we will assume that the default barrier, K, needed in the formula has been set at $60 million. Note how this default barrier is lower than the principal value of the debt. (This follows a standard approach that calculates the default barrier as recovery rate times principal debt to the exponential value of −rT, which always leads to a default barrier that is lower than the principal debt value. A longer discussion of why this has become a standard way to set the default barrier is beyond the scope of this book.)

FINDING THE DEFAULT PROBABILITY

We start by finding the default probability. We plug the given values into equations 39 and 40, which gives us

$$h_1 = \frac{In(\frac{K}{e^{r(T)}A_t})+\frac{\sigma_A^2}{2}\times T}{\sigma_A\sqrt{T}} = \frac{In(\frac{60}{e^{0.05\times4}\times100})+\frac{0.2^2}{2}\times4}{0.2\times\sqrt{4}} = 1.577 \quad [42]$$

$$h_2 = h_1 - \sigma_A\sqrt{T} = -1.577 - 0.2\times\sqrt{4} = -1.977 \quad [43]$$

We then use a normal distribution to find the values of N(h$_1$) and N(h$_2$).

$$N(h_1) = N(-1.577) = 0.0574 \quad [44]$$

$$N(h_2) = N(-1.977) = 0.0240 \quad [45]$$

Plugging these two values into equation 38 gives us the default probability

$$P = N(h_1)+\exp\{2(r-\frac{\sigma_A^2}{2})In(\frac{K}{A})\frac{1}{\sigma_A^2}\}N(h_2) \quad [46]$$

$$= 0.0574 +\exp\{2(0.05-\frac{0.2^2}{2})In(\frac{60}{100})\times\frac{1}{0.2^2}\}\times 0.0240 = 0.0686$$

We obtain that the default probability of ABC Corp. is 6.86 percent.

We then plug the default probability into preceding equation 41, which gives the price of a zero-coupon risky bond that pays off $1 at maturity. This gives us

$$e^{-rT}(1-P) = e^{-0.05 \times 4}(1-0.0686) = 0.7626 \qquad [47]$$

The market value of ABC Corp's debt is then calculated as

$$\$70 \text{ million} \times 0.7626 = \$53.38 \text{ million} \qquad [48]$$

We have now caught up with the Merton model in so much as that we have values for the same parameters. We have a face value of $70 million, a newly computed market debt value of $56.38 million (compared to the $56.21 million that the Merton model gave us in equation 22) and a time to maturity of 4 years. To calculate the credit spread, we need to find a value for the yield to maturity, y. Using the values we do know, we can solve for y using the equation

$$53.238 = 70 \times e^{-4y} \qquad [49]$$

Solving for y gives us

$$y = 0.0678 = 6.78\% \qquad [50]$$

Because our aim is to find the credit spread, we need to subtract the risk-free interest rate from the yield to maturity. Consequently, the credit spread is calculated by

$$6.78\% - 5\% = 1.78\% \qquad [51]$$

Under the Black and Cox model, the credit spread for the risky debt of ABC Corp. is 1.78 percent or 178 basis points.

For the same risky debt, recall that the Merton model gave us a credit spread of 49 basis points in equation 25. In other words, the Black and Cox model's result is 129 basis points higher. It should have been expected, though, that Black and Cox would deliver a higher credit spread than Merton. The early default arrival, which the Black and Cox model allows for, accelerates default probability, and as we know from our sensitivity analysis of the Merton model, the higher the default probability, the higher the credit spread. This in part explains the higher credit spread. The other part of the explanation lies in the default barrier function. As we mentioned earlier, the Merton model can be seen as a special case of the Black and Cox model in which the default barrier is zero up until the maturity of the debt, at which point it becomes equal to the debt's principal amount. This is actually just another way of saying that the Merton model does not allow default prior to maturity. However, Black and Cox allows for early default, which also speeds up the default probability. Again, a higher default probability results in a higher credit spread.

Comparing Black and Cox to the Merton Model

Now that we have covered the basic distinction between the Merton model and the Black and Cox model, let us compare the two models in greater depth. We will do this by considering the case where K equals the principal value of the debt. As we have stated, the Merton model allows for default if the asset value is below the principal value of the debt, but only at expiration. In the Black and Cox scenario, however, default can occur at anytime that the asset value drops below a certain threshold. In this example, we assume this threshold is K, the principal value of the debt.

In comparing this special case of the Black and Cox model to the basic Merton model, we can make the intuitive guess that the credit spread resulting from the Black and Cox model will always be higher than that coming out of the Merton model. In the Black and Cox model, not only can the firm default at the debt's expiration if the asset value is below the principal value of the debt, but it can also default at *any* point in the life of the debt. The probability of default is therefore always greater than in the Merton model, meaning investors should ask for a higher credit spread as compensation for taking on this extra risk.

Let us verify this by graphing the default probability coming out of both the Merton model and Black and Cox's extended version of the Merton model. We will compare how the models rate the same debt, described in Table 3-7 and reproduced in Table 3-9.

Table 3-9 Baseline data for comparing the Merton and Black and Cox models

Asset value	$100 million
Principal value	$40 million
Risk-free rate	5%
Volatility	40%
Time to maturity	Variable parameter from 1 to 20 years

We will compare the two models against the same set of variables for which we compared our initial sensitivity analysis of the Merton model:

- Asset volatility
- Interest rate
- Asset value
- Principal value of debt

We start by comparing the two models according to asset volatility.

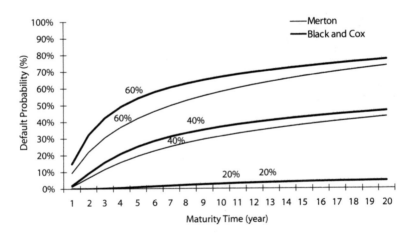

Figure 3-23 Default probability comparison by asset volatility between Merton model and Black and Cox model

We then continue with a comparison of the two models by interest rate.

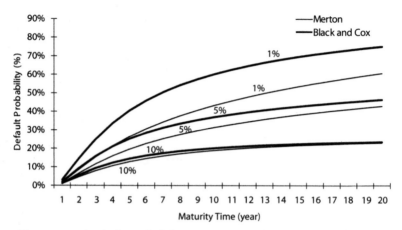

Figure 3-24 Default probability comparison by interest rate between Merton model and Black and Cox model

Third, we compare the two models by asset value.

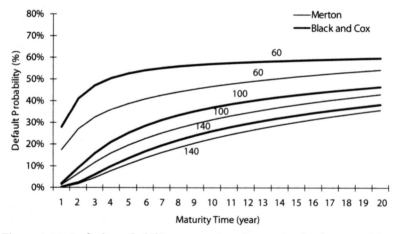

Figure 3-25 Default probability comparison by asset value between Merton model and Black and Cox model

Finally, we compare the two models by the principal value of the debt.

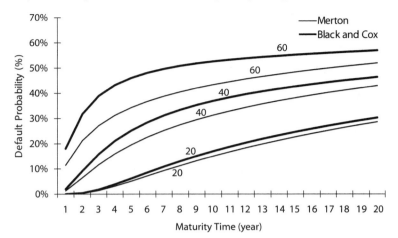

Figure 3-26 Default probability comparison by principal value of debt between Merton model and Black and Cox model

The preceding graphs verify our intuition: The default probability coming out of the Black and Cox model is higher than that of the Merton model. This makes sense because the Black and Cox extension is closer to the real-world behavior of firms and their defaults. Professionals thus prefer to use the more realistic Black and Cox model. However, Black and Cox's extension comes with the drawback that it is analytically and mathematically more complex to implement, especially its barrier function. For the working professional, Merton remains much simpler to apply, even if it comes with more limiting assumptions than Black and Cox.

Further Extending the Merton Model: Longstaff and Schwartz

In the previous section about Black and Cox's extension to the Merton model, we relaxed an important assumption in the Merton model, namely that firms can only default on the maturity date of the debt. There are two more assumptions that another extension to the model addresses; this extension is known as the Longstaff and Schwartz model.[12] The first of Merton's assumptions that the model addresses is that the risk-free rate is constant, meaning that throughout the lifespan of the debt the rate remains the same. The other assumption is that the term structure of interest rates is flat, meaning that the yield curve is perfectly flat—that is, that yield for all maturities is the same.

The model as such is rather complicated mathematically, which is why the interested—and mathematically apt—reader can find it in the appendix to this chapter. For other readers, it is enough to note that the assumptions of the Merton model make for a simple-to-use approximation of reality, but that if we want to use a model that is more realistic—and also more complicated—when it comes to interest rate behavior, one could turn to the Longstaff and Schwartz model.

APPENDIX TO CHAPTER 3

THE LONGSTAFF AND SCHWARTZ MODEL

The Longstaff and Schwartz model, first presented in 1995, accommodate time varying interest rates in that it allows for a stochastic, mean-reverting interest rate process, which among other things means that the yield curve is not flat. A word of caution: When discussing Longstaff and Schwartz's extension, we use a rather high-level and mathematical approach. The fundamental approach to using Longstaff and Schwartz remains the same as for the other structural models: looking at the firm's balance sheet to see when the asset value falls below the debt value.

Defining the Longstaff and Schwartz Model

When using the Longstaff and Schwartz model, we take the previous Black and Cox model with the constant barrier function, K, and instead of using a constant interest rate, we allow for a time-varying interest rate. The interest rate process is described as

$$dr = \beta (\alpha - r)dt + \sigma_r dW \qquad [52]$$

where

- dr = Interest rate process
- α = Long-run average short-term interest rate
- β = The rate of mean-reversion
- r = Short-term interest rate
- σ_r = Volatility of the short-term interest rate

The preceding equation is known as a **diffusion process**. It is simply a way of specifying how the short-term interest rate, r, moves through time. The coefficient in front of dt, **the drift**, specifies the predictable component of interest rate movements. The coefficient in front of dW, **the diffusion**, specifies the unpredictable component of the movement of the interest rate through time. Important to keep in mind when using the formula are the three parameters determining the drift and diffusion coefficients: α, β, and σ.

There is an additional parameter that we need to consider but that is *not* present in the preceding equation. In the Longstaff and Schwartz model, there are two stochastic factors. The first is the asset value of the firm, which is also a factor in both the Merton and Black and Cox models. The second is the short-term interest rate. In a two-factor model, we also need to specify how the two factors interact with each other. Specifically, we will assume that the two factors are related through a constant correlation defined by ρ (rho).

An Example of Applying Longstaff and Schwartz

In the Longstaff and Schwartz model, the formula for default probability can be shown to be

$$P(A, D, r, T, n) = \sum_{i=1}^{n} q_i \qquad [53]$$

where the parameters are defined as

$$q_1 = N(a_1) \qquad [54]$$

$$q_i = N(a_i) - \sum_{j=1}^{i-1} q_j N(b_{ij}), i = 2,3K \ ,n \qquad [55]$$

$$a_j = \frac{-\ln(A/D) - M(iT/n, T)}{\sqrt{S(iT/n)}} \qquad [56]$$

$$b_{ij} = \frac{M(jT/n, T) - M(iT/n, T)}{\sqrt{S(iT/n) - S(jT/n)}} \qquad [57]$$

And also

$$M(t,T)=\left(\frac{\alpha-\rho\sigma_A\sigma_r}{\beta}-\frac{\sigma_r^2}{\beta^2}-\frac{\sigma^2}{2}\right)t+\left(\frac{\rho\sigma_A\sigma_r}{\beta^2}+\frac{\sigma_r^2}{2\beta^3}\right)\exp(-\beta T)[\exp(\beta t)-1]+$$

$$\left(\frac{r}{\beta}-\frac{\alpha}{\beta^2}+\frac{\sigma_r^2}{\beta^3}\right)[1-\exp(-\beta t)]-\left(\frac{\sigma_r^2}{2\beta^3}\right)\exp(-\beta T)[1-\exp(-\beta t)] \qquad [58]$$

$$S(t)=\left(\frac{\rho\sigma_A\sigma_r}{\beta}+\frac{\sigma_r^2}{2\beta^3}+\sigma_A^2\right)t-\left(\frac{\rho\sigma_A\sigma_r}{\beta^2}+\frac{2\sigma_r^2}{\beta^3}\right)[1-\exp(-\beta t)]+$$

$$\left(\frac{\sigma_r^2}{2\beta^3}\right)[1-\exp(-2\beta t)] \qquad [59]$$

In the Longstaff and Schwartz model, the value of a zero-coupon bond paying \$1 at maturity is given by the following formula:

$$D_{risky}=D_{riskless}-\omega\times D_{riskless}\times P \qquad [60]$$

where

- D_{risky} = Current value of risky debt
- $D_{riskless}$ = e^{-rT}
- r = Risk-free interest rate
- T = Time to maturity
- P = Probability of default as defined by the preceding formula
- ω = The loss rate of a default occurs

The parameter ω, the loss rate, simply indicates what fraction of the principal value of the debt the bond holder loses when default occurs. For example, if ω is 2 percent, the bond holder loses 20 cents for every dollar of principal that he is owed—that is, he recovers 80 cents on the dollar.

As a final comment, it should be said that it is difficult to do a direct comparison of the Longstaff and Schwartz, Black and Cox and Merton models. The Longstaff and Schwartz has many more parameters, and depending on the choice of parameters, the probability of default coming out of the Longstaff and Schwartz model can be higher or lower than the Black and Cox model. A full comparison/sensitivity analysis therefore falls outside of the scope of this book.

Endnotes

1 See the original papers: Black, Fischer and Myron S. Scholes, "The Pricing of Options and Corporate Liabilities," *Journal of Political Economy*, 1973, volume 81, pages 637-654; Merton, Robert C., "A Dynamic General Equilibrium Model of the Asset Market and Its Application to the Pricing of the Capital Structure of the Firm," 1970 (unpublished manuscript available in Merton, Robert C., *Continuous-Time Finance*, Blackwell Publishing, 1992); and Merton, Robert C., "On the Pricing of Corporate Debt: the Risk Structure of Interest Rates," *Journal of Finance*, 1974, volume 29, pages 449-470. (For their work, Scholes and Merton received the 1997 Nobel Prize in Economics. Black passed away in 1995, and the Nobel Prize is not awarded posthumously.)

2 Note that in this example, you have speculated against stock that you already own, which is known as having a **covered option**. You can actually trade options for stock that you do not own, which is referred to as having a **naked option**. If you exercise the put option and have to deliver the actual stock, you have to purchase the stock in a separate transaction.

3 The original Black-Scholes model defines stock price and the volatility of stock prices, calling them σ_S. Here, however, because we are applying the Black-Scholes model to the Merton model on credit risk, we have modified the variables to define asset price and the volatility of asset prices, respectively. The connection allowing this modification is shown in Table 3-4.

4 The expression **random walk** is used in mathematics to describe a function that takes a number of successive steps, each in a random, different direction.

5 If you have an equation such as $a^n = x$, you would use a logarithm to obtain the exponent n. This is normally expressed as $\log_a x = n$. As an example, $3^5 = 243$ and thus $\log_3 243 = 5$.

6 Another common use of Black-Scholes is to compute the implied volatility for two equity options on the same stock, and then to compare those implied volatilities. In theory, because the underlying stock is the same, the volatility should be the same. In practice, those two volatilities are usually different. Investors, such as hedge funds, often use these two implied volatilities to compare prices for these two options to find out which one is expensive and which one is cheap.

7 There is a rather complicated formula that one can use to translate the risk-neutral probability of default into the actual probability of default. However, this requires understanding an investor's risk tolerance, or put differently, knowing how much premium an investor demands for bearing a unit of default risk. As such, it falls outside the scope of this book.

8 The risk premium can be determined in many ways. The most common way is to use a Capital Asset Pricing Model (CAPM) type model.

9 For the original paper, see Fischer Black and J. C. Cox, "Valuing Corporate Securities: Some Effects of Bond Indenture Provisions," *Journal of Finance*, 1976, volume 31, pages 351-367.

10 An **indenture** is another term used for a bond contract, or for the document that states the terms under which a security, such as a bond, is issued.

11 In the original Black and Cox paper (1976), they chose a barrier function given by $e^{-\gamma(T-t)}K$ where γ is a constant. In our example, we consider that γ (gamma) equals zero.

12 For the original paper, see Francis A. Longstaff and Eduardo S. Schwartz, "A Simple Approach to Valuing Risky Fixed and Floating Rate Debt," *Journal of Finance*, University of California at Los Angeles, 1995, Vol. L, No. 3, pages 789-819.

4

MODELING CREDIT RISK: ALTERNATIVE APPROACHES

In Chapter 3, "Modeling Credit Risk: Structural Approach," we discussed the structural approach to credit risk modeling. We discussed primarily one application of that approach, the Merton model, which also is the main credit risk model used in this book. In practice, however, a wide variety of models are used for pricing and hedging credit risk. You now know that these models can be grouped into three large categories: **structural models of default** (such as those we covered in Chapter 3), **empirical models** (also known as credit scoring models), and **reduced form models**. Whereas the structural approach proposes that firms never default by surprise, and that their default probability can be modeled from looking at the structural values of the company—primarily at its balance sheet—the two other approaches assume that there is no reliable method of predicting when default will happen. In their view, there is no relationship between the firm's asset value and default. Instead, defaults "just happen"; they are unpredictable events that either can be estimated based on historical data or for the sake of modeling can be tied to some external signal. In this chapter, we provide an overview of the two approaches that we have not yet discussed: empirical models and reduced form models.

Empirical Models of Default, or Credit Scoring Models

As we demonstrated in Chapter 3, the structural models attempt to model the economics underlying a default. In the case of the Merton model, the basic economic factor driving default is a drop in equity value to zero. Thus, equity is a signal, or indicator, of default. Empirical models, however, do not try to model the underlying drivers of default. The defining characteristic of the empirical model is that it identifies the possibility of default with a **quantitative score**. Instead of modeling the underlying default drivers, a credit scoring model simply compares companies that defaulted in the past with companies that did not. The comparison is based on financial data such as balance sheet and income statement data, and uses financial ratios to indicate profitability, solvency, and liquidity. These financial ratios are valued against size, industry, and other company features. All values are combined to create a score for the firm. When properly calibrated, the model should then simply enable us to look at the financial data of any company in the selected group and accurately tell whether the firm defaulted. Defaulted companies should receive a lower score than those that did not default in the historical control group—and these scores become the basis against which to evaluate new companies. Companies that have higher scores than the firms that historically defaulted are considered financially sound, whereas those with lower scores than the defaulted companies are considered not creditworthy, and in fact are very likely to go bankrupt themselves.

Because of their focus on producing scores, the empirical models of default are (not surprisingly) often referred to as **credit scoring models**.

As an example, let's picture a bank that receives a loan application from a small business owner. Instead of using the Merton model or another structural approach model, the bank decides to assign the applicant a simple credit score from which it can evaluate whether to grant the loan. The bank collects some basic information about the business— for example, its annual revenues, existing debts, and real estate costs— and converts this data into values that it plugs into a credit score formula. (The formula that the bank uses can be a generic one, or it can be a proprietary formula that the bank has developed itself.) The formula produces a number, which becomes the applicant's score. The score is then compared to a cut-off value, which has been estimated using either historical default rates (as we described earlier) or historical credit ratings by one of the major credit rating agencies. If the credit score is higher than the cut-off value determined by the model, the bank grants the loan. If the score is lower than the cut-off point, the loan application is declined.

Because empirical models do not try explicitly to capture the economics of default, they have the potential—depending on the model chosen—to be much simpler than structural models. As the preceding small example shows, credit scoring models tend to be highly standardized, and the process of applying them can be very formulaic. Credit scoring models are statistical in their mathematical approach, regressing instances of default against various risk indicators.

It is also worth noting that credit scoring models do *not* produce probabilities of default on which to base pricing activities. The benefit of the approach lies instead in its simplicity and that it quickly allows for a comparison of a new debt to historical ones.

Z-Score Model

Edward I. Altman of New York University's Stern School of Business introduced the first scoring model in 1968.[1] He laid the basis for the whole approach by defining his so-called **Z-score model**. He chose a group of companies from a specific time period and separated defaulting (or distressed) firms in that group from nondefaulting (or nondistressed) ones on the basis of certain financial ratios. The ratios are standard ones, focusing on liquidity, profitability, leverage, solvency, and activity. Altman's econometric model is a linear analysis that weights and sums up these five ratios to arrive at an overall score. This score should predict whether a company is in the default or nondefault group based on historical data. With that data confirmed, scores from current-day companies can be calculated, and the results can be used to indicate whether a company is about to default.

Equation 1 presents the Z-score model as Altman defined it, along with the five financial ratios he chose, marked as X_1 through X_5. Note that other empirical models might use other financial ratios and that the ratios here are the ones selected specifically for the Z-score model:

$$Z = \beta_1 X_1 + \beta_2 X_2 + \beta_3 X_3 + \beta_4 X_4 + \beta_5 X_5 \qquad [1]$$

where

- Z = Overall score
- $\beta1$ through $\beta5$ = Coefficients
- X_1 = Working capital / total assets
- X_2 = Retained earnings / total assets
- X_3 = Earnings before interest and taxes / total assets
- X_4 = Market value equity / book value of total liabilities
- X_5 = Sales / total assets

Let us discuss in more detail each of Altman's five financial ratios:

- **X_1, Working Capital/Total Asset (WC/TA)**
  This variable indicates the firm's net liquidity against the firm's value. **Working capital** is defined as current assets minus current liabilities. This ratio reflects both liquidity and size features, and is preferred to other liquidity ratios such as quick ratio and current ratio.

- **X2, Retained Earnings/Total Assets (RE/TA)**
  Retained earnings shows the firm's total reinvested earnings and/or losses over its entire life. A high ratio of retained earnings over total assets indicates that the company has built up considerable cumulative profit, and thus is less likely to default. As Altman points out, companies that have been in existence for a long time have naturally had more time to build up their retained earnings, and therefore the ratio could be seen as penalizing young companies. However, argues Altman, it mirrors the real world: Young firms are more likely to default or go into bankruptcy than older companies. In addition, the ratio measures the firm's leverage.

A high RE/TA ratio shows that the company has financed its assets by keeping its profits and not by taking on more debt.

- **X3, Earnings Before Interest and Taxes/Total Assets (EBIT/TA)**
  This variable measures the firm's productivity and profitability against its assets. A company's existence is ultimately based on how much revenue it can take in, given its asset base, making this ratio particularly appropriate to include in the formula, argues Altman.

- **X4, Market Value of Equity/Book Value of Total Liabilities (MVE/TL)**
  This measure indicates the company's solvency, in that it looks at how much the firm's assets can decline in value (measured by market value of equity plus debt) before the liabilities exceed its assets and the firm becomes insolvent.

- **X5, Sales/Total Assets (S/TA)**
  This ratio, also known as the capital-turnover ratio, is commonly used to represent the sales-generating capability of the firm's assets. In short, it reflects how active the company is.

The values for the ratios come directly off the financial statements of a company. For the model to work, you also need values for coefficients β_1 through β_5. To find those values, you can proceed as follows.

Select a number of companies for your baseline data. (The more the better, but this ultimately depends on the sector or industry that you are using for your baseline data.) Take the historical data on all the companies in the selected group and calculate the financial value of each of the five ratios, as X_1 through X_5, for every single quarter. You then assign a large positive value, such as 5, to firms that did not default and a low value, such as 0, to firms that defaulted. For every quarter, you calculate each of these five financial ratios for firms in both categories. Thus, for each firm and for each quarter, you have the firm's default score—5 or 0—and you have the value of the five financial ratios. You now run a regression[2] using the default score as the dependent variable and the five financial ratios as the independent variables. The regression generates numerical values for the coefficients β_1 through β_5. Your model is then ready to be used to forecast default.

Altman performed exactly such a regression, using a set of data from 66 corporations, with 33 firms that had defaulted and 33 that had not, between the years of 1946 and 1965. To come up with values for the coefficients β_1 through β_5, he assigned high and low values for the default and nondefault groups, respectively. He then derived the following formula:

$$Z = 0.012\,X_1 + 0.014\,X_2 + 0.033\,X_3 + 0.006\,X_4 + 0.999\,X_5 \qquad [2]$$

where the values X_1 through X_5, remain the same as in equation 1.

Worth noting is that Altman's original formula, as presented in equation 2, mixes absolute values (for variables X_1 to X_4) and ratios (variable X_5). A more convenient format of the formula, which only uses ratios, was introduced as

$$Z = 1.2\,X_1 + 1.4\,X_2 + 3.3\,X_3 + 0.6\,X_4 + 1.0\,X_5 \qquad [3]$$

Now that you have the values for β_1 through β_5, you can use the model to forecast default. Using the numbers that Altman found, you can do this as follows.

For any current company, you can go to its annual report and calculate the values of the five financial ratios. You input the values of these financial ratios into the model, which in our case is equation 2 and calculate the Z-score. You then compare that Z-value to the Z-values of companies that historically have been in default. If the Z-value is sufficiently low, you can conclude that the company at this time probably has a high probability of default. If the Z-value is sufficiently high, you can conclude that the firm has a fairly low probability of default.

However, this begs the question: What are high and low values for Z? The cut-off level for the Z-score depends on the historical data you originally used. For example, the results that Altman derived from his data in 1968 are shown in Table 4-1.

Table 4-1 Altman's Z-score interpretation in his 1968 paper

Default group	Z < 1.81
Grey zone	1.81 ≤ Z ≤ 2.99
Nondefault group	Z > 2.99

Altman found that the high value for the Z-score, given his data, was 2.99. A company with a Z-score higher than 2.99 could then be considered unlikely to default. Similarly, he found the low value for his group to be 1.81. Companies with a score lower than 1.81 would be considered to have a high probability of default. However, companies with a value between 1.81 and 2.99 were more difficult to categorize. Altman therefore placed these firms in what he referred to as a **grey zone**.

In addition to developing the default classification featured in Table 4-1, Altman also showed the relationship between his Z-score results and standard bond ratings from rating agencies. Table 4-2 shows the bond rating equivalents of Altman's Z-scores based on data from Standard & Poor's (S&P).

Table 4-2 Average Z-scores by S&P bond rating, 1995-1999

Bond Rating	Average Annual Number of Firms	Average Z-Score	Standard Deviation
AAA	11	5.02	1.50
AA	46	4.30	1.81
A	131	3.60	2.26
BBB	107	2.78	1.50
BB	50	2.45	1.62
B	80	1.67	1.22
CCC	10	0.95	1.10

Source: Edward I. Altman. "Revisiting Credit Scoring Models in a Basel 2 Environment." May 2002. Paper available at /www.stern.nyu.edu/fin/workpapers/papers2002/pdf/wpa02041.pdf. Accessed May 2005. Paper originally prepared for M. Ong, "Credit Rating Methodologies, Rationale, and Default Risk." London Risk Books, 2002.

Based on Altman's formula in equation 2, let's now demonstrate how to use the Z-score with a real-world example. We are going to figure out the creditworthiness of the world's largest retailer, Wal-Mart. Table 4-3 shows a summary of Wal-Mart's 2003 and 2004 financials.

Table 4-3 Wal-Mart 2004 and 2004 financials, summarized

1. Balance Sheet (amounts in $ million)

	2003	2004	Average
Assets			
Current assets	30,722	34,421	32,572
Fixed assets	64,086	70,491	67,289
Total assets	94,808	104,912	99,860
Liabilities and equity			
Current liability	32,519	37,418	34,969
Long-term liability	22,828	23,871	23,350
Equity	39,461	43,623	41,542
Total liability and equity	94,808	104,912	99,860

Additional data:

- Number of shares as of January 31, 2004: 4,311 million

- Share price on January 31, 2004: $53.85 / share

- Average retained earnings: $38,891 million

2. Income Statement (amounts in $ million)

	2004
Sales	258,681
Costs and expenses	244,488
Income before income taxes and interest	14,193

Source: Adapted from Wal-Mart 2004 Annual Report.

We begin by calculating each financial ratio that is needed in the formula. Note that you should average the data you use from the balance sheet between the current fiscal year and last fiscal year so that the ratio captures the financial performance of the entire year. The calculations for our ratios are as follows:

$$X_1 = \text{working capital / total assets} \qquad [4]$$

$$= (\text{current asset} - \text{current liability}) / \text{total asset}$$

$$= (32{,}572 - 34{,}969)/99{,}860 = -0.024$$

$$X_2 = \text{retained earnings / total assets} \qquad [5]$$

$$= 38{,}891 / 99{,}860 = 0.390$$

$$X_3 = \text{earnings before interest and taxes / total assets} \qquad [6]$$

$$= 14{,}193 / 99{,}860 = 0.142$$

$$X_4 = \text{market value equity / book value of total liabilities} \qquad [7]$$

$$= \text{number of shares} \times \text{share price} / (\text{current liabilities} + \text{long-term debt})$$

$$= 4{,}311 \times 53.85 / (34{,}969 + 23{,}350) = 4.350$$

$$X_5 = \text{sales / total asset} \qquad [8]$$

$$= 258{,}681 / 99{,}860 = 2.590$$

We then take these values and plug them into our equation 2. This gives us

$$Z = 1.2X_1 + 1.4X_2 + 3.3X_3 + 0.6X_4 + 1.0X_5 = \qquad [9]$$

$$= 1.2 \times (-0.024) + 1.4 \times 0.39 + 3.3 \times 0.142 + 0.6 \times 4.35 + 1.0 \times 2.59 = 6.186$$

The score indicates that if we were a lending institution, we would approve a loan application from Wal-Mart because its score of 6.186 is higher than the 2.99 level designated by Altman's findings. We can further validate this by comparing the score with standard results from credit rating agencies, as in Table 4-2. As the figure shows, Wal-Mart would receive an AAA-rating because its score is greater than 5.02.

A Revised Z-Score Model: Z'-Score

One of the major limitations of the original Z-score model was that it allowed only for evaluating public companies, whose equity was traded and easily measured. However, the Z-score model quickly became a popular tool to use for medium and small firms with little or no publicly traded equity. Altman therefore developed a revised Z-score model, which modified the fourth financial ratio (market value equity / book value of total liabilities) so that it could use the **book** value of the firm's equity instead of the **market** value. The revised model was dubbed **Z'-score**[3] and was useful for firms in the private sector. The revision led to a change in the coefficients before each variable. The resulting Z'-formula thus became

$$Z' = 0.717\ X_1 + 0.847\ X_2 + 3.107\ X_3 + 0.420\ X_4 + 0.998\ X_5 \qquad [10]$$

where all variables are the same as for equation 1 except the following:

- X_4 = Book value equity / book value of total liabilities

The cut-off point between defaulted and nondefaulted companies also changed with Altman's new interpretation. We replicate his findings in Table 4-4.

Table 4-4 Altman's Z'-score interpretation

Default group	$Z < 1.23$
Grey zone	$1.23 \le Z \le 2.90$
Nondefault group	$Z > 2.90$

A Z'-SCORE EXAMPLE

Although the Z'-score was developed for private companies, for simplicity's sake, we will reuse our Wal-Mart example to exemplify the method. Remember that the Z'-score shares the same parameters as the Z-score, except X_4, which means we can reuse the calculations we did earlier, with the exception of the fourth financial ratio (which was market value equity / book value of total liabilities, but now should be book value equity / book value of total liabilities).

X_4, calculated with book value of equity, is then calculated, based on the data in Table 4-3 as

$$X_4 = \text{book value equity / book value of total liabilities} \qquad [11]$$

$$= 41,542/ 58,319 = 0.7123$$

The Z' score is then given by

$$Z' = 0.717 \, X1 + 0.847 \, X2 + 3.107 \, X3 + 0.420 \, X4 + 0.998 \, X5 \qquad [12]$$

$$= 0.717 \, (-0.024) + 0.847 \, 0.390 + 3.107 \, 0.142 + 0.420 \, 0.7123 + 0.998 \, 2.59$$

$$= 3.638$$

The result shows again that Wal-Mart is not a likely candidate for default, because its score is greater than 2.90, the nondefault limit found by Altman for his Z'-score reference group.

A Further Revision of Z-Score: Z"-Score

Later on, Altman saw a further need to revise the Z-score model. He observed that the financial ratios that he had developed differed significantly between industries, and he wanted the Z-score model to take this into consideration. Specifically, he noted that asset turnover, or sales divided by total assets, varied from one industry to another. The manufacturing industry, for instance, traditionally required more assets in the form of factories and equipment than the financial industry, which could generate larger sales on smaller assets. To reduce the sensitivity of the Z-score model to industry factors, Altman further revised the model, changing coefficients and variables.[4] One of the simplest variations of the model meant simply removing the last variable, X_5, or sales over assets. He called the new model the Z"-score and made it applicable to all nonmanufacturing companies.

Thus, for nonmanufacturers, the Z"-score model became

$$Z'' = 6.56 \, X_1 + 3.26 \, X_2 + 6.72 \, X_3 + 1.05 \, X_4 \qquad [13]$$

Where the variables are the same as for equation 1, and where the default/nondefault cut-off interpretation is presented in Table 4-5.

Table 4-5 Altman's Z"-score interpretation

Default group	Z < 1.10
Grey zone	1.10 ≤ Z ≤ 2.60
Nondefault group	Z > 2.60

A Z"-SCORE EXAMPLE

Reusing our Wal-Mart example, we can now show how to apply the Z"-score model. We already know the value of the coefficients from the preceding, and so the calculation becomes

$$Z" = 6.56\ X1 + 3.26\ X2 + 6.72\ X3 + 1.05\ X4 \qquad [14]$$

$$= 6.56\ (-0.024) + 3.26\ 0.390 + 6.72\ 0.142 + 1.05\ 0.7123$$

$$= 2.96$$

Again, Wal-Mart is not likely to default on its liabilities because its score is higher than the cut-off point for the nondefault group.

Reduced Form Modeling

After looking at structural and empirical models of default, we now turn our attention to reduced form models, the third and final class of default models that we cover in this book. In this section, we lay out the principles of the approach. There is then one implementation of the approach known as the Jarrow-Turnbull model. Describing this particular model is done in the appendix to this chapter, and is meant for the mathematically apt reader, because explaining the Jarrow-Turnbull model requires a rather advanced understanding of mathematics.

We have just seen how empirical models assign a score to a company, based on the financials of that company. Structural models, as we know from Chapter 3, take a different approach: They try to capture the economics of the actual default event. Default occurs in the structural approach when the company's equity value has essentially dropped to zero. This event, which we catch from looking at the balance sheet, is the signal that tells us default has occurred.

By contrast, reduced form models do not model the balance sheet like the structural approach, nor do they try to capture a default indicator from the financial statements of the company like the empirical approach. Instead, the reduced form approach supposes that there is no relation between the firm value and default. Default is instead seen as completely unpredictable, and results from a sudden, inexplicable loss in the company's market value. This means that the approach also assumes that there is no such thing as gradual default, but that default is by definition an abrupt event. The approach still asks for a signal to indicate that default has occurred—and the reduced form models therefore simply assign an external signal to serve this purpose. When this exogenous variable—which normally is a statistical or econometric number—hits a certain value, we simply assume the company has defaulted. It is worth noting that no economic modeling goes into developing the external signal; we simply pick an easily observed signal that for some reason we feel is adequate for our model as a sign that default has occurred.

The abrupt event of default represented in the model by the external signal can be described in mathematical terms as a **Poisson event**. Because Poisson models look at the arrival rate, or intensity, of a specific event, this approach to credit risk modeling is also referred to as **default intensity modeling**. There are several types of reduced form or default intensity models including Duffie and Singleton (1995) and Madan and Unal (1994). In this book, we will look at just one example of a commonly used reduced form model, known as the Jarrow and Turnbull (1995) model. Before we discuss their model, however, we cover the fundamental concept of default intensity in more detail.

Default Intensity

We just stated that reduced form models typically assume an external signal or statistical process for determining default. Using a signal builds on the approach's assumption that default arrives suddenly and unexpectedly for no reason; it is a random event. In probability theory, there are distribution models to describe how discrete, random events occur over time. One such model is the Poisson distribution that refers to these random occurrences as **arrivals**.[5] Think of it this way: There are constant draws from the Poisson distribution, and each draw either brings up a 0 or a 1. Most of the draws come up with 0. However, every once in a while, the draw comes up with a 1. This represents a default, and it makes the Poisson distribution a key building block of the reduced form approach.

The Poisson distribution mandates that the time between the occurrence of this particular event and the previous occurrence of the same event has an exponential distribution. Like all distribution models, the Poisson model has parameters defining its distribution. However, the Poisson model only has *one* such parameter, known as the **arrival rate**. The arrival rate explains how often an event actually happens, or arrives. When the Poisson process is used for credit risk, the arrival rate is more often referred to as **default intensity** and normally represented by λ (lambda). Put in more technical terms, when trying to model defaults as random repeated events, the occurrence of defaults is determined by a Poisson distribution with the mean arrival rate λ. This means that the expected time to default can be described as $1/\lambda$. λ can then also be thought of as the default rate or frequency—or simply the default intensity. Yet another way to think of the parameter λ in this modeling scheme is that $1\text{-}e^{-\lambda t}$ gives the probability that a default will occur sometime in the next t years. Let's summarize what we just stated.

- λ: Default intensity

- The probability of default at time t years: $1-e^{-\lambda t}$

- The expected time to default: $1/\lambda$

Here is a simple example of default intensity: Suppose that a newly founded venture company has a constant default intensity, λ, of 0.05. This means that the probability that this new company will default within the next year is

$$1 - e^{-0.05 \times 1} = 4.88\% \qquad [15]$$

In terms of the expected time to default, 1/0.05 is exactly twenty years. In other words, it is likely that this new company will default in twenty years, which also then can be seen as the life expectancy of the company.

Coming up with an actual value for default intensity is difficult (we cover some of the reasons why in the appendix in this chapter, which is meant for the mathematically interested reader). Still, though, we can discuss how default intensity might change over time.

Default Intensity over Time

The preceding section describes the Poisson process as a continuous draw from a distribution, where every now and then the draw returns a 1 instead of the customary 0. The 1 then becomes the signal for default. From a mathematical point of view, you can choose to keep the distribution the same over time by always applying the same mean and variance. You can also allow for the distribution to change over time. Within the framework of the Poisson process, taking the latter approach makes the model more realistic because a company's default probability changes over time based on its financial results and business news. On the flip side, however, letting default intensity change over time adds a level of complexity when we apply the model to real-world situations. Let's use an example to understand this complexity.

Every so often, new information about a company becomes available; stock prices might change or new business events unfold. These new pieces of information affect the likelihood that the company will default. If you are looking to calculate average default intensity for a company over an extended period of time, you have to take such changes into consideration. Here's a simple situation: We are looking for the average default intensity of company ABC Inc. over two years. For each year, the company might either default or continue to exist. If it survives, its default intensity might either increase or decrease. We further assume that no new information arrives during the first year, and that default intensity doesn't change for two years. This can be shown in a binomial tree diagram, as in Figure 4-1.

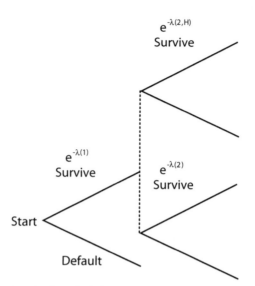

Figure 4-1 Survival probabilities with randomly changing intensity

Source: Adapted from Darrell Duffie and Kenneth J. Singleton. *Credit Risk: Pricing, Measurement, and Management*. New Jersey: Princeton University Press, 2003.

where

- $\lambda(t)$ = Default intensity at time t

- $\lambda(t,H)$ = The higher default intensity at time t

- $\lambda(t,L)$ = The lower default intensity at time t

- $P(t)$ = Survival probability at time t

The company comes into existence at time t=0. The probability of survival one year from now, T=1, can be represented as

$$e^{-\lambda t} \qquad [16]$$

Let's assume that it survives its first year of operations; in the binomial tree in Figure 4-1, we arrive at time t=1. As the tree shows, at t=1, we have three possible cases for the next year. First, the company could default. Second, it could survive with increased default intensity, denoted as $\lambda(2,H)$. The probability of this is denoted as q. Third, the firm could survive but with lower default intensity, denoted as $\lambda(2,L)$ with the probability of $(1 - q)$.

Taking all these options into consideration, the survival probability for the company after the second year, p(2), would be

$$p(2) = e^{-\lambda(1)} \times [qe^{-\lambda(2,H)} + (1-q)e^{-\lambda(2,L)}] \qquad [17]$$

Note that the default intensity changes for every time interval. In the case where the time interval is one year, it can be shown that a more general way to express survival probability for year t, P(t), is

$$P(t) = E[e^{-[\lambda(1)+\lambda(2)+\cdots+\lambda(t)]}] \qquad [18]$$

With continual change of default intensity for year t, the survival probability is rewritten as follows:

$$p(t) = E[e^{-\int_0^t \lambda(s)\,ds}] \qquad [19]$$

where

- s = Short time

- $\lambda(s)$ = The default intensity during the very short time s

Of course, the time frame needed to measure survival probability is not necessarily from time 0 to time t. We can generalize the formula to describe any time frame from a current time t to a further future time T as follows:

$$p(t, T) = E[e^{-\int_t^T \lambda(s)\,ds}] \qquad [20]$$

EXAMPLE OF DEFAULT INTENSITY OVER TIME

Let us exemplify. Suppose that ABC Inc. plans to issue a two-year bond. As an investor, you want to examine ABC Inc.'s survival probability over two years. Is the company going to be around in two years to honor its obligations? As the basis, we will simply assume a few default intensities that you need to carry out the calculations. (In the appendix to this chapter, we discuss how values for default intensities can be obtained, based on advanced mathematics.) The values you need are given in Table 4-6.

Table 4-6 Default intensity for ABC Inc.

$\lambda(1) = 0.1$
$\lambda(2,H) = 0.15$
$\lambda(2,H) = 0.15$
$\lambda(2,L) = 0.05$
Probability for higher default intensity year 2 = 0.4

Plugging these values into the formula gives us

$$p(2) = e^{-0.1} \times [0.4 \times e^{-0.15} + (1 - 0.4) \times e^{-0.05}] = 0.828 \qquad [21]$$

The survival probability of ABC Inc. over two years is 82.8 percent. You have an 82.8 percent chance of receiving the full principal back from ABC Inc. at maturity. Conversely, the default probability for ABC Inc. (which is what we have calculated in previous examples) is 17.2 percent.

APPENDIX TO CHAPTER 4

In this chapter, we have introduced two approaches to credit risk modeling, in addition to the structural approach that we covered in Chapter 3. The last approach that we covered in this chapter—the reduced form approach—built on the concept of default intensity. The first model that actively used the concept of default intensity came from Robert Jarrow and Stuart Turnbull in 1995.[6] This appendix gives a quick overview of their model, which in itself is rather mathematically advanced and thus requires a greater level of mathematical analysis.

The Jarrow-Turnbull Model

Jarrow and Turnbull constructed their model based on two classes of zero-coupon bonds: a risk-free zero-coupon bond and a risky zero-coupon bond. The value, D, of these two debt classes was denoted as

$$D_{riskfree}(t, T) \text{ and } D_{risky}(t, T) \qquad [22]$$

where

- t = Current time

- T = Maturity time

Jarrow and Turnbull showed that when default intensity was held constant, the risky debt's value could be calculated as

$$D_{risky}(t, T) = [e^{-\lambda \mu (T-t)} + (1 - e^{-\lambda \mu (T-t)})\delta] \times D_{riskfree}(t, T) \qquad [23]$$

where

- t = Current time

- T = Maturity time

- λ = Default intensity

- μ = Market price of default risk (positive constant less than 1)

- δ = Recovery rate

Finding Default Intensity

One parameter that naturally is difficult to estimate in the Jarrow-Turnbull model, as in all reduced form models, is the default intensity, λ, itself. This complicates things as it is the foundation of the whole model. The reason why it is difficult to observe is fairly straightforward: A firm that is currently active has by definition never defaulted, and because default intensity is really a measurement of something that has happened (or an event that has arrived, to put it in Poisson distribution terms), it can hardly be observed. There are of course exceptions—some bankrupt companies are restructured and brought back—but if you look at historical data, most companies have no record of default. A very limited number have one default in their past, and an even more limited number have more than one. Think of this in practical terms: U.S. computer giant IBM has been around since 1911 and has never defaulted. Neither has French car manufacturer Renault, which was founded in 1898. If you want to estimate the default intensity for these two companies, there would be no historical data telling you how often defaults occur for them. In almost all such cases, you cannot estimate the default intensity parameter by looking directly at the default data of the companies you are analyzing.

However, we have come across this problem of unobservable parameters before. We had the same problem when estimating asset volatility in the Merton model. The solution then was to try and imply the value we needed from other existing data. We reuse that idea here, and look for implied default intensity in already traded securities. For example, if a company has two bond issues outstanding, and we can observe the spread of one bond issue, but not of the other, which has not been traded in a while, we can use the Jarrow-Turnbull model to calculate the implied default intensity for the bond issue whose credit spread we do observe. We then apply that default intensity to the company's other bond issue. Put differently, we take the Jarrow-Turnbull formula and solve for the parameter λ such that the formula comes up with the same price that the bond is traded at in the market. Using industry lingo, we calibrate the formula so that it perfectly prices the bond issue we observe. We then use this value for λ for calculating the spread of the other bond issue.

This is but one example of how the Jarrow-Turnbull model is used. An even more common way is to find the implied default intensity for a company's bond issue and use that value to price the derivatives written on the credit risk of that company such as credit default swaps.

Example Using Jarrow-Turnbull

Let's demonstrate how to use the Jarrow-Turnbull model. The company Bacme Ltd. has a single bond issue outstanding. For every $1,000 US of that bond issue, it has a market value of $792.87. The bond has four years to maturity, and it is not giving any coupons. The firm's investment bank has told the firm that the market price of default risk, μ, for all firms in that industry is 0.5 and that the expected recovery rate, δ, for firms in that industry is 0.8. The risk-free rate at this time is constant at 5 percent.

Bacme Ltd. is now considering issuing another bond and would like to calculate the marginal credit spread on that bond. In other words, what would be the credit spread for the first dollar issued on that new bond issue? Compared to the already issued bond, the new bond issue has a maturity of 8 years and is senior to the first issue, so the expected recovery rate is higher, assumed at 0.85.

To calculate the marginal credit spread, Bacme Ltd. can use any one of a number of credit risk models, such as the Merton or Z-score models. However, the company has decided to use the Jarrow-Turnbull model. It has all the parameters for that model to price the new issue—except for default intensity. Bacme therefore starts by calculating the implied default intensity, using its outstanding bond issue. Plugging the numbers it has into equation [23] gives the following:

$$792.87 = [e^{-\lambda x 0.5(4-0)} + (1 - e^{-\lambda x 0.5(4-0)})0.8] \times 1000 e^{-5\% x 4}{}^{7} \qquad [24]$$

Solving for λ, the default intensity, provides Bacme with a λ of 0.0859. Armed with this default intensity, Bacme can now use the same formula once more to come up with market price for its new bond issue:

$$D_{risky}(0,7) = [e^{-0.0859 x 0.5(7-0)} + (1 - e^{-0.0859 x 0.5(7-0)})0.85] \times 1000 e^{-5\% x 8} = \$677.22 \quad [25]$$

With this implied market price, Bacme can then calculate the marginal credit spread, which is what it is after in the first place. First, it calculates the yield of the new risky bond (see Chapter 3 to recall how to do this) as follows:

$$\frac{-1}{7}\ln(677.22/1000) = 0.0557 = 5.57\% \qquad [26]$$

The credit spread on the risky zero-coupon bond is calculated as yield on risky bond minus yield on risk-free bond, or expressed in numbers:

$$5.57\% - 5\% = 0.57\% \qquad [27]$$

The credit spread for this particular debt, in a Jarrow-Turnbull economy, is therefore 0.57 percent or 57 basis points.

Just to compare the two bond issues, Bacme Ltd. uses the same formula to calculate the spread for the original bond:

$$\frac{-1}{4}\ln(792.87/1000) = 0.0580 = 5.80\% \qquad [28]$$

This gives a credit spread of 0.80 percent or 80 basis points.

The numbers tell us that—given the parameters we have set up—we obtain a slightly downward sloping credit curve. Because we also have a higher recovery rate for the second bond, we also consequently get a lower credit spread on the new debt.

Sensitivity Analysis of Jarrow-Turnbull Model

In Chapter 3, we submitted the Merton model to a number of so-called sensitivity tests. We saw how the outcome of the model reacted as we changed the values of its underlying parameters. Let us now submit the Jarrow-Turnbull model to the same type of sensitivity tests. We will look at how the credit spread that the model produces changes as we change the baseline parameters described in Table 4-7.

Table 4-7 Baseline data for the Jarrow-Turnbull sensitivity analysis

Risk-free interest rate	5.00%
Current time (t)	0
Market price of default risk (μ)	0.5
Default intensity (λ)	0.2
Recovery rate	0.8

As a starting point, the credit spread sensitivity given this baseline data is shown in Figure 4-2.

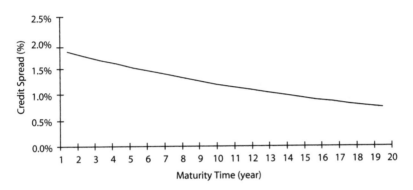

Figure 4-2 Credit spread sensitivity for Jarrow-Turnbull example

Credit Spread Sensitivity Against Maturity Time by Default Intensity

The aim of our first sensitivity test is to see how the credit spread reacts to changes in default intensity. We use three different default intensity levels, which we plug into the Jarrow-Turnbull formula shown earlier in equation 23. In addition to our baseline default intensity level of 0.20, we look at default intensity levels 0.10 and 0.05 over maturities that run from 1 year to 20 years. Figure 4-3 shows the resulting graph.

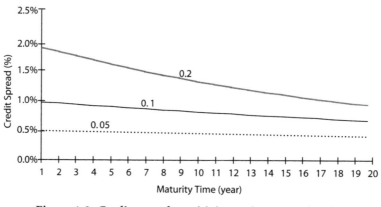

Figure 4-3 Credit spread sensitivity against maturity time
by default intensity

As we can tell from the graph, the greater the default intensity, the greater the credit spread. This is hardly surprising: A higher default intensity by definition renders the default event more likely, making the bond riskier and forcing investors to ask for more compensation to invest in that bond.

The graph also illustrates that no matter what the default intensity is, the credit spread declines for the longer maturities. Intuitively, this might appear strange: Holding on to a debt for longer times increases the risk exposure, and so investors should be asking for a higher return, which should be demonstrated by a higher credit spread. However, the opposite occurs because of a Jarrow and Turnbull assumption: The recovery rate is constant against the face value of risky debt. As a default occurs, the actual loss is then given by multiplying the debt's face value by one minus the recovery rate. Because the recovery rate is the same for a 1-year bond as it is for a 20-year bond, the present value of the loss is smaller for longer maturities than for shorter ones—thus, the smaller the potential loss, the lower the credit spread requested by the investor.

The figure also shows us that all curves have an inverse shape—and that they in fact converge to about 1 percent as maturity times start to exceed 20 years. In other words, the curves tell us that the higher the default intensity, the higher the credit spread sensitivity. Low default intensity levels, such as 0.05 in the preceding figure, are not affected much by increased length in time to maturity.

Credit Spread Sensitivity Against Maturity Time by Recovery Rate

Figure 4-4 shows how the credit spread reacts over maturity times as we change the recovery rate. This sensitivity test has been run under the same conditions used in the previous sensitivity test in Figure 4-3 except this time, the default intensity has been kept constant at 0.20. The recovery rate levels we test the model against are 0.1, 0.5, and 0.8.

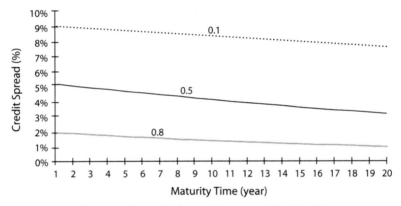

Figure 4-4 Credit spread sensitivity against maturity time by recovery rate

The graph illustrates that the smaller the recovery rate, the greater the credit spread. This is as one would expect: The lower the potential recovery, the more money will be lost by the lenders, who in turn will ask for higher compensation.

The graph also shows that the credit spread decreases as times to maturity increase. The explanation is the same as for Figure 4-3: Because the model assumes a constant recovery rate no matter the maturity, the present value of losses is smaller for longer maturities than for shorter ones. Note, however, that unlike in our previous example, the lines, although still inverse, are now more linear. In other words, the slope of the curves is driven almost exclusively by the recovery rate, and not by the maturity time.

Endnotes

1   For the original seminal paper, see Edward I. Altman, "Financial Ratios, Discriminant Analysis and the Prediction of Corporate Bankruptcy," *Journal of Finance* (September 1968), pages 589-609.

2   Regression analysis refers to methods that determine how a dependent variable and one or more independent variables are associated to each other. Regression analysis helps to model and explore the relationship between several variables.

3   For instance, see Altman, E.I., "Corporate Financial Distress: A Complete Guide to Predicting, Avoiding and Dealing with Bankruptcy," (New York: Wiley & Sons, 1983), page 122.

4   Ibid.

5   The distribution model is named after its discoverer, the French mathematician Siméon-Denis Poisson (1781–1840).

6   For their paper, see Robert Jarrow and Stuart Turnbull, "Pricing Derivatives on Financial Securities Subject to Credit Risk," *Journal of Finance* (1995), volume 50 (1), pages 53-86.

7   The variable e represents **the exponential function**, one of the most important functions in mathematics. It can be written either as $\exp(x)$ or e^x.

Part III

TYPICAL CREDIT DERIVATIVES

Chapter 5   Credit Default Swaps   147

Chapter 6   Collateralized Debt Obligations   191

5

CREDIT DEFAULT SWAPS

Part I, "What Is Credit Risk?" established the foundations of credit risk, discussing concepts such as default, probabilities of default, and credit spreads. Part II, "Credit Risk Modeling," then focused on how credit risk models can be used to describe defaults and default probabilities. We focused on the structural approach to credit risk modeling, most notably the Merton model, and also looked at examples of empirical and reduced form models.

In the third and final part of this book, "Typical Credit Derivatives," we now look at credit derivative instruments that help us manage credit risk. Chapter 2, "About Credit Risk," contained a quick overview of credit derivatives, and we now focus on two specific instruments: credit default swaps (CDSs) and collateralized debt obligations (CDOs), devoting a chapter to each. As we know from earlier chapters, the main objective of credit derivatives is to transfer credit risk from those that have it but do not want it, to those that are willing to accept it for a fee. In the coming chapters, we are not only going to describe the mechanics of the instruments, but we will also use the credit risk models from Part II to calculate a fair value of that fee.

What Are Swaps?

One of the most fundamental credit derivative instruments in the market is **credit default swaps** or **CDSs**. Conceptually, CDSs build on a financial technique known quite simply as a **swap**. Before we launch into a discussion on CDSs, let's review the traditional swap.

A swap is exactly what it sounds like: an exchange of one thing for another. In a financial context, the exchange typically consists of one cash flow being exchanged for another cash flow. Put more generally, a financial swap is the exchange of one security's return for another security's return. Typical financial swaps include interest rate swaps (where one party normally exchanges a fixed-rate interest stream for another party's floating-rate interest stream) and total return swaps, where party A pays the total return of a security—for example, the S&P 500—to party B and party B pays the total return of another security—for example, the Nasdaq 100—to party A.

A Typical Swap: Interest Rate Swap

Interest rate swaps are generally used by companies that want to change their exposure to interest rate fluctuations. A company that believes interest rates will drop, and that wants to benefit from that drop, can enter into a swap whereby it exchanges the cash flow of any fixed-rate bonds it has issued for the cash flow of floating-rate bonds. The floating-rate leg of the swap is tied to a reference interest rate in the international financial markets, such as LIBOR.[1] The party offering the floating-rate bonds in exchange for the fixed-rate bonds is looking to avoid any exposure to interest rate fluctuations. Generally speaking, a swap can involve any combination of fixed-to-floating, fixed-to-fixed, or floating-to-floating rate.

Let's exemplify. Figure 5-1 shows a swap between AAA Corp and BBB Corp, in which AAA Corp agrees to pay a fixed rate of 5 percent semiannually on $100 million for three years. In return, BBB Corp agrees to pay the going LIBOR rate semiannually on the same $100 million, also for three years.

Figure 5-1 Diagram of interest rate swap

Every six months for the three years of the swap contract, AAA Corp gives BBB Corp $2.5 million, and BBB Corp gives AAA Corp the amount due given the LIBOR at that time. Practically speaking, the two companies do not exchange the full cash flows. Instead, they determine the difference to see who owes who money. Any actual cash payment between two companies is thus determined by the difference in cash flows. It is this net difference that is actually paid.

Table 5-1 gives an example of how the cash flow payments could look between the two firms, based on assumptions of how the LIBOR evolved over time. The figure shows the cash flows to BBB Corp from AAA Corp.

Table 5-1 Cash flows for an interest rate swap
(from BBB Corp's perspective)

Time	6-Month LIBOR (%)	Fixed Cash Flow ($ Million)	Floating Cash Flow ($ Million)	Net Cash Flow ($ Million)
6 months	4.60%	2.50	-2.30	0.20
12 months	4.70%	2.50	-2.35	0.15
18 months	5.00%	2.50	-2.50	0.00
24 months	5.30%	2.50	-2.65	-0.15
30 months	5.40%	2.50	-2.70	-0.20
36 months	5.70%	2.50	-2.85	-0.35
Total				-0.35

As the figure shows, after the first six months, AAA Corp owes BBB Corp $2.5 million, and BBB Corp owes AAA Corp $2.3 million, given a LIBOR at the time of 4.6 percent. AAA Corp pays the difference of $0.2 million to BBB Corp. After the next six-month period, LIBOR has increased to 4.7 percent, decreasing the payment from AAA Corp to BBB Corp to $0.15 million. The figure shows the net payments for every period during the three years of the swap contract between the two companies. As it shows, in the end, BBB Corp ends up having paid AAA Corp $0.35 million.

Theoretically, you could swap any type of cash flows. Instead of the interest rates used in the preceding example, you could have a monthly swap of the return of the S&P 500 Index[2] for the return on a three-month U.S. Treasury Bill. Each month, you would look at the return of the three-month T-Bill and at the last month's return on the S&P 500 index, and you would exchange the difference between these two. Put differently, the net receiver is paid by the other party. Because the returns on the S&P 500-index and the three-month T-Bill are expressed in percentage points, the net difference is by default also expressed in percentage points. We want to arrive at a money value, so we multiply the percentage difference by some **notional amount**. In our previous example of AAA Corp and BBB Corp, the notional amount was $100 million. The size of the notional amount is defined in the swap contract.

A Comment on Pricing Swaps

Our preceding AAA Corp and BBB Corp example covers the mechanics of a swap. However, we left out one important aspect: how to price a swap. Suppose you were asked to pay the return on the S&P 500 in exchange for the one-month return on the three-month T-Bill. (This is the scenario we just described.) Would you be happy with that arrangement as it is or would you like an up-front payment before agreeing to the contract? In other words, what is the fair value of the swap? If it is unfavorable to you to give the counterparty payments based on the S&P 500, the swap has negative value to you and positive value to the counterparty. If it is favorable to you to pay the counterparty based on the S&P 500, the opposite is true.

This example illustrates that every swap has an implicit value to each party. Normally, in a fixed-for-floating swap, the fixed portion—or the fixed **leg**—is set such that the overall value for both parties is zero. It doesn't have to be that way, but then one party has to make an up-front payment. If the fixed amount is set too low, the swap has a positive value to the person receiving the floating end, and he has to make an up-front payment to the person receiving the fixed leg to convince him to enter into the swap.

Returning to our S&P 500-for-a-T-Bill example, what is the value of that swap? Should one of the parties make a payment to the other? Most people would guess that the person receiving the S&P 500 returns is better off, because returns on stocks often are higher than the coupons paid on Treasury Bills. However, let's decompose the swap and fully examine the situation. We know that party A is paying S&P 500 return to party B. In return, party B is paying the one-month return on a three-month U.S.

Treasury Bill. It appears that party A is worse off, and that the swap has negative value to him. If this is true, party A should ask for a compensating up-front payment from party B. However, before we ask party B to pay that fee, let's look at the swap from another perspective. Imagine that, instead of using a swap, parties A and B do the following: First, party A buys $100 million in S&P 500 stocks and hands that stock over to party B. Party B now receives the return on S&P 500 stocks worth a notional of $100 million. In exchange, party B gives party A $100 million worth of three-month T-Bills. Party A now receives the return on these T-Bills every month, based on a notional of $100 million. We have **replicated** the swap. We let each party buy $100 million worth of stock or Treasury Bills and hand those securities over to the other party. The replication shows that the swap actually has a value of zero. Each party spends $100 million, which makes them even; it is a fair swap that needs no up-front payment.

Whether or not the stocks will have a higher return than the bonds is of no interest to pricing the swap. However, the difference in return is the speculative basis on which both parties choose to enter the contract; they just happen to take the opposing view on which of the two instruments that will have the higher return. Without different views on that matter, there would be no need for a swap.

Note that our discussion here centers on whether one of the parties wants an up-front payment to enter into the contract. Naturally, a swap generally includes a fee that the protection buyer pays the protection seller; how to determine the fee that is paid for the protection that a CDS gives is the topic of the section "Pricing Single-Name CDSs Using the Structural Approach" later in this chapter.

Credit Default Swaps Defined

Now that we have established how swaps work and introduced their pricing aspect, we are ready to address the focus of this chapter: credit default swaps. Like any swap, the CDS is an exchange of two payments: on the one hand a fee payment and on the other a payment that only occurs if a credit default event happens. As a tool, the CDS is written to cover against the event that an entity or reference asset defaults on its obligations. A comparison with insurance coverage is natural: You pay for home insurance to reimburse any lost value if you are the victim of burglary or damage; and you pay a fee for health and life insurance to pay a sum in the event of injury or death. Insurances use burglary, injury, or death as the events that prompt compensation, where the CDS uses default of the underlying security to trigger payment.[3]

A Standard Credit Default Swap (CDS)

CDSs exist in many variants, and we start with the basic, **plain vanilla**, credit default swap. The plain vanilla CDS involves two parties that enter into an agreement whereby one party pays the other a periodic fee during a specified time in exchange for a much larger payment should a predefined credit event occur during that time period. If the credit event never occurs, the other party does not have to make any payment. Figure 5-2, repeated from Chapter 2, shows the relationship.

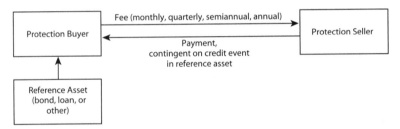

Figure 5-2 Diagram of plain vanilla credit default swap

The fee that the protection buyer pays the protection seller is calculated as a fraction of the notional amount of the reference asset. The fee is often referred to as the **credit default swap spread** or **credit default spread premium**, and is paid periodically (monthly, quarterly, semiannually, or yearly).

The credit event is tied to the development of a reference asset such as a bond, loan, or another financial liability. It is easy to think of a typical credit event as a default on a bond, bankruptcy by a firm, or debt restructuring in a company, but the credit event can also be defined more loosely—as a credit spread widening, a rating downgrade, or any other exogenous event. The two swap counterparties can define the credit events as they see fit in the contract that binds them. As an aid, the International Swaps and Derivatives Association (ISDA) has developed standard definitions and documentation to simplify the use of CDSs.

The first party in a CDS swap is looking for protection against a default; we'll refer to him as the **protection buyer** or **risk hedger**. The other party offers that cover for a fee; let's call her the **protection seller** or **risk buyer**. (Returning to the option terminology we developed in Chapter 3, "Modeling Credit Risk: Structural Approach," the protection buyer could be said to be going short the credit, and the protection seller is going long the credit.)

If the credit event occurs, the CDS contract is terminated and the termination payment takes place. The CDS contract defines one of two payment scenarios. The first option is to use **physical settlement**, through which the protection buyer has to present the defaulted asset to the protection seller to obtain the termination payment. If a physical settlement is required, the termination payment becomes the full face value of the asset reference. The second option is **cash settlement**, whereby the protection buyer keeps the asset. In this case, the payment becomes the difference between the face value of the reference asset and its recovery value. The recovery value and the value of the asset after default are then normally assessed by an independent assessor.

Let's exemplify. Suppose the protection buyer enters into a five-year CDS for a $1,000 bond. He agrees to pay a semiannual fee of $5 to the protection seller; the fee equals a 1 percent annual premium on the notional amount. In return, the protection seller compensates the protection buyer if the bond issuer fails to make its coupon interest payments. As it turns out, the bond issuer does fail to make coupon payments after three years (or 36 months). Because the CDS contract does not specify physical settlement, an independent party is called to assess the recovery value of the bond. The assessor sets the recovery value to $400. The protection seller then pays the difference between the face value and the recovery value—in this case, $600. (If the contract had specified physical settlement, the protection buyer would have delivered the defaulted asset to the protection seller and received the full face value, $1000, as termination payment.) Table 5-2 outlines the cash flow for this example.

Table 5-2 Cash flows for a plain vanilla CDS ($ million) where default occurs after 36 months

Time	Recovery Value of $1,000 Bond	Fee to Protection Seller	Contingent Payment to Protection Buyer	Net Cash Flow to Protection Buyer
6 months	NA	$5	$0	-$5
12 months	NA	$5	$0	-$5
18 months	NA	$5	$0	-$5
24 months	NA	$5	$0	-$5
30 months	NA	$5	$0	-$5
36 months	$400	$5	-$600	$595
Total				$570

Having looked at the simplest form of a CDS, we can now present some variations on credit default swaps.

Digital Credit Default Swaps

Digital CDSs are almost identical to normal CDSs. The exception is that the recovery rate is fixed beforehand, regardless of the real value of the underlying asset at the time of default. Digital CDSs are therefore also known as **fixed-recovery CDSs** (and sometimes also referred to as **binary CDSs**). In other words, the payoff in case of default is independent of the market value of the reference asset at default. Through their construction, digital CDSs eliminate any uncertainty about the recovery rate and the payoff.

Given their distinguishing feature, digital CDSs are typically settled through cash settlement, whereby the protection seller pays out the difference between the asset's principal value and the predefined recovery value. Studies have shown that the predetermined recovery rate normally ends up being lower than the market value of the asset at the time of default. Expressed differently, the protection buyer receives a larger contingent payment with digital CDSs than for a standard CDS. This increased exposure for the protection seller normally makes the seller ask for a higher fee for a digital CDS than for a standard CDS.

Consequently, the digital credit default swap is normally viewed as more costly in hedging credit risk than a normal CDS.

Figure 5-3 shows the difference of settlement between a plain vanilla CDS and a digital credit default swap.

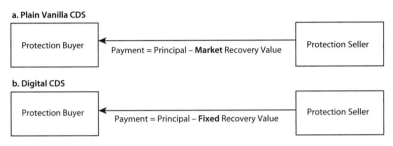

a. Plain Vanilla CDS

Protection Buyer ← Payment = Principal – **Market** Recovery Value → Protection Seller

b. Digital CDS

Protection Buyer ← Payment = Principal – **Fixed** Recovery Value → Protection Seller

Figure 5-3 Cash settlement of plain vanilla CDS versus digital CDS

To exemplify how a digital CDS works, we return to our plain vanilla CDS example from earlier. You have just bought protection from a five-year CDS for a $1,000 notional and a 1 percent credit spread. The difference this time is that your digital CDS contract predefines the recovery rate to be $350. After year three, the bond does default on its coupon payments, and the CDS goes into effect. The protection seller pays you the difference between the principal value and the predetermined recovery rate—that is, $650. Table 5-3 outlines the cash flow for this example.

Table 5-3 Cash flows for a digital CDS ($ million) where default occurs after 36 months

Time	Recovery Value of $1,000 Bond	Fee to Protection Seller	Contingent Payment to Protection Buyer	Net Cash Flow to Protection Buyer
6 months	$350	$5	$0	-$5
12 months	$350	$5	$0	-$5
18 months	$350	$5	$0	-$5
24 months	$350	$5	$0	-$5
30 months	$350	$5	$0	-$5
36 months	$350	$5	-$650	$645
Total				$620

Basket Credit Default Swaps

The plain vanilla CDS we started with in the section "A Standard Credit Default Swap (CDS)" was a **single-name** CDS, meaning that the CDS contract was written on just one single reference asset. The reference asset can also be a portfolio or group of reference assets such as several bonds or debts. The resulting CDS is then known as a **multiname** CDS. There exist several types of multiname CDSs; we can think of them as variations on the same CDS theme. One of the more common variations is the **basket CDS**, where the protection buyer is looking for protection against default on any one of the securities in the basket. A basket swap in which the protection seller has to pay the protection buyer as soon as any of these securities defaults is known as a **first-to-default** (FTD) basket CDS. The CDS contract may also define a different default security in the basket, such as the second or third security to default. The basket CDS is then known as **second-to-default** (STD) or **third-to-default**—and it can more generally be referred to as an **n^{th}-to-default** basket CDS. As we can see, these variants are similar to the plain vanilla CDS with the exception that the pay-out trigger is the nth credit event in a specified basket of reference entities. Basket CDSs are best suited for protection buyers who may tolerate one or a few defaults, but only up to a certain level.

The basket CDS is a useful instrument for protection buyers looking to shield more than one reference asset from default. As it turns out, the fee on the basket default swap is normally lower than the sum of the fees for individual CDSs on the same reference assets. From a protection seller's point of view, the basket CDS is also an attractive instrument given the limited exposure to only one of several default probabilities. This leaves the protection seller with the same exposure as in an individual CDS, but on the receiving end of a higher premium fee and thus a higher yield.

Figure 5-4 shows the general structure of a basket CDS and the relationship between the protection buyer and seller.

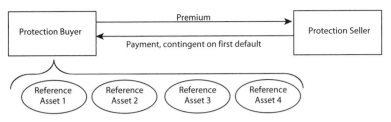

Figure 5-4 Diagram of a basket default swap

Using the figure, let's demonstrate how a basket CDS works. Assume that there is a protection buyer who seeks protection against default in any one of four different reference assets. Pooling these together as one group, she looks for a five-year protection scheme. The notional amount for each asset is $25 million and the recovery rates for all assets in this example are (for the sake of simplicity) $0.

The protection buyer enters into a CDS contract with a protection seller, who charges a fee quoted as 3 percent per year, due in semiannual payments. The semiannual payment to the protection seller becomes

$$\$25\,\text{million} \times 0.03 \times 0.5 = \$375,000 \qquad [1]$$

Note that the equation quotes the notional amount of only one asset, rather than that of all four assets. This follows the definition of this particular CDS: It is a first-to-default CDS and thus only covers the first credit event. After a default has occurred, the basket contract is terminated, and the protection buyer stops paying the fee. Like the plain vanilla CDS, settlement can be either physical or cash. In this example, we assume that the contract specifies cash settlement.

Three years into the five-year contract, one of the reference assets defaults. As specified in the contract, the basket CDS expires and the protection seller makes the termination payment. The payment is only for the defaulted asset, because the other reference assets are still non-defaulted and still generate income for the protection buyer. Table 5-4 shows the total cash flows for this basket default swap.

Table 5-4 Cash flows for a basket default swap ($ million)

Time	Fee to Protection Seller	Contingent Payment to Protection Buyer	Net Cash Flow to Protection Buyer
6 months	$0.375	$0.00	-$0.375
12 months	$0.375	$0.00	-$0.375
18 months	$0.375	$0.00	-$0.375
24 months	$0.375	$0.00	-$0.375
30 months	$0.375	$0.00	-$0.375
36 months	$0.375	-$25.00	$24.625
Total			$22.750

Portfolio Credit Default Swaps

A portfolio CDS is similar to a basket default swap in that it also references a group of reference assets. However, a portfolio CDS is different from a basket default swap in that it covers a prespecified *amount* rather than a prespecified sequential default *number* (first, second, and so on). For example, in a portfolio CDS where the prespecified amount is $10 million and the first default loss is only $5 million, the protection seller pays the $5 million to the protection buyer—and the contract is still active. Just one default does not terminate the contract, unless that default happens to match the predefined amount. A second default with a value of $5 million brings the total default to $10 million, and the contract terminates as soon as the protection seller has paid out the additional $5 million. If the CDS had been a basket swap instead of a portfolio, the contract would have terminated already after the first default.

Figure 5-5 shows a diagram of a portfolio credit default swap. It is almost identical to the diagram of a basket CDS, with the difference that it does not cease to exist until the predefined payment level has been reached.

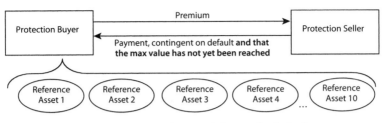

Figure 5-5 Diagram of a portfolio credit default swap

To exemplify, suppose that the protection buyer in the preceding figure is a bank with a $10 million portfolio, consisting of 10 reference assets, each valued at $1 million with a zero recovery rate. The bank enters a portfolio CDS contract, covering against the first 20 percent default losses in the portfolio. The contract is valid for five years. For this, the bank pays a 2 percent annual premium. In dollars, the premium is calculated as the premium percentage times the covered portion in the portfolio, or

$$2\% \times (20\% \times \$10,000,000) = 2\% \times \$2,000,000 = \$40,000 \qquad [2]$$

The protection seller thus receives $40,000 annually in return for covering the first 20 percent of default losses or $2 million.

Now, at the end of year two, one of the reference assets defaults, causing a loss of $1 million. The protection seller pays out the $1 million, but the CDS contract does not expire, because it has not yet reached the $2 million limit. The protection that it provides is still in place, but the premium fee does change, because 10 percent of the default limit has already been paid out. The new premium payment is calculated as

$$2\% \times (10\% \times \$10,000,000) = 2\% \times \$1,000,000 = \$20,000 \qquad [3]$$

No more defaults occur after that, and the portfolio CDS expires after five years, as agreed upon in the contract. Table 5-5 shows the total cash flows in this example.

Table 5-5 Cash flows for a basket default swap ($ million)

Time	Fee to Protection Seller	Contingent Payment to Protection Buyer	Net Cash Flow to Protection Buyer
1 year	$0.04	$0.00	-$0.04
2 years	$0.04	-$1.00	$0.96
3 years	$0.02	$0.00	-$0.02
4 years	$0.02	$0.00	-$0.02
5 years	$0.02	$0.00	-$0.02
Total			$0.86

CDS Indices: iTraxx

Traditionally, traders quote prices, credit spreads, and trading volume of individual CDSs. On an aggregate, **indices** track the development of prices and volumes for parts or all of the CDS market. Such CDS indices work like all financial indices: Their statistics reflect the combined value of a number of components. Common financial indices are stock market indices, such as the S&P 500 or Dow Jones Industrial Average, which show the composite value of a number of stocks. This value is then often used as a benchmark against which to compare the performance of other instruments or portfolios. More importantly, from a trading point of view, indices can also be used as the underlying collateral against which to write new derivative instruments.

Indices for CDSs were properly introduced in 2003, when investment banks J.P. Morgan and Morgan Stanley launched the market's first index, known as Trac-X. Trac-X built on the banks' experience with products known as synthetic TRACERS, tradable baskets of 50 investment-grade CDSs. Soon after the launch of Trac-X, a rival CDS index called iBoxx appeared on the market, launched by a group of American and European banks. In the spring of 2004, Trac-X and iBoxx merged, and management of the new combined index was given to Dow Jones & Company, Inc. The index has since been known as **Dow Jones iTraxx** (primarily for regional indices for Europe and Asia) or **Dow Jones CDS indices** (for North America).

The arrival of these CDS indices helped push the market's liquidity and transparency, because prices and products were now more readily available for all market participants. It also helped widen the product range, because derivative instruments could now be created off the index. Already at the end of their first year of operation in 2003, indices accounted for 11 percent of the credit derivative market in 2003.[4]

iTraxx contains 125 equally weighted default swaps, composed of both investment grade CDSs and speculative, high-yield CDSs. CDSs are chosen to be part of the index based on their liquidity (the higher their liquidity, the more likely they are to be included in the index), credit quality (a sufficient number of both investment and noninvestment grade CDSs has to be included), and lack of counterparty conflict (CDS issuers that are also large users of the index should not be included in the index, if possible).

USING A CDS INDEX: A NUMERICAL EXAMPLE

Just like instruments derived from stock indices, CDS indices are tradable, meaning that they can be used to write derivative instruments. For an iTraxx note, the typical maturity time is between five and ten years, and the notes are normally issued every six months by index note issuer International Index Company Ltd.[5] A typical iTraxx note is shown in Figure 5-6.

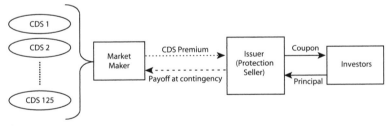

Figure 5-6 Diagram of iTraxx index note

As seen in the figure, investors enter into a contract whereby they receive coupon payments in exchange for paying a principal investment. In case of a default event in one of the underlying CDSs, the issuer pays the investors based on the weight of the defaulted CDS. The contract does not expire, because all the remaining CDSs are still part of the index. However, the principal value of the note does decrease to adjust for the removal of the defaulted CDS. This also affects the coupon payments, which are set as a percentage of the principal.

The left part of Figure 5-6 shows the market maker can view the issuer as a CDS protection seller. The market maker pays the issuer premiums in exchange for a payoff in case one of the reference entities defaults. If a default occurs, the issuer/protection seller then pays the asset's par value to the market maker while the market maker delivers the actual asset to the issuer. The total notional amount of the index note decreases by the notional amount of the defaulted CDS, and the fee that the protection seller receives is revised accordingly.

For a numerical example, suppose that an issuer launches an iTraxx Europe note with a principal (or par) value of €100 million and a maturity of five years. The note pays a quarterly coupon of three-month Euro LIBOR + 40 basis points (or 0.40 percent) per year on a notional amount of €100 million. We assume that the three-month Euro LIBOR is 4 percent annually, which means that the annual coupon becomes 4.4 percent. In money value, investors who purchase the note then receive a coupon of €4.4 million per year (or €1.1 million every quarter) from the issuer.

The issuer in turn receives a fee from the market maker (the left side of Figure 5-6). We'll say that this fee is three-month Euro LIBOR plus 36 basis points per year, still on a principal of $100 million. In money terms, the annual fee becomes 4.36 percent times €100 million, or €4.36 million, which per quarter becomes €1.09 million. (The difference of €0.01 million is the gain that the issuer makes on the transaction.)

Now, at the end of year two, a credit event occurs on one of the reference entities in the index. The credit event results in the termination of that CDS, which has been included in the note together with iTraxx's 125 default swaps, all equally weighted. This gives the defaulted reference entity a weighting of 0.8 percent (or 1/125). We assume that the recovery rate of this particular reference entity is 20 percent. Based on the amount of the asset's value that can be recovered, the investor is awarded a certain cash settlement. Given the numbers, this settlement becomes:

$$0.8\% \times €100,000,000 \times 20\% = €800,000 \times 20\% = €160,000 \qquad [4]$$

The default also means that the notional amount that the investor has put into the note will drop to

$$(100\% - 0.08\%) \times €100,000,000 = €99,200,000 \qquad [5]$$

The coupon rate stays the same (three-month Euro LIBOR + 40 basis points per annum) but because the notional amount now has changed, the money value of the quarterly coupon also drops and becomes €1.091 million.

The CDS default also affects the relationship between the issuer (or protection seller) and the market maker that holds the CDSs. The default provokes the contingent payment from the protection seller, calculated as

$$0.8\% \times €100,000,000 = €800,000 \qquad [6]$$

In return for the payoff, the market maker delivers the obligations at their face value to the protection seller who can thereby recover as much as possible. From the beginning of year three, the protection seller's notional amount then drops to

$$(100\% - 0.08\%) \times €100,000,000 = €99,200,000 \qquad [7]$$

After the default event, the CDS premium remains at 36 basis points on the new notional amount of €99,200,000 until the maturity time of five years. The new quarterly CDS premium payment that the market maker pays the protection seller drops to €1.081 million.

No more credit event occurs after that, and the iTraxx index note expires at maturity after five years. Table 5-6 shows the total cash flows in this example.

Table 5-6 Cash flows for the iTraxx index note (€ million)

Time	Notional Principal	Recovery Rate	Cash Flow to Investor	Cash Flow from Issuer	Net Cash Flow to Investor
0 month	€100	20%	€0.00	-€100.00	-€100.00
3 months	€100	20%	€1.10	€0.00	€1.100
6 months	€100	20%	€1.10	€0.00	€1.100
9 months	€100	20%	€1.10	€0.00	€1.100
12 months	€100	20%	€1.10	€0.00	€1.100
15 months	€100	20%	€1.10	€0.00	€1.100
18 months	€100	20%	€1.10	€0.00	€1.100
21 months	€100	20%	€1.10	€0.00	€1.100
24 months	€100	20%	€1.10+€0.16	€0.00	€1.260
27 months	€99.20	20%	€1.081	€0.00	€1.081
30 months	€99.20	20%	€1.081	€0.00	€1.081
33 months	€99.20	20%	€1.081	€0.00	€1.081
36 months	€99.20	20%	€1.081	€0.00	€1.081
39 months	€99.20	20%	€1.081	€0.00	€1.081
42 months	€99.20	20%	€1.081	€0.00	€1.081
45 months	€99.20	20%	€1.081	€0.00	€1.081
48 months	€99.20	20%	€1.081	€0.00	€1.081
51 months	€99.20	20%	€1.081	€0.00	€1.081
54 months	€99.20	20%	€1.081	€0.00	€1.081
57 months	€99.20	20%	€1.081	€0.00	€1.081
60 months	€99.20	20%	€1.081+€99.2	€0.00	€100.281
Total					€21.132

Pricing CDSs

From Part II of this book, we know that credit risk models can be divided into structural models, empirical models, and reduced form models. The first two approaches especially help us arrive at probabilities of default for risky debt—and they thus form the basis for pricing the derivative instruments that enable us to transfer credit risk. (As we showed in Chapter 4, "Modeling Credit Risk: Alternative Approaches," the third approach with empirical models such as the Z-score is best suited for categorizing companies as more or less likely to default. By itself, the approach does not generally produce a default probability for a company or for a liability.)

In this section, we look at how structural and reduced form credit risk models help us price credit default swaps. We first look at how they can be used to price single-name CDSs (swaps written with just one single reference asset as collateral). We then move on to a discussion of various techniques for pricing multiname CDSs (such as basket or portfolio CDSs, which are written on a group of reference assets). Our discussion on multiname CDSs continues in more detail in Chapter 6, "Collateralized Debt Obligations," which is fully devoted to this particular multiname instrument.

Pricing Single-Name CDSs Using the Structural Approach

When single-name CDSs are priced, the underlying reference asset can be one of many instruments such as a bond, a loan, or any other potentially risky debt. The fee that the protection buyer pays the protection seller is calculated based on the default probability of that one reference asset. As we know by now, we use credit risk models to arrive at default probability values. We'll now look at how to use both structural and reduced form models to price single-name CDSs, starting with the structural approach.

Pricing CDSs involves making a distinction between the payment stream going from the protection buyer to the protection seller and the stream going in the opposite direction. (Refer to Figure 5-2 for a graphic illustration of the two streams.) Each stream is often referred to as a **leg** of the CDS. The periodic fee or premium that is paid by the protection buyer is known as the **premium leg**. The payment that the protection seller has to pay the protection buyer in case of a credit default is called the **protection leg**. Each leg in the CDS has to be priced individually to come up with the full pricing picture of the CDS.

PRICING THE PREMIUM LEG

We start by pricing the premium leg. For this, we need the default probability as defined in the structural approach. Using the Merton model, we recall that default probability, P, in a risk-neutral world can be defined as[6]

$$P = N(-d_2) \qquad [8]$$

where the factor d_2 is given by

$$d_2 = \frac{\ln(A_0/D) + (r - \sigma_A^2/2)T}{\sigma_A \sqrt{T}} \qquad [9]$$

And where

- N(.) = Cumulative probability distribution function for a standard normal distribution
- D = Debt value
- A_0 = Asset value at time 0
- T = Maturity time
- σ_A = Asset volatility
- r = Risk-free interest rate

We can then convert the probability of default, P, at maturity T years to an annual default probability, called q. Assuming that the annual default probability is constant for each year until maturity, the probability that the obligor will not default before maturity can be written as

$$1 - (1 - q)^T \qquad [10]$$

Although deriving it is beyond the scope of this book, it can be shown that this probability is in fact the same as the P we defined in equation 8. Hence, we can solve for q and show that it is the same as

$$q = 1 - (1 - P)^{1/T} \qquad [11]$$

As we now set out to price the premium leg of our single-name CDS, let us look at the cash flow from the protection buyer to the protection seller. We know that this cash flow comes in periodic payments. For simplicity, let's assume that the payments are annual, denoting them as f, and that they are paid up-front at the beginning of the year. The fee for the first year then becomes f. The fee for the second year becomes the fee times the probability that there has been no default, or f(1-q). For the third year, the fee is f(1-q)^2, and so on. Table 5-7 shows the expected fee payment flows.

Table 5-7 Expected fee payment cash flow

Time (Year)	Expected Fee Payment
1	F
2	$f(1-q)$
3	$f(1-q)^2$
4	$f(1-q)^3$
:	
:	
T	$f(1-q)^{T-1}$

In other words, Table 5-7 shows how we take the expected fee payment for every year between year one and the last year, T. To arrive at the total expected fee payment, we then total up the fee for each year. This can be put into a general formula for the expected total fee payment from a protection buyer to a protection seller as

$$\sum_{t=1}^{T}\left[(1-q)^{t-1} * f\right] \qquad [12]$$

The formula then shows us the cash flows from the premium leg.

PRICING THE PROTECTION LEG

Let's now turn to the cash flows coming from the protection leg, which is the payment that the protection seller has to give the protection buyer if the credit event occurs. Just like the premium leg, the payment leg depends on the probability of default. The final value also depends on how much principal value can be recovered, if a default indeed occurs.

Let's denote the notional principal of the debt as D. We also denote the recovery rate as δ, and we assume that it is constant up until the debt's maturity. The difference between the two, or $1 - \delta$, is the loss rate, which we denote as L. The expected loss at default can therefore be expressed as the debt times the loss rate, or

$$D \times (1-\delta) = D \times L \qquad [13]$$

We established in our calculation for the premium leg that the default probability for the first year is q. Adding q to the expected loss at default that we just defined gives us the expected cost for the first year for the protection buyer, or the following:

$$D \times L \times q \qquad [14]$$

Because default in the second year would only occur if default did not happen in the first year, the expected cost in the second year would be

$$D \times L \times q(1-q) \qquad [15]$$

For all following years up until the year of maturity, T, the expected cost can be computed in the same way. Table 5-8 summarizes the expected costs for various years.

Table 5-8 Expected cost of default

Time (Year)	Expected Cost of Default
1	DLq
2	$DLq(1-q)$
3	$DLq(1-q)^2$
4	$DLq(1-q)^3$
:	
:	
T	$DLq(1-q)^{T-1}$

Based on Table 5-8, the expected total cost of default from the protection seller can then be summarized as

$$\sum_{t=1}^{T}[DL \times q(1-q)^{t-1}] \qquad [16]$$

Matching the Premium and Protection Legs
We now have formulas for cash flows for both legs in the credit default swap. For the CDS to be fairly priced, the total fee payment should equal the total default cost. In other words, the formulas for the premium and protection legs should match

$$\sum_{t=1}^{T}\left[(1-q)^{t-1} * f\right] = \sum_{t=1}^{T}\left[DL \times q(1-q)^{t-1}\right] \qquad [17]$$

Given values of annual default probability, maturity time, risky debt value, and loss rate or recovery rate, the preceding equation can be solved for the expected fee, denoted as f.

Let's demonstrate how to price a CDS using the structural approach. Suppose that ABC Corp issues a $100 million bond with a one-year maturity. The bond has semiannual coupon payments, and it is assumed that in case of a default, there is no recovery to be made. To fully paint the scenario, assume further that the current prevailing risk-free interest rate is 5.0 percent. The bond is summarized in Table 5-9.

Table 5-9 ABC Corp's one-year bond

Notional principal	$100 million
Recovery rate	0%
Maturity time	1 year
Payment frequency	Semiannual
Risk-free rate	5.0%

Now, suppose further that there is a bank, Secure Bank Ltd., that buys ABC's bond and then plans to enter into a CDS contract as protection in case ABC Corp defaults on the bond. (Secure Bank thus becomes the protection buyer.) The CDS premium payments are semiannual, just as for the underlying security. To gather background information on the company, Secure Bank Ltd. studies ABC Corp's balance sheet, shown in Table 5-10.

Table 5-10 ABC Corp financials (in USD millions)

Asset	150	Debt	100
		Equity	50
	150		150

Secure Bank assumes that ABC Corp's asset volatility is 40 percent.

Secure Bank now needs to determine what a fair price would be for the CDS that it wants to buy. We have all the information we need to calculate the fee that the protection seller is likely to charge, and we start by calculating the default probability for ABC Corp, using earlier equations 8 and 9. They give us [18]

$$P = N(\frac{-\ln(A_0/D)+(r-\sigma_A^2/2)T}{\sigma_A\sqrt{T}}) = N(\frac{-\ln(150/100)+(0.05-0.4^2/2)\times1}{0.4\times\sqrt{1}}) = 0.138$$

This default probability is on an annual basis. Because the CDS premium payments are semiannual, the default probability has to be converted into a six-month probability, as follows:

$$q = 1 - (1-P)^{1/t} = 1 - (1-0.138)^{1/2} = 0.0716 \text{ or } 7.16\% \qquad [19]$$

Based on this default probability, the expected total fee payment, f, to the protection seller—or the premium leg—for two payments (semiannual payments for a one-year maturity) can be calculated using equation 12 as

$$f + f(1-0.0716) = 1.9284f \qquad [20]$$

We now have the premium leg. Let's match it with the protection leg payment to obtain a value for f. Given what we know about the CDS from Table 5-9, the expected total contingent payment can be calculated using equation 16. This gives us

$$100 \times 0.0716 + 100 \times 0.0716 \times (1-0.0716) = \$7.227 \text{ million} \qquad [21]$$

Remember that to arrive at a fair price, the expected total fee payment and expected contingent payment should be equal. Hence, the expected fee payment can be obtained by solving the equation we presented in equation 17.

$$1.9284 \; f = \$7.227 \text{ million} \qquad [22]$$

$$f = \$3.748 \text{ million}$$

$3.7 million is then the total fee that the protection seller will charge for this CDS.

As a final point, we should note a key difference between calculating a credit spread for risky debt and calculating a credit premium for a CDS: The recovery rate is not required for calculating the credit spread according to the Merton model, but is an important input value for calculating the CDS's credit premium.

Pricing Single-Name CDSs Using the Reduced Form Approach

Let's now see how we can price a single-name CDS using a reduced form model instead of a structural model. Recall that to produce a credit spread or other price quote, the reduced form model requires default intensity data. (The default intensity value is used to arrive at a default probability, which is the foundation for pricing the derivative.) We'll apply this knowledge to price the same ABC Corp-based CDS that we just used, and that we defined in Table 5-9. For the reduced form model, we need one additional value that we did not already specify: We will now assume that the default intensity, λ, is constant at 0.05.

Again, we calculate the value of each of the CDS's two legs, starting with the premium leg. Recall that the probability of default at time t under the simple reduced form approach is given by

$$P = 1 - e^{-\lambda t} \qquad [23]$$

Hence, the probability that ABC Corp will default on its bond at its first payment after six months—or at time t = 0.5—with a default intensity of 0.05, is calculated as

$$P = 1 - e^{-0.05 \times 0.5} = 0.0247 \text{ or } 2.47\% \qquad [24]$$

Because we have assumed that the default intensity is constant over time, the same default probability of 2.47 percent applies for the next six months.

Armed with the default probability for each payment period, we know from equation 20 how to calculate the expected total fee payment to the protection seller. Using our new default probability, we calculate this over two semiannual payments as

$$f + f(1 - 0.0247) = 1.9753f \qquad [25]$$

We then calculate the expected total contingent payment just as we did in equation 21. It becomes

$$100 \times 0.0247 + 100 \times 0.0247 \times (1 - 0.0247) = \$4.879 \text{ million} \qquad [26]$$

And again, just as before, we match these two formulas, and solve for f.

$$1.9753f = \$4.879 \text{ million} \qquad [27]$$

$$f = \$2.480 \text{ million}$$

The protection fee, using the reduced form approach, is thus $2.5 million.

This value can be compared to the $3.7 million fee that we determined using the structural approach. As we know from earlier chapters, the approaches vary in their approach to determining defaults, and thus a difference in price should be expected. Practically, the structural approach depends much more heavily on balance sheet data than does the reduced form approach. The reduced form approach instead relies on finding a value for default intensity, which as we know from Chapter 4 is rather difficult. If we had assumed a higher or lower value for default intensity in our preceding example, the result would have been quite different—and the difference vis-à-vis the structural model's result would have changed accordingly. Therefore, we'll refrain from comparing the two results, because they depend on highly variable inputs to generate their outputs.

Pricing Multiname CDSs: Basic Concepts

We have now looked at how to price credit default swaps that are based on one reference asset. However, as we know from earlier in this chapter, there are several types of CDSs that are based on more than one reference asset. Typical examples of such multiname CDSs are basket and portfolio default swaps. Pricing a multiname CDS is intuitively more complicated than pricing a single-name CDS. First, picture a CDS based on one reference asset. The default pattern for this CDS is easy: It either defaults or it does not. Add one more reference asset, though, and the default pattern immediately gets more complicated: either both reference assets survive, both default, one defaults but not the other, or the other defaults but not the first. In total, there are four possible outcomes. Now, picture a portfolio with ten reference entities. The default pattern has 1,204 possible outcomes (or 2^{10}). To price a CDS with this number of possible outcomes using the same technique as for single-name CDSs would require calculating default probabilities for each possible outcome and then adding them up. This would be a rather time-consuming approach. Now, luckily, there exist some statistical techniques that make valuing multiname CDSs easier. We will look at two of these techniques, where the reference assets may or may not be linked to each other. If they are linked, this means that if one asset defaults, several others might be "drawn into" the default as well; we refer to this as **default correlation**. Calculating the default probabilities of reference assets given their default correlation gives us something known as the **loss distribution** of the CDS. Both default correlation and loss distribution are important concepts when valuing multiname CDSs, so before we look at how to actually price a multiname CDS, let's spend some time on these two concepts.

DEFAULT CORRELATION

The distinguishing features of a multiname CDS are that it has more than one reference asset, and that it might face more than one default in any given time horizon. Knowing the probability of any of the underlying entities defaulting lays the groundwork for determining the premium to pay for a multiname CDS. Knowing the probability of more than one default occurring at any given time helps further to set the premium. An even more important measurement is that of how likely two default events are to occur at the same time, known as **default correlation**. Figure 5-7 gives a visual representation of default correlation.

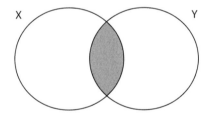

Figure 5-7 Diagram of default probabilities of two entities

Using the figure, suppose that there are two reference assets, X and Y. The circles X and Y in the preceding figure represent the default probability of assets X and Y, respectively. This default probability can also be denoted as ω_X and ω_Y. The overlap between the two circles, colored in grey, marks the probability of a joint default, denoted as $\omega_{X\&Y}$. We can now use these values to create a formula for the probability that X or Y defaults, denoted as ω_{XorY}. The formula becomes

$$\omega_{XorY} = \omega_X + \omega_Y - \omega_{X\&Y} \qquad [28]$$

Now, suppose circle X is greater than circle Y, or $\omega_X > \omega_Y$. As shown in the left panel of Figure 5-8, if the default correlation is equal to 1, circle X includes the full circle Y. This means that $\omega_{X\&Y} = \omega_X$ and $\omega_{XorY} = \omega_X$. If the default correlation is equal to zero, circle X and circle Y do not share any area, as shown in the right panel of Figure 5-8. This means that $\omega_{X\&Y}$ is zero and $\omega_{XorY} = \omega_X + \omega_X$.

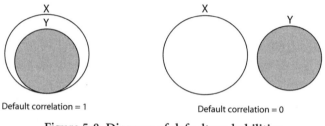

Default correlation = 1   Default correlation = 0

Figure 5-8 Diagram of default probabilities

The figure illustrates that the default probability for any of the two individual reference assets increases as default correlation decreases. Applied to a portfolio default swap, for instance, the default probability of the portfolio increases if the default correlation of the two entities approaches zero. There are simply more factors that can cause any one of the assets to default, if the reference assets don't share the same default factors. This naturally translates into a higher premium to pay for the protection buyer.

Based on equation 28 for ω_{XorY}, it can be shown that the joint default correlation of X and Y, denoted as $\rho_{X,Y}$, can be written as

$$\rho_{X,Y} \int \frac{\omega_{X\&Y} - \omega_X \omega_Y}{\sqrt{\omega_X\,(1-\omega_X)}\,\sqrt{\omega_Y\,(1-\omega_Y)}} \qquad [29]$$

where the default correlation has to be equal to or larger than -1 and equal to or smaller than 1. (In other words, $-1 \le \rho_{X,Y} \le 1$.)

LOSS DISTRIBUTION FUNCTION
When valuing multiname CDSs, it is also essential to understand the **loss distribution function**. Let's use a simple example to explain the loss distribution function by itself (before we add default correlation to the picture). Suppose that we have two reference assets. Asset A has a 100 percent default probability for a loss of 10 percent, and asset B has a 50

percent default probability for two potential losses, one of 5 percent and one of 15 percent. Both assets then have the same average expected loss of 10 percent. However, the losses are distributed differently, which has an effect on the fee that the protection seller wants to charge.

Assume now that our two assets are part of a basket default swap defined as a first-ten-percent loss default swap. For asset A, the protection seller knows she has to compensate for a 10 percent loss with 100 percent probability. For asset B, however, she has a 50 percent probability of a 5 percent loss, and a 50 percent probability of a 15 percent loss. Should the default loss of 15 percent occur, the protection seller does not have to compensate for all 15 percent, because the limit of the contract is set to 10 percent. The default probability of asset B then stays at 50 percent for the same potential loss of 10 percent. Consequently, the protection seller should ask for a lower premium for asset B than for asset A. Despite the fact that the two portfolios have an identical expected loss of 10 percent, the loss distribution gives them different credit spreads.

Let's look at another example, to which we add the concept of default correlation that we discussed in the previous section. Consider two portfolios that have the same expected loss but different default correlations: one with high default correlation and one with a low default correlation. Figure 5-9 shows possible loss distributions for these two hypothetical portfolios.

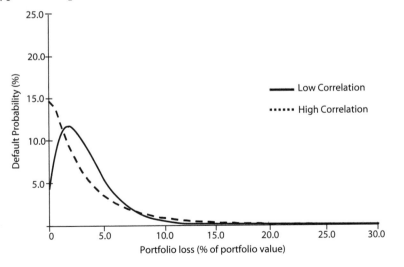

Figure 5-9 Loss distribution for two portfolios

The high correlation portfolio (represented by the dotted line) shows high probability of small losses, with the probability decreasing for higher losses. The low correlation portfolio (shown as the solid line) has a slightly different distribution profile: It has a lower probability than the other portfolio for small losses, but at around the level of 2 percent loss, its probability actually exceeds the high correlation portfolio's probability. Now, if you were the protection seller, offering a first-two-percent loss basket swap, and the fee payment on both contracts was the same, which portfolio would you choose? Naturally, you'd pick the low correlation portfolio because its probability of loss up to 2.0 percent is smaller than that of the other portfolio.

Pricing Multiname CDSs: A Basket Default Swap

As we just established, both default correlation and loss distribution affect the pricing of a multiname CDS. This section exemplifies how to price a specific type of a multiname CDS, namely the basket default swap. In fact, we use two pricing examples of two completely opposite types of basket default swaps: one with perfect positive correlation between its reference assets and one with zero correlation. In a real-world situation, it would be close to impossible to trade basket CDSs under any one of these two extremes. Most reference assets show some sort of default correlation, and the calculations would have to be adopted to handle such portfolios. Here, however, we satisfy ourselves by looking at these extreme cases, because they help us understand how default correlation affects loss distribution and consequently the CDS protection seller's payment. We will see how a portfolio with lower correlation has a higher expected loss, and consequently requires a higher fee, than a portfolio with a higher correlation. (These concepts—especially default correlation—are crucial to understanding collateralized debt obligations and are covered more extensively in Chapter 6.)

As the basis for both examples, we take a portfolio that consists of ten reference assets. Each reference asset has a value of $1 million, a risk-neutral default probability of 10 percent and a zero recovery rate. The total size of the portfolio ends up as $10 million. Table 5-11 summarizes the portfolio's profile.

Table 5-11 **Portfolio for basket default swaps**

Number of assets	10
Value of each asset (N)	$1 million
Total portfolio value	$10 million
Default probability for each individual asset (ω)	10% (identical for all assets)
Recovery rate for each individual asset	0%

Two basket default swaps are written on this portfolio: a first-to-default (FTD) swap and a second-to-default (STD) swap. Their contract term is one year, and we assume for simplicity that default can only occur at the maturity date. We will now calculate the premium fee that the protection sellers of either the FTD or STD swap would charge, for both of the two extreme cases of either full or zero default correlation.

THE ONE EXTREME: A PERFECT DEFAULT CORRELATION PORTFOLIO

We start with the example of a portfolio with perfect default correlation between its reference assets. Perfect default correlation means that if one reference asset defaults, all reference assets default. This all-for-one-and-one-for-all assumption is not far from the behavior of many CDS baskets, where reference entities tend to default or survive together as a group simply because they have similar credit quality.

The general perfect default correlation case can be described as a portfolio composed of N reference assets, where each asset has an individual default probability, ω, that is identical to all other default probabilities in the portfolio over a given time horizon. The notional principal amount of each reference asset, V, is also assumed to be identical. The default event pattern of such a portfolio is simple to describe: Either all reference assets default at the same time, or they don't. The premium fee that the protection seller requests can then be calculated as expected cost if all assets survive to maturity (survival probability times 0) plus expected cost if all assets default before maturity (default probability times value of each reference asset). Put in a formula, this becomes

$$\text{FTD premium fee} = [(1-\omega) \times 0] + [\omega \times V] \qquad [30]$$

where

- ω = Individual default probability

- V = Notional principal amount of each reference asset

Using the numbers of our sample portfolio in Table 5-11, the value of each reference asset is $1 million and the default probability is 10 percent. This gives us the information we need to calculate FTD premium fee using equation 30.

$$[(1-10\%)\times 0] + [10\% \times \$1,000,000] = \$0.1 \text{ million} \qquad [31]$$

The protection seller is thus likely to charge $100,000 for a CDS written on this particular portfolio.

Theoretically, investors in a second-to-default swap (or any other number-to-default swap) end up paying the same fee as first-to-default swap investors, because the fee is calculated from the individual amount of one reference asset. However, this is based on our assumption of complete correlation; when the first reference asset defaults, the whole portfolio defaults, and thus the risk profile and associated fee is the same no matter which number default the CDS specifies.

THE OTHER EXTREME: A NONDEFAULT CORRELATION PORTFOLIO
The other extreme case for a basket default swap is when there is no default correlation at all between the reference assets. Calculating the premium fee for investors in first- and second-to-default swaps is more complicated than in our perfect default correlation example, because the number of possible default outcomes grows exponentially. In the perfect correlation case, we had two possible outcomes: survival or default of the whole group. In the zero default correlation case, we have the number of reference assets plus one as possible default outcomes. (Either no asset defaults, or one asset defaults, or two default, or....) In our example, this generates 11 possible default outcomes.

Note that one of our assumptions is that defaults can only occur at maturity of the one-year contract. This means that if several defaults happen, they all occur jointly at the same time. We further assume that all assets are identical in terms of asset value and recovery rate. This limits the number of possible default outcomes. If we relaxed this assumption to allow for defaults to occur at any time and for longer maturities, we would theoretically end up with a maximum of 2^{10} or 1,024 possible default outcomes.

The starting point for our price calculation is to find the default distribution of our portfolio; what is the likelihood that we will have between 0 and 10 defaults at the end of the year? If one assumes that the default probabilities follow a binomial distribution, it can be shown that the probability of joint defaults i among N assets in a portfolio, or $P(i)$, can be expressed as

$$P(i) = \frac{N!}{i!\,(N-i)!} \times \omega^i \times (1-\omega)^{N-i} \qquad [32]$$

where

- ω = Individual default probability
- i = Joint default
- $i!$ = i factorial[7]
- N = Number of assets

We plug the data that we have about our sample portfolio (as presented in Table 5-11) into equation 32 to calculate the loss distribution of the ten reference assets. For each of the 11 default outcomes (for i=0 to i=10), the equation gives us the probability of that particular outcome. For instance, the probability of one default is 38.7 percent, and that of two simultaneous defaults is 19.4 percent. We then plot all the outcomes on a curve, as in Figure 5-10.

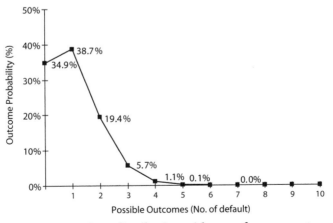

Figure 5-10 Loss distribution with ten reference assets

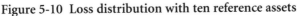

Using the default distribution, we can complete the picture by looking at the payment that the protection seller has to make in the case of a default. We do this for both our first-to-default and our second-to-default investor. Table 5-12 shows the payments, along with the outcome probabilities represented graphically in Figure 5-10.

Table 5-12 Loss distribution of ten reference assets basket swap

Outcome (Number of Simultaneous Defaults)	Probability of Outcome	Payment from First-to-Default Protection Seller	Payment from Second-to-Default Payment Seller
0	34.9%	0	0
1	38.7%	$ 1 million	0
2	19.4%	$ 1 million	$ 1 million
3	5.7%	$ 1 million	$ 1 million
4	1.1%	$ 1 million	$ 1 million
5	0.1%	$ 1 million	$ 1 million
6	0.0%	$ 1 million	$ 1 million
7	0.0%	$ 1 million	$ 1 million
8	0.0%	$ 1 million	$ 1 million
9	0.0%	$ 1 million	$ 1 million
10	0.0%	$ 1 million	$ 1 million

Note how the first-to-default investor or protection seller makes a payment directly when the first default occurs, whereas the second-to-default seller does not pay until at least two defaults occur simultaneously.

We now have the data we need to calculate the actual premium fee that the investors would charge for these basket CDSs. First, let's establish the formulas needed for both the protection and premium legs of the basket CDS. As the table in Table 5-12 shows us in numbers, the protection payment, given the recovery rate of zero, is equal to the notional amount of one reference asset, V. The expected loss, L, is then calculated as the sum of all outcome probabilities times the reference asset value

$$L = \sum_{i=1}^{N} [P(i) \times V] \qquad [33]$$

Because the protection leg has to match the premium leg in a CDS, the premium for the first-to-default (FTD) swap should be equal to the expected loss.

$$\text{FTD Premium} = L = \sum_{i=1}^{N}[P(i) \times V] \qquad [34]$$

For the second-to-default (STD) swap, the premium should be equal to the expected loss excluding the events of no default and one default.

$$\text{STD Premium} = L = \sum_{i=1}^{N}[P(i) \times V] \qquad [35]$$

Given the loss distribution that we just calculated in Table 5-12, we can calculate the expected loss of the first-to-default swap from equation 33—which is the same as its fee shown in equation 34—and which becomes

$$(38.7\% + 19.4\% + 5.7\% + 1.1\% + 0.1\%) \times \$1 \text{ million} = \$0.65 \text{ million} \qquad [36]$$

In the same way, the expected loss—and fee—for the second-to-default swap is given by equation 35.

$$(19.4\% + 5.7\% + 1.1\% + 0.1\%) \times \$1 \text{ million} = \$0.26 \text{ million} \qquad [37]$$

COMPARING THE TWO EXTREMES

We have now calculated the prices for two types of basket CDSs (first- and second-to-default) for two default correlation variations on the same basket: either perfect correlation or zero correlation. Table 5-13 summarizes what we have found.

Table 5-13 Summary of expected loss

Expected Loss and Fee to	Portfolio with	
	Zero Correlation	Perfect Correlation
First-to-default investor	$0.65 million	$0.1 million
Second-to-default investor	$0.26 million	$0.1 million

As the preceding table shows, the expected loss—and consequently the fee—of first-to-default swap investors is much lower under perfect correlation than under zero correlation. The same holds true for second-to-default investors. Intuitively, this makes sense: If the entire portfolio behaves as one asset, and all default for the same event, there must be fewer credit factors that can influence the default, and thus less credit risk. The investor or protection seller consequently asks for less of a premium. By contrast, if the reference assets have no default correlation—meaning they all default for different reasons—the level of credit risk increases, because it is more likely that one of the assets— any asset—will default; as a result, the premium fee increases as well.

In the real world, of course, no basket CDSs are based on reference assets with either perfect or zero default correlation. A normal basket CDS has a default probability somewhere between the two extremes, which in turn affects the shape of its loss distribution curve. More advanced statistical approaches than those we have shown here exist for calculating the expected loss and premium fee of these basket CDSs. However, they fall outside of the scope of this book. Our main goal here is to show how the basic concepts of loss distribution and default correlation affect the price of a basket CDS.

Pricing Multiname CDSs: A Portfolio Default Swap

Just as we priced a basket CDS, we will also show how to price another multiname CDS: the portfolio default swap. Recall from earlier in this chapter that the portfolio CDS shares many similarities with the basket CDS, with one major difference: The portfolio CDS covers a prespecified amount rather than a prespecified default number. For example, a first-ten-percent loss portfolio CDS continues to offer protection even after a default occurs, as long as that default has a value that is less than 10 percent of the portfolio. It is when the *total* default value—irregardless of the number of defaults—reaches 10 percent that the CDS terminates.

We base our example on a portfolio that consists of 20 reference assets, each with a notional amount of $1 million and an individual default probability of 10 percent. We assume that there is zero default correlation between the assets. The portfolio CDS contract is written as a first-10%-loss default swap, and it has a maturity of one year. Table 5-14 summarizes the portfolio's profile.

Table 5-14 Sample portfolio default swap

Number of assets	20
Value of each asset (N)	$1 million
Total portfolio value	$20 million
Default probability for each individual asset (ω)	10% (identical for all assets)
Recovery rate for each individual asset	0%
CDS contract protection	First 10% loss
Default correlation between reference assets	Zero

Put more generally, our sample portfolio CDS relies on some simplifying assumptions. For instance, the individual default probabilities and notional amounts are treated as identical, and the maturity time is limited to only one time period, with defaults only occurring at the end of that time period. Pricing "real-world" portfolio CDSs, which almost never meet these assumptions, would involve more complicated mathematical operations. Such an example becomes so mathematically complicated that it falls outside of the scope of this book.

Under the preceding assumptions, however, the reference assets in this sample portfolio have the same loss distribution as the basket CDS we priced earlier, because the only difference between them lies in the payoff flows. We can thus reuse equation 32 to calculate the probability of joint default outcomes with i references, denoted as $P(i)$. For simplicity, we repeat that equation:

$$P(i) = \frac{N!}{i!\,(N-i)!} \times \omega^i \times (1-\omega)^{N-i} \qquad [38]$$

where

- ω = Individual default probability

- i = Joint default

- N = Number of assets

Because the portfolio has 20 reference assets, there are 21 possible default patterns, from no default to 20 joint defaults. Using equation 38, the probability of i simultaneous defaults among 20 assets in a portfolio with individual default probability of 10 percent is calculated as

$$P(i) = \frac{20!}{i!(20-i)!} \times 0.1^i \times (1-0.1)^{20-i} \tag{39}$$

For each of our 21 default outcomes (for i=0 to i=20), we use this equation to arrive at a default probability. The result can then be plotted on a loss distribution graph, as shown in Figure 5-11.

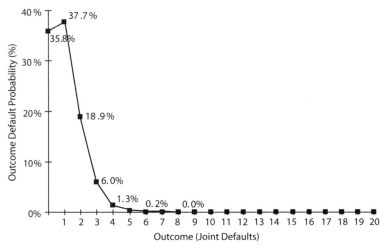

Figure 5-11 Loss distribution with 20 reference assets

Now, given the probabilities of joint default outcomes, the expected loss on a portfolio CDS can be calculated by adding up the expected loss for each of the outcomes. For each outcome, the expected loss is calculated as the default probability times the lower of two values: the default value or the remaining value up until the protection cap. As a formula, this gives us

$$FTD_{y\%} = \sum_{i=0}^{N} P(i)\, Min\big[L(i), NV \times \frac{y}{100}\big] \tag{40}$$

where

- y = Protection percentage for default loss
- $L(i)$ = Total loss in a portfolio with i defaults

- Min[L(i), NV x y/100] = Selection of the lower value between L(i) and the loss maximum level (expressed as the number of default references, N, times the notional amount, V, times the protection level)

For each of the outcomes, we then calculate the expected loss for the protection seller. Table 5-15 shows the results of those calculations.

Table 5-15 Loss distribution of 20 reference assets portfolio swap

Possible Outcomes (Number of Defaults)	Outcome Probability	Portfolio Loss ($ Million)	Payment by First-10%-Loss Protection Seller ($ Million)	Expected Loss for Protection Seller ($ Million)
0	35.8%	0	$0.00	$0.000
1	37.7%	$1.00	$1.00	$0.377
2	18.9%	$2.00	$2.00	$0.378
3	6.0%	$3.00	$2.00	$0.120
4	1.3%	$4.00	$2.00	$0.026
5	0.2%	$5.00	$2.00	$0.004
6	0.0%	$6.00	$2.00	$0.000
7	0.0%	$7.00	$2.00	$0.000
8	0.0%	$8.00	$2.00	$0.000
9	0.0%	$9.00	$2.00	$0.000
10	0.0%	$10.00	$2.00	$0.000
11	0.0%	$11.00	$2.00	$0.000
12	0.0%	$12.00	$2.00	$0.000
13	0.0%	$13.00	$2.00	$0.000
14	0.0%	$14.00	$2.00	$0.000
15	0.0%	$15.00	$2.00	$0.000
16	0.0%	$16.00	$2.00	$0.000
17	0.0%	$17.00	$2.00	$0.000
18	0.0%	$18.00	$2.00	$0.000
19	0.0%	$19.00	$2.00	$0.000
20	0.0%	$20.00	$2.00	$0.000
				$0.905

Table 5-15 shows, for each of the outcomes, first the outcome probability (which we saw graphically represented in Figure 5-11) and then the portfolio loss (which is obtained simply by multiplying the number of simultaneous defaults by the notional value of $1 million). The fourth column shows the payment that the protection seller has to make; because the protection is capped at 10 percent of the value of the $20 million portfolio, the payment never exceeds $2 million. The final column shows the expected loss for the protection seller, as computed by multiplying the default probability by the payment. As it turns out, the expected loss value is always lower than the payment. Therefore, we sum up those values to arrive at the total expected loss for the protection seller: $905,000.

As in our basket default swap example, we assume that the expected loss equals the premium fee that the protection seller will charge (for instance, refer to equation 34). In other words, the fee should cover at least the expected loss for the protection seller—who ends up charging a premium fee of $905,000, in this example.

The CDS Market

As we stated in the introduction, a credit default swap can be likened to an insurance policy; it protects against credit events and becomes a sort of default insurance. In theory, any assets that generate cash flows have a credit risk built into them—but they can all be underlined in a CDS. This flexibility, combined with the fact that a CDS can cover any amount and maturity time, explains the growing popularity of the credit default swap as a financial instrument and credit derivative.

Since 1996, the credit default swap market has seen almost 100 percent annual growth, even during the difficult financial years of the late 1990s. It is by far the largest part of the overall credit derivatives market, as shown in Figure 5-12.

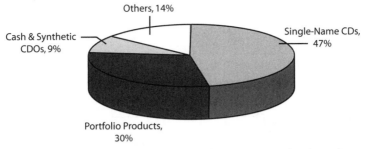

Figure 5-12 Breakdown of credit derivatives market (2003)

Source: Fitch Ratings, as referenced on http://db.riskwaters.com/public/
showPage.html?page=168496. Accessed June 2005.

It is worth noting that in addition to having a 47 percent market share in 2003 for single-name default swaps, portfolio products, as well as cash and synthetic[8] collateralized debt obligations (CDOs), use default swaps as building blocks for their instruments. In 2003, Fitch Ratings estimated the market for single-name CDSs at $1.9 trillion and portfolio products at $754 billion.[9]

The trend over the past decade has been to use increasingly diverse asset types as underlying securities for CDSs. According to the British Bankers' Association (BBA), the major type of underlined assets in 1996 was sovereign debt, which stood at 46 percent. By 2001, the percentage of sovereign debt had decreased to 15 percent as more and more corporate assets were used to create default swaps. Overall, the number of market participants has increased in the past years, resulting in increased liquidity, which in turn has attracted more market participants. The arrival of CDS indices such as iTraxx has also helped to improve the liquidity and transparency of the market.

On the buy-side of the market, the largest group of protection buyers using CDSs is the banks. (As you may recall from Chapter 2, banks are the largest protection buyers in the credit derivatives market.) Figure 5-13 shows the overall breakdown of the market by type of protection buyer.

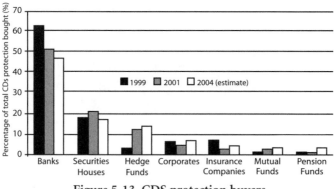

Figure 5-13 CDS protection buyers

Source: Calyon, British Bankers' Association, Fitch Ratings, as shown on
http://db.riskwaters.com/public/showPage.html?page=168229. Accessed June 2005.

Given the importance of CDSs in the credit derivatives market, other leading CDS buyers rank among the major overall buyers in the credit market. What the preceding figure shows is that, except for the top two groups of banks and securities houses, each group's market share has increased over the past few years. In absolute terms, all groups are buying more, confirming the picture of an increasingly diversified CDS market.

It is clear that banks and other entities operate on both sides of the market. In some cases, they buy protection to transfer default risk off their balance sheets, and in other cases, they act as protection sellers to earn a premium spread. On the sell-side, banks also dominate as sellers of CDS protection. This is shown in Figure 5-14.

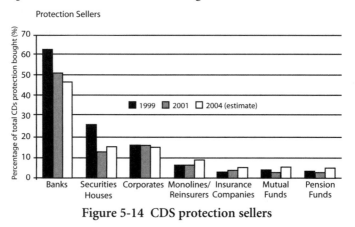

Figure 5-14 CDS protection sellers

Source: Calyon, British Bankers' Association, Fitch Ratings, as shown on
http://db.riskwaters.com/public/ showPage.html?page=168229. Accessed June 2005.

Endnotes

1   As stated in Chapter 2, LIBOR, London Inter Bank Offered Rate, is the interest rate at which London banks borrow funds from other banks. LIBOR is a widely used reference rate not only for interest rate swaps but also for other derivative instruments such as forward rate agreements.

2   The Standard & Poor's (S&P) 500 Index is an equity index that measures the collective performance of 500 leading U.S. stock companies. (Other common equity indices include the Dow Jones Industrial Average, the British FTSE 100, or the German Dax 30.) If you invest $1 in the S&P 500 at the start of the month, your *monthly return on the S&P 500* would include appreciation in stock prices plus any dividends that are paid during that month, minus the initial $1 dollar.

3   Given this definition, it is worth noting that the credit default swap is not a "pure" swap, because only one of the two cash flows is dependent on an underlying credit security. Several industry participants argue that a CDS could more accurately be referred to as a **credit default option** (see Janet Tavakoli, "Credit Derivatives and Synthetic Structures" (New York: Wiley, 2001)). However, the nomenclature in the securities market has developed to call even these types of protection-buying instruments for swaps.

4   British Bankers' Association (BBA), Credit Derivatives Report 2003/2004, page 21.

5   International Index Company Ltd. is a joint venture between several large banks. In June 2005, the financial institutions included ABN Amro, Barclays Capital, BNP Paribas, Deutsche Bank, Deutsche Börse, Dresdner Kleinwort Wasserstein, HSBC, JP Morgan, Morgan Stanley, and UBS Investment Bank.

6   We discussed this in the section, "Using Risk-Neutral Probability to Calculate Default Probability," in Chapter 3.

7   In mathematics, n! (pronounced *n factorial*) represents the factorial of a natural number, which is the product of the positive integers less than or equal to n. Here, we use the letter i, but the factorial principle remains the same. For example, if i = 5, then 5! is 5×4×3×2×1 = 120.

8   One way to define CDOs are as cash or synthetic CDOs. If the assets that underlie the CDO are acquired using cash, it becomes a cash CDO. If the assets are acquired by selling protection rather than buying assets, this is seen as a synthetic acquisition, and thus the CDO becomes a synthetic CDO.

9   Fitch Rating's "Global Credit Derivatives Survey," September 7, 2004, page 3.

6

COLLATERALIZED DEBT OBLIGATIONS

The previous chapter looked at credit default swaps (CDSs), those written on one reference asset (single-name CDSs) and those written on several reference assets (multiname CDSs). The benefit of a multiname product such as a basket or portfolio default swap is that they allow investors to invest in a combined portfolio; individual credit risk is often difficult to assess, but in a pooled group of assets, the individual risk matters less.

For credit instruments backed by a pool of assets, one of the most popular derivatives in the market is the **collateralized debt obligation** (CDO). A CDO gathers reference assets such as loans, bonds, or other debt instruments and sells of pieces of the interests from the pool—or tranches—to investors. In this way, a CDO allows you to redistribute the credit risk in any given portfolio into new tranches with risk profiles that are different from the underlying assets.

Depending on which type of debt instrument the CDO holds, it can also be referred to as a **collateralized loan obligation** (CLO), a **collateralized bond obligation** (CBO), or a **collateralized mortgage obligation** (CMO). The CDO as a concept applies to a large spectrum of credit instruments; practically any type of risky debt can become collateral for a CDO.

The CDO idea also intersects with another financial notion: theoretically, any asset with a revenue stream—and not just debt instruments—can be transformed into a marketable security. Known as **asset-backed securities** (ABSs), such instruments could use as collateral not only mortgage loans and corporate bonds, but also credit card receivables, car payments, leasing payments, project finance loans, student loans, or home-equity loan cash flows. ABSs, just like CDOs, apply the same method of packaging a group of securities in order to issue new securities, also known as **securitization**. The investor who purchases the securitized instrument then has a claim against the cash flow generated by the original pooled assets; it is just the type of asset that differs between the instruments.

In this chapter, we give an introduction to the mechanics, structure, and pricing of CDOs. Compared to previous chapters, the reader should note that in the following we make more use of mathematical and statistical approaches. In a separate appendix to the chapter, we also discuss how to price a CDO. The chapter is thus the most "numbers heavy" in the book.

The Mechanics of CDOs

Let us start by looking at the inner workings of a CDO.

A Traditional CDO

At first glance, the CDO may look like a very theoretical construct. Let's try to ground it in reality through the use of an example. Assume you run a bank and that you have some loans or debt that you want to remove from the bank's balance sheet. If you were looking to remove just the risk of default for some of your loans, you could use CDSs. However, you want to off-load large pools of debt from your balance sheet so you decide to issue a CDO. (Balance sheet off-loading is one reason to use a CDO; we'll look more at this and other motivations in the section "Motivation for Using CDOs: Balance Sheet or Arbitrage" of this chapter.)

In a CDO, you have the originating bank on one hand and the investors willing to take on the credit risk on the other. However, a third party plays an important role in CDOs: the **special purpose vehicle** (SPV) or **special purpose entity** (SPE). The SPV is a legal entity that has been created for just this CDO transaction; it is a small company complete with assets, liabilities, and management. Although the SPV might originally be established by you and your bank, it is run separately with no shared management and no legal ties between it and the originating financial institution. Practically, it is the SPV that takes over the loans from your bank and issues the CDOs; its assets become the risky debt it takes on and its liabilities are the CDO notes. The separation between the originator and the issuer assures that the loans cannot be consolidated back onto the originator's balance sheet.[1] The separation also brings with it a protection for CDO investors: Should the originator go bankrupt, the SPV still lives on and honors its obligations; this is known as the **bankruptcy** or **default remoteness** of an SPV.

Figure 6-1 lays out the relationship between the originating financial institution, the issuing SPV, and the investors.

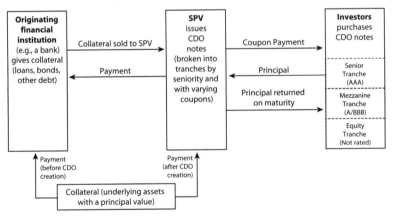

Figure 6-1 Cash-flow diagram of sample CDO

Figure 6-1 shows us that at the outset, the originating financial institution—such as your bank in the preceding example—sets up an SPV to which it sells the underlying assets at their principal value. (Because there is a payment involved, this basic CDO type is often referred to as a cash CDO.) The collateral has now been moved off the balance sheet of the originator and belongs to the SPV. The coupon payments from the collateral—for instance, mortgage payments, bond coupons, or loan payments—which used to go to the originating institution, now go to the SPV.

The SPV then pools all the assets and sells them off in pieces as notes to investors. Taken together, the investors pay a price equal to the principal value of the assets and receive in return a regular coupon payment, up until the CDOs mature. The notes are grouped in so-called tranches, which in turn are ranked by how likely they are to default and when repayment takes place; this ranking is known more generally as seniority of debt (recall our discussion on the topic from Chapter 2, "About Credit Risk"). The tranche's risk profile determines its order of seniority: More risk means a lower ranking, whereas almost no risk means a senior ranking. By distributing the risk between the tranches, senior tranches end up with considerably less risk than the underlying collateral, and the lower ranked tranches end up with more risk than the underlying reference assets. Linked to the difference in risk profiles, the tranches also receive differing coupon payments.

The tranches are also often examined by rating agencies and then receive different ratings, given their varying characteristics. In our example in Figure 6-1, there are three levels of tranches: a senior tranche (with a top AAA rating), a mezzanine tranche (with a rating between A or BBB), and a third tranche consisting of the remainder of the collateral, which is not rated and normally referred to as the equity tranche. The varying risk profiles and coupon payments naturally give the tranches different values to investors, and consequently they are sold at different prices and traded at varying credit spreads.

This flexibility to provide investors with various products depending on their risk propensity is a key feature of collateralized debt obligations. By being able to better target investors with different risk preferences, credit holders can sell off credit in pieces rather than trying to find investors who accept the full risk. Risk-adverse investors can turn to stable senior tranches, whereas more risk-willing investors look to the mezzanine or equity tranches with their higher potential payoff.

As we stated, the SPV receives payments from the collateral on a regular basis, and it passes this payment stream on to the CDO investors in the form of coupon payments on the notes. (The coupon payment is normally equal to the underlying payment of the assets, minus an administrative fee.) In the basic case, the payments from the collateral are sufficient to pay the coupon payments of all the investors. However, assume one of the reference assets defaults and the underlying payments are no longer enough for the full coupon payments. Investors are then paid in order of seniority: The senior tranche investors are paid before the mezzanine tranche investors, and the equity tranche investors are paid only if both the senior and the mezzanine tranche investors have received their coupon payments. (Again, recall our discussion in Chapter 2 on the debt waterfall.) In industry parlance, we say that the first loss is absorbed by the lowest tranche; it is often referred to as the first-loss position in the collateral portfolio. If the loss exceeds the total amount of the lowest class, the remaining loss is then compensated by the mezzanine class, and so on.

At maturity, the investors are paid back their principal investment. If there have been no changes to the underlying assets, the full principal is paid back. However, if some of the underlying assets have defaulted, only a part of the principal is returned. Again, whether an investor is paid back the principal in that case is determined by the seniority of the debt.

A CLOSER LOOK AT TRANCHES

As we mentioned earlier, a key feature of a CDO is the possibility that it gives an asset holder to redistribute risk of a pool of assets through the use of tranches. Therefore, let's look a little closer at how tranches are issued. Suppose that the CDO that you as a bank manager issued via an SPV in Figure 6-1 built on a collateral portfolio with a value of $1 billion. The CDO consists of three tranches, and each tranche is defined by a lower and an upper attachment point. Of the three tranches, the equity tranche consist of the first 4 percent of the portfolio (its attachment points were 0 percent and 4 percent), the mezzanine tranche of 6 percent (with attachment points 4 percent and 10 percent), and the senior tranche of the last 90 percent (with attachment points 10 percent and 100 percent). Table 6-1 summarizes this information and also includes the notional amount, credit rating, and spread for each tranche.

Table 6-1 Tranches of sample CDO

Tranche	Attachment Points	Notional Amount ($ million)	Credit Rating	Spread (Basis Points)
Equity	0%–4%	40	Not rated	1400
Mezzanine	4%–10%	60	A	150
Senior	10%–100%	900	AAA	10
Entire portfolio	0%–100%	1,000	A	74

Source: Table format based on Basel Committee on Banking Supervision. "Credit Risk Transfer." Bank for International Settlements. Basel: 2005. Table 1, page 45. Available at /www.bis.org/publ/ joint13.pdf. Accessed July 2005.

For example, if the portfolio has an 8 percent loss after a default event, the investors in the equity tranche would bear the first 4 percent (which would completely wipe out their investment) and the mezzanine investors would bear the remaining 4 percent.

As the figure further shows, the unrated equity tranche has a notional amount of $40 million, the A-rated mezzanine tranche one of $60 million, and the triple-A rated senior tranche carries $900 million. The credit spreads are the inverse of the ratings: the lower the rating, the higher the spread, with, for example, the equity tranche given a spread of 1,400 basis points spread over a reference interest rate, such as LIBOR. The credit spread for the total portfolio is calculated as the sum for all tranches taking the notional amount times the basis points, divided by the full notional amount for the portfolio. In Table 6-1 (where mn stands for million and bps stands for basis points), this becomes

$$\$40 \text{ mn} \times 1400 \text{ bps} + \$60 \text{ mn} \times 60 \text{ bps} + \$900 \text{ mn} \times 10 \text{ bps})/\$1000 \text{ mn} = 74 \text{ bps} \qquad [1]$$

The portfolio's average spread is 74 basis points.

As we stated, given their different profiles, the tranches are sold to investors with different risk appetites. For instance, the equity tranche can be sold to a professional asset manager or a hedge fund because they are willing to take the high risk in exchange for the high return. It is worth noting that the equity tranche is also often bought back by the originating financial institution. For instance, there might be a lack of investors interested in the high-risk equity tranche, forcing the originator to take on the debt itself. Often, however, the bank wants to show that it is not privy to some hidden information about the debt and that it is not "dumping bad debt" on the market. To avoid this moral hazard dilemma, the originator then buys back the equity trance to show the market its good faith. The mezzanine tranche is often bought by investors that desire to diversify their credit exposure, and who are appealed by the medium-risk and medium-return of the tranche. Lastly, the senior tranche's low-risk, low-return profile often appeals to large, institutional investors, such as reinsurers.

THE CDO LIFE CYCLE

A CDO does not just spring into existence, live for a while, and then expire at maturity. It is worth noting that the lifespan of a typical CDO actually revolves around three periods:

- **Ramp-up period**, when the collateral portfolio is gathered and formed.

- **Cash-flow period**, the major part of the CDO's life. This is when the collateral portfolio is in place; it can then either be actively managed by the CDO manager for changes in the composition of the collateral (the period is known as **reinvestment period**) or just left to generate its cash flows based on its collateral.

- **Unwind period**, when the investors are repaid their principal investment in order of seniority using the collateral principal proceeds.

Motivation for Using CDOs: Balance Sheet or Arbitrage

In the preceding example, we assume that you as a bank manager are looking to off-load some debt from your balance sheet and that you pick CDOs as the tool to help you do this. This is not an uncommon scenario. **Balance sheet motivated CDOs** help banks transfer risky debt off their balance sheets, which in turn helps them improve their equity/debt ratio, one of the key measurements for banks. The underlying risky debt that is being securitized through the CDO is usually poorly traded on the market by itself, and the CDO construction, with its reorganization and reshuffling of risk profiles, thus helps create a more liquid market.

A CDO that is purely motivated by balance sheet off-loading normally passes on the underlying coupon payments to the investors. By contrast, **arbitrage motivated CDOs** look to extract value by repackaging the collateral into tranches. Although theoretically the securities of a CDO should have the same market value as its underlying portfolio, this is often not the case in practice. The difference results in an arbitrage possibility for the originator, who is looking to create a collateral with a funding cost lower than the returns expected from the CDO notes issued.

To exemplify, assume that an SPV purchases bonds and loans in the market to a value of $50 million. These debt instruments come with a monthly coupon payment of 300 basis points over LIBOR. The SPV then issues CDO notes off this portfolio for a total value of $50 million, and it divides the notes into three tranches. Table 6-2 summarizes the CDO and its tranches.

Table 6-2 Tranches of arbitrage motivated CDO

Tranche	Attachment Points	Notional Amount ($ million)	Credit Rating	Spread (Basis Points)
Equity	0%–10%	$5	Not rated	300
Mezzanine	10%–40%	$15	A/BB	200
Senior	40%–100%	$30	AAA	100
Entire portfolio	0%–100%	$50		150

Of the tranches, as shown in Table 6-2, the equity tranche pays 300 basis points over LIBOR in coupon on a total notional amount of $5 million; the mezzanine tranche pays 200 basis points on $15 million; and the senior tranche pays 100 basis points on $30 million. On average, the SPV then pays 150 basis points over LIBOR every month—compared to the 300 basis points it receives from the underlying collateral. The originator behind the SPV is thus looking to make a profit by obtaining the difference between the received coupons from the collateral and the paid coupons to the investors. Figure 6-2 (where mn stands for million and bps stands for basis points) shows the cash-flow diagram of this arbitrage motivated CDOs.

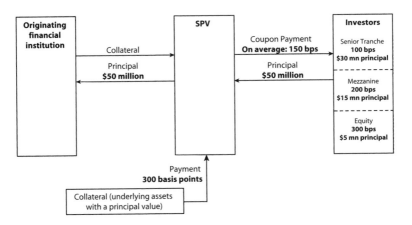

Figure 6-2 Cash-flow diagram of arbitrage motivated CDOs

The difference between the received payment and the coupon payment due is 150 basis points. In money terms, this becomes $0.75 million, calculated as 150 basis points times the notional value of the full portfolio at $50 million. It can also be calculated by taking the full value of the received coupon minus the value of the due coupons. The received coupon can be calculated as

$$\$50 \text{ million} \times 300 \text{ bps} = \$1.5 \text{ million} \tag{2}$$

And the coupon payment due to the investors can be calculated as

$$\$30 \text{ million} \times 100 \text{ bps} + \$15 \text{ million} \times 200 \text{ bps} + \$5 \text{ million} \times 300 \text{ bps} = \$0.75 \text{ million} \tag{3}$$

Again, the SPV makes an arbitrage profit of $0.75 million.

Synthetic CDOs

The type of CDO we have been discussing so far, whether it was balance sheet or arbitrage motivated, has been the original, most basic type of CDO. It is primarily characterized by the fact that the SPV takes over ownership of the collateral assets. Because there is a payment involved, these types of CDOs are also known as **cash CDOs**. In paying for the collateralized assets, the purchasing SPV takes on their principal value and recurring payments—and also any credit risk that they might have.

What if the originating financial institution, which we assume is a bank (for simplicity), only wants to get rid of the credit risk of the reference assets, and not the assets themselves? We devoted the entire previous chapter to an instrument that fits this situation: the credit default swap. However, assume further that the bank at the same time wants to issue CDO notes based on this particular collateral. This is where combining CDSs with the CDO structure brings us to what is called **synthetic CDOs**. Synthetic CDOs use credit default swaps (both single-name and portfolio based) as the collateral instead of the reference assets themselves. The SPV that issues the CDOs does not take ownership of the reference assets but only takes on their credit exposure, by being the bank's counterparty in the CDS contract. (The term *synthetic* is used because the risk is synthetically but not truly removed from the originator's balance sheet and thus technically is still present in the company's financials.)

Because the SPV does not hold the assets themselves, it finds itself lacking in funds to pay both the coupon payments to its investors as well as the principal value upon maturity. However, compared to the cash CDO, it does have cash flow in the form of the principal paid by the investors. The SPV then normally invests in high-grade, low-risk assets. The structure of a sample synthetic CDO is shown in Figure 6-3.

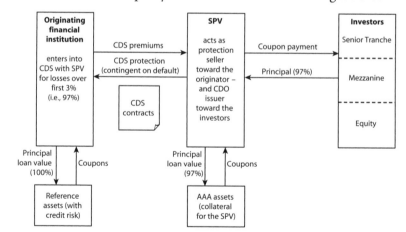

Figure 6-3 Cash-flow diagram of sample synthetic CDO

The figure shows us how the originating financial institution (which we assume is a bank) enters into a CDS contract with the SPV. The CDS gives the bank credit protection for all credit losses exceeding 3 percent of the value of a group of reference assets. For this protection, the bank pays the SPV a regular premium fee.

The SPV now uses the CDS contract as collateral to issue CDO notes. The issuance of synthetic CDOs is similar to that of traditional cash CDOs: In exchange for a principal payment, the investors receive coupon payment on notes grouped by tranches. Because the CDS contract does not cover the first 3 percent of losses, the investors pay 97 percent of the collateral's principal value.

In a cash CDO, the investors' payments are used by the SPV to purchase the collateral from the originator. The issuer of a synthetic CDO does not have to do this, because the collateral remains with the originator. No transfer of the underlying assets takes place. The sum of payments from the investors instead becomes the funding source for the SPV's payment if a default occurs. In the meantime, to protect the investors' principal from loss, the SPV uses the principal to purchase its own high-grade reference assets. Any cash flow that these assets might generate can be added to the coupon payments; thus, the coupons are often a combination of the return on the SPV collateral and the premium fees on the CDS contracts.

In case of default, the assets are sold off to generate funds for the contingent default payment that the SPV—in its role as protection seller—is due the bank. Upon maturity, the assets are sold off and the profit from the sale returned to the investors as principal-back payment. If a default event has occurred during the lifespan of the CDO, and the SPV issuer lacks funds to fully repay all investors their principal amount, the order of payment follows the tranches' seniority of debt.

In our example of a synthetic CDO, we have used CDS as the collateral. More generally speaking, a synthetic CDO can be based on a number of different credit instruments. In addition to using CDSs, a synthetic CDO can also use credit linked notes or total return swaps as its collateral.

Synthetic CDOs normally appeal to investors that look to trade "pure credit" in a diversified portfolio. These investors seek to avoid using cash CDOs, which mix the credit of the assets with the ownership aspect of the same asset; they just want to involve themselves with the credit aspect of an investment and not with actually owning it. Investors are also drawn to synthetic CDOs because their spread is generally greater than that of high-yield cash CDOs.

Even More CDO Types

As we wrote in the beginning of this chapter, CDOs are a prime example of how securitization works: packaging a group of securities in order to issue new securities. So far, we have seen how to use the securitization process to create cash CDOs out of a bank's transferred collateral, or synthetic CDOs out of CDS contracts. Along that same line of reasoning, it is easy to see how other types of underlying assets or collateral also can be used to form CDOs. As collateralized debt obligations become more and more common, issuers look for new assets against which to collateralize them. To exemplify, we'll look at two more types of CDOs: CDO squared (which are CDOs based on CDOs) and CDOs of EDSs (equity default swaps).

CDO SQUARED

A CDO squared note, also known as a **CDO2** note, is simply a CDO issue using other CDO notes as its collateral. (The process is also referred to as **resecuritization**.) Although initially typically issued as a single-tranche CDO, the CDO squared is now increasingly similar to the standard CDO in its issuance of tranched notes. Figure 6-4 shows the cash-flow diagram of a sample CDO squared.

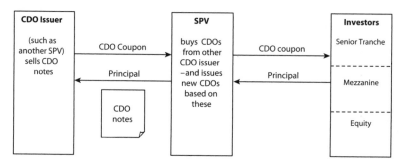

Figure 6-4 Cash-flow diagram of sample CDO squared

The figure shows how the SPV issues three classes of notes, and uses the principal payment of its investors to fund the purchase of CDO notes from another CDO issuer. The coupon payment that the SPV receives from the underlying CDO notes is passed on, minus an administrative fee, to its own CDO investors. In case of default among any of the underlying CDOs, the SPV loses its corresponding principal investment—and in response passes this loss on to its own investors, so that they lose their principal, in order of seniority.

In Figure 6-4, we assume the underlying collateral for the CDO squared is a set of other CDO notes, with varying risk profiles. One can imagine any combination of CDOs for the collateral, however, such as using only one CDO tranche as the collateral or a pool of mixed CDO tranches that also includes other types of asset backed securities.

Generally, a CDO squared has low volatility and low correlation to other assets—and thus looks at first glance to be an ideal instrument for an investor looking to create a diversified portfolio. However, investors should beware of the overlap that might occur between credit derivatives. Because CDOs squared redistribute credit risk of other CDOs, which in turn redistribute credit risk of a portfolio of assets, chances are that the same fundamentally underlying credit risk might appear several times in a CDO squared. This overlap causes a default on that underlying credit risk to propagate through the chain and effects more than just one credit derivative. This problem of overlap among the underlying portfolios is all the more acute because there still are only a limited number of liquid CDSs in the market.

CDOs of EDS

Just like credit default swaps, equity default swaps (EDSs) serve as protection. Where the CDS protects against a default event in an underlying asset, the EDS is a contract in which the protection buyer receives a payment from the protection seller should a predefined equity event take place. The equity event is normally tied to the equity's price falling below a predetermined level; the drop in stock price thus becomes analogous to a default event in a CDS.

As a variation on the CDO theme, EDSs can be used as collateral for creating CDO notes. These CDO notes then give investors exposure to equity risk, as an alternative to the credit risk in CDO structures. Figure 6-5 shows the cash-flow diagram of sample CDOs of EDS (which is strikingly similar to the structure for synthetic CDOs shown in Figure 6-3 earlier).

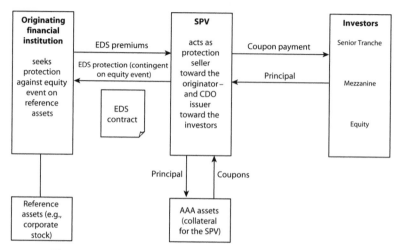

Figure 6-5 Cash-flow diagram of sample CDOs of EDS

As Figure 6-5 shows, an originating financial institution seeks protection against an equity event (for instance, a price drop by more than 50 percent of its initial value) in an underlying reference asset (such as a stock or a combination of stocks). For this protection, the originator enters into an EDS contract with the SPV and pays a premium fee. The SPV then uses the EDS contract as collateral for issuing CDO notes. The cash flows between the SPV and its CDO investors become the same as for the synthetic CDO we discussed earlier in this chapter; and just like with the synthetic CDO, the SPV buys AAA-rated assets to serve as collateral to protect the investors' principal. These assets also serve as a funding source in case an equity event does take place and the SPV has to make the contingent payment to the protection buyer.

Figure 6-5 shows a CDO created of pure EDSs. The market has seen variations on this theme, with hybrid deals where the CDO notes offered exposure to a combination of EDSs and CDSs. (For example, in January 2004, investment bank JP Morgan issued a hybrid CDO called Odysseus, which consisted of 10 percent EDSs and 90 percent CDSs.)

CDO Credit Enhancement

To make derivative instruments based on credit risk even more interesting to investors, an issuer can implement a number of so-called **credit enhancement** provisions. These serve to further reduce the credit risk of an obligation. Some common practices are in essence credit enhancement techniques without effectively carrying that label. For instance, if you apply for a loan from a bank and give the bank a third-party guarantee, where another person promises to meet your obligations if you default on the loan, you have then given the bank a credit enhancement provision. Rephrased, the guarantee enhances your credit profile in the eyes of the bank. Another technique is to take out a credit insurance, which provides compensation in the event that a party defaults.

In addition to such business practices, credit enhancement provisions can also be built into contracts, as key ratios or threshold values. In this section, we discuss how such provisions can improve the credit profile of CDOs, making these instruments even more interesting to investors. Before we describe the actual techniques, however, we first need to look at two fundamentally different so-called credit structures for CDOs.

Two Credit Structures: Cash-Flow and Market-Value CDOs

As we know, CDOs can be classified based on underlying collateral (resulting in cash CDOs, synthetic CDOs, CDOs squared, and so on) and by the motivation of its issuer (balance sheet or arbitrage). Yet another way to look at a CDO is whether it is structured as a **cash-flow** or **market-value** CDO. These two types of **credit structures** differ in how they shield the tranches of the CDO from credit losses in case of default events, especially the more senior notes.

The cash-flow CDO has been the implicit credit structure in the CDOs we have looked at so far in the chapter. The fundamental building block of this credit structure is that the cash flow from the collateral is used to pay the CDO investors. If one of the underlying assets defaults and the cash flow proves inadequate to pay off all tranches, payments are made to the tranches according to seniority. Obligations to senior tranches are thus met before any payments are made to less senior tranches.

The market-value CDO also uses the cash flow from the underlying collateral as the source for payments to the CDO investors—but in addition, the CDO manager can also sell the underlying collateral itself to generate even more cash to meet the CDO's liabilities toward its investors.[2] Because the collateral is traded on the financial markets, the portfolio's assets have to be assigned a market-value rather than using their principal, or par, value—hence, the structure's label as a market-value CDO. The manager of the CDO frequently adjusts the value of the portfolio given the market value of the assets; in industry jargon, we say that the value of the assets is **marked-to-market** periodically. The credit structure of the market-value CDO thus centers on making sure the market value of the collateral does not drop below a certain level. If it does, payments are suspended to the most subordinate tranche, the equity tranche. If the market value falls even further, more senior tranches are affected. CDO assets are then sold and debt tranches repaid until the market value of the collateral once again exceeds the designated level.

In other words, for market-value CDOs, the payments to the investors do not depend on the adequacy of the collateral's cash flow but on its market value. The market-value structure depends on the ability of the asset manager to maximize the portfolio's market value, while the cash-flow structure depends on the ability of the asset manager to control its cash flows. Yet another way to phrase it is to say that the market-value CDO focuses on the volatility of the collateral's market value, whereas the cash-flow CDO looks at the collateral's credit quality.

In both types of credit structures, the senior CDO note holders are shielded from default events impacting their payments simply by the fact that they are the last to be affected by decreased payment streams. For both types, a number of methods exist to further enhance the credit protection of the senior notes. These methods are put in place to ensure that a collateralized instrument has sufficient capacity to handle default events and build on specifying minimum levels of credit quality in the derivative contracts. For CDOs, if these levels—which normally are expressed as ratios or thresholds—are not maintained, the CDO manager might be required to sell off parts of the collateral to restore the ratios to an acceptable level. When we talk about such credit protection methods, we commonly talk about **coverage tests**, especially overcollateralization (O/C) and interest coverage (I/C) ratios for cash-flow CDOs, and advance rate mechanisms and market overcollateralization tests for market-value CDOs. The following looks at these specific methods for both types of credit structures, starting with the ones for cash-flow CDOs.

Credit Enhancement for Cash-Flow CDOs

To understand the concept of coverage tests, recall our discussion of debt and cash-flow waterfalls based on seniority from Chapter 2. Figure 6-6 takes this discussion as its basis and exemplifies the cash-flow waterfall for a specific CDO issue with four tranches (A, B, C, and a fourth equity tranche, also referred to as D).

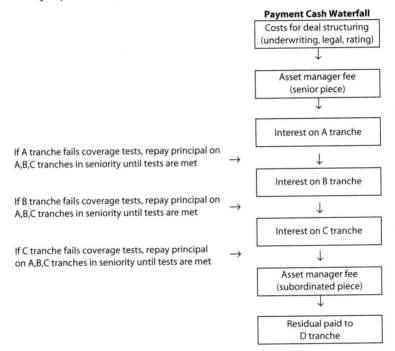

Figure 6-6 Cash-flow waterfall

Source: Format based on example in Basel Committee on Banking Supervision. "Credit Risk
  Transfer." Bank for International Settlements. Basel: 2005, page 59. Available at
  www.bis.org/ publ/joint13.pdf. Accessed July 2005.

Figure 6-6 outlines how the cash flow (in the form of coupon or interest payments) that comes from the underlying collateral is distributed to the various debt holders. The distribution is done in order of seniority:

tranche A has to receive payment in full before tranche B receives its share, and so on. In addition to the liabilities owed to the tranche holders, the cash flow also has to pay for the deal structuring (or setup) and administrative fees for CDO. Normally, these fees take seniority over all tranches, are quoted as a share of the underlying collateral's principal value, and are paid in amortizations over the lifespan of the CDO.

Figure 6-6 also shows the role of the coverage tests in the waterfall structure. For each tranche, coverage tests are run to see if the credit structure of the CDO still meets its obligations. As the figure shows, if any tranche fails its coverage tests, the rest of the interest cash flow is diverted to pay down the principal value of the tranches, starting with the most senior tranche, and continuing until all tranches again meet their coverage tests.

OVERCOLLATERALIZATION (O/C) AND INTEREST COVERAGE (I/C)

There are traditionally two types of coverage tests: overcollateralization (O/C) and interest coverage (I/C) tests. The **overcollateralization test** is designed to monitor the general robustness of the CDO's tranches and ensures that the principal value of the notes is at least a certain percentage of the value of the underlying collateral. The test consists of calculating an O/C ratio for each tranche in order to compare it to a trigger ratio set for that tranche. The O/C ratio is the ratio of the CDO's total par value divided by the par value for the tranche and any senior tranches, or

$$O/C = \frac{\text{Principal value of collateral portfolio}}{\text{Principal for tranche} + \text{Principal for all tranches senior to it}} \quad [4]$$

Should the calculated ratio fall below the trigger value, the tranche has failed the test. If the ratio is greater or equal to the threshold ratio, the test is passed for the concerned tranche.

The **interest coverage test** is designed to monitor the robustness of the tranches specifically for interest (or coupon) proceeds. It ensures that there is sufficient collateral interest income to cover losses and still make interest payments to the more senior notes; the amount by which the tranche exceeds the threshold value is at times referred to as an excess spread. Again, the test consists of calculating a ratio for each tranche that is measured against a preset target ratio.

The I/C ratio for a tranche is calculated as [5]

$$I/C = \frac{\text{Scheduled interest due on underlying collateral portfolio}}{\text{Scheduled interest to that tranche} + \text{Scheduled interest to all tranches senior}}$$

The outcome of the I/C test is measured in the same way as the O/C test: If the result is greater or equal to the threshold ratio, the tranche passes the test; otherwise, it fails.

In the event that a tranche fails a coverage test, cash flows from the subordinate tranches is diverted and the more senior tranches are paid down, in order of seniority, until all tranches again meet their coverage test ratios.

A NUMERICAL EXAMPLE OF O/C AND I/C TESTS

Let's exemplify how to use the O/C and I/C tests.[3] Assume that there is a standard CDO, using as collateral high-yield bonds with a combined a value of $100 million. The CDO and its tranches are summarized in Table 6-3.

Table 6-3 Structure of hypothetical CDO tranche

Tranche Class	Notional Amount	Rating	Spread	O/C Target	I/C Target
A	$60 million	AAA	50 bps	1.350	1.600
B	$10 million	BBB	200 bps	1.250	1.400
C	$10 million	BB	500 bps	1.130	1.200
Equity	$20 million	Not rated	N.A.		
	$100 million				

Note how the final tranche—the equity tranche—does not have any coverage targets. As the residual class that receives what remains of the cash flow, it is generally considered a high-risk investment and does not benefit from the additional protection of coverage tests.

We assume further that the collateral has a weighted average coupon rate of 10.0 percent. The CDO itself has a five-year maturity with semi-annual coupons paid to the investors; the notes are grouped in four tranches. In addition, the SPV charges a deal structuring fee of 100 basis points of the notional amount, which is amortized over the life-span of the CDO at 5 percent. The current prevailing risk-free interest rate is otherwise at 6 percent. The yearly asset manager fee is 40 basis points per year for the senior tranche and 20 basis points for the subordinate tranches.

As the time for the first semiannual coupon payment approaches, we take this information and submit each tranche to the two types of coverage tests. For the overcollateralization test, we calculate the value for each tranche as

O/C Tranche A	= 100 / 60	= 1.667	[6]
O/C Tranche B	= 100 / (60+10)	= 1.429	[7]
O/C Tranche C	= 100 / (60+10+10)	= 1.250	[8]

For the interest coverage test, we make sure to include the deal structuring and management costs associated with CDO, because the I/C ratio calls for the inclusion of all scheduled interest (or coupon) payments:

- The deal structuring fee, given a five-year maturity and a 5 percent annual rate on 100 basis points of the collateral's principal, can be calculated to be $0.11 million using the general formula

$$100 \times (100bp) = \sum_{t=1}^{10} \frac{F}{(1+0.5\times5\%)^t}$$

and solving for F, which denotes the deal structuring fee.

- The asset management fee for the senior tranche becomes $0.2 million (= $100 million × 0.4 percent × 0.5) and for the subordinated debt $0.1million (= $100 million × 0.2 percent × 0.5).

As preparation, we also need to calculate the semiannual coupon (or interest) payments for each tranche, and the full underlying portfolio.

Interest collateral portfolio	= $100 million × 10% × 0.5	= $5.0 million	[9]
Interest on Tranche A	= $60 million × (6.0% + 50 bp) × 0.5	= $1.95 million	[10]
Interest on Tranche B	= $10 million × (6.0% + 200 bp) × 0.5	= $0.4 million	[11]
Interest on Tranche C	= $10 million × (6.0% + 500 bp) × 0.5	= $0.55 million	[12]

We can now use this information in addition to calculate the I/C ratios for each tranche.

I/C Tranche A = $5.0M / ($0.11M + $0.2M + $1.95M) = 2.212 [13]

I/C Tranche B = $5.0M ($0.11M + $0.2M + $1.95M + $0.4M) = 1.879 [14]

I/C Tranche C = $5.0M ($0.11M + $0.2M + $0.4M + $0.55M) = 1.557 [15]

We can now compare the calculated O/C and I/C ratios with the trigger values that were set, as done in Table 6-4.

Table 6-4 Coverage tests at launch of CDO

Tranche Class	O/C		I/C	
	Trigger	Initial Value	Trigger	Initial Value
A	1.350	1.667	1.600	2.212
B	1.250	1.429	1.400	1.879
C	1.130	1.250	1.200	1.557

As Figure 6-7 shows, all values are above the assigned trigger values, and so the credit structure of the CDO has met the requirements set up in its contract. The interest can be divided up according to the waterfall structure. Figure 6-7 shows how the money flows between the recipients according to seniority and based on our preceding calculations.

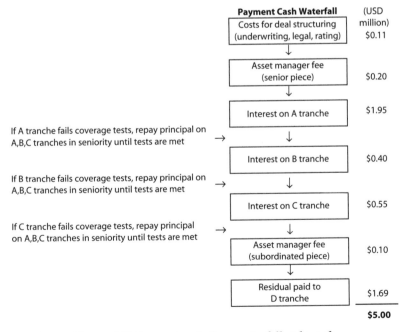

Figure 6-7 Interest cash-flow waterfall at launch

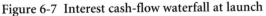

However, let's now assume that the collateral portfolio suffers a default event in one of its reference assets before the next coupon payment. The default event makes the notional amount of the underlying portfolio drop from $100 million to $90 million. The notional decline of $10 million is taken from the equity tranche. This naturally affects the interest cash-flow waterfall. However, the first question is if the default event impacted the coverage ratios. To find out, we recalculate the O/C and I/C ratios.

The O/C ratios are now calculated as

O/C Tranche A	= 90 / 60		= 1.500	[16]
O/C Tranche B	= 90 / (60 + 10)		= 1.286	[17]
O/C Tranche C	= 90 / (60 + 10 + 10)		= 1.125	[18]

For the I/C ratios, we first state that the deal structuring fee is not affected; after it is set at the launch of the CDO, it does not change regardless of changes to the underlying collateral, and thus remains at $0.11 million. However, the asset management fee is impacted because it is based on the notional value of the collateral. The fee for the senior tranche becomes $0.18 million (= $90 million × 0.4 percent × 0.5) and for the subordinate tranches $0.09 million (= $90 million × 0.2 percent × 0.5), respectively.

The dollar value for the coupon payments for each tranche remains the same as before, but the coupon on the underlying collateral portfolio changes.

Interest collateral portfolio = $90 million × 10% × 0.5 = $4.5 million   [19]

With these new values, the I/C ratio for each tranche can be calculated as

I/C Tranche A	= $4.5M ($0.11M + $0.18M + $1.95M)		= 2.009	[20]
I/C Tranche B	= $4.5M ($0.11M + $0.18M + $1.95M + $0.4M)		= 1.704	[21]
I/C Tranche C	= $4.5M ($0.11M + $0.18M + $1.95M + $0.4M + $0.55M)		= 1.411	[22]

We now compare the calculated O/C and I/C ratios with the trigger values, as done in Table 6-5, to see how the default event impacts our coverage ratios.

Table 6-5 Coverage tests after default event in CDO

Tranche Class	O/C		I/C	
	Trigger	Current Value	Trigger	Current Value
A	1.350	1.500	1.600	2.009
B	1.250	1.286	1.400	1.704
C	1.130	1.125	1.200	1.411

As Table 6-5 shows us, the C tranche did not pass its O/C test. The waterfall cash flow has to be adjusted, so that the C tranche again meets both coverage tests. As the coverage test in Figure 6-7 states: "If C tranche fails coverage tests, repay principal on A, B, and C tranches in seniority until tests are met." We now have to figure out how much to repay to meet the O/C test. If we denote the repayment as y, the following equation for the C tranche's O/C test should hold:

$$90 / (60 + 10 + 10 - y) \geq 1.130 \qquad [23]$$

Solving for y in equation 23 gives us $0.354 million. Thus, we have to divert $354,000 of the interest payments to the tranches in order to meet the O/C test for the C tranche. Because the repayment is done in order of seniority, the sum goes to paying back the principal of the A tranche. As a result, the principal amount of the A tranche decreases from $60 million to $59.646 million.

It is important to note that although the A tranche's principal amount drops, the overall notional amount of the portfolio remains at $90 million. Intuitively, one might think that the overall value should also drop by $0.354 million. However, because that payment originated with the cash-flow payments and not from a liquidation of any assets, the overall portfolio value remains the same. You can think of it as the SPV buying back notes to a value of $0.354 million from an A tranche holder; the SPV now holds those notes itself and they are still part of the overall portfolio. This means that, for example, the overall interest payment on the portfolio does *not* change but remains at $4.5 million.

However, the change in the A tranche's nominal value does affect the following calculations and ratios.

Tranche A O/C $\quad$ = 90 / 59.646 $\qquad$ = \$1.509 million $\quad[24]$

Tranche A interest $\quad$ = \$59.646 mn $\times$ (6.0% + 50 bp) $\times$ 0.5 $\qquad$ = \$1.94 million $\quad[25]$

Tranche A I/C $\quad$ = \$4.5M / (\$0.11M + \$0.18M + \$1.94M) $\qquad$ = \$2.019 million $\quad[26]$

We then compare the new overall O/C and I/C ratios for all tranches, as shown in Table 6-6.

Table 6-6 Coverage tests after default event in CDO

Tranche Class	O/C		I/C	
	Trigger	Current Value	Trigger	Current Value
A	1.350	1.509	1.600	2.019
B	1.250	1.292	1.400	1.704
C	1.130	1.130	1.200	1.416

The C tranche now meets the trigger level for the O/C ratio; it has been restored to the credit-enhancing overcollateralization level it had before the default. With all tranches meeting their coverage tests, the coupon cash flow from the collateral can now be divided up according to the waterfall structure, as shown in Figure 6-8 (amounts that changed from Figure 6-7 are marked in bold).

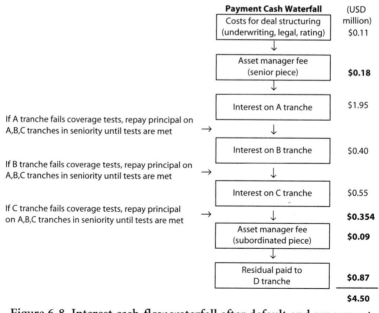

Figure 6-8 Interest cash-flow waterfall after default and repayment

To recapitulate, we launched a CDO with four tranches. Before distributing the first coupon payment to the investors, we submitted all tranches to so-called coverage tests. Because all tranches passed the tests, we could pay out the coupon interests due to our investors. However, before the next coupon payment, a default event occurred in one of the assets. This affected the coverage tests; in particular, the C tranche did not pass the O/C test any longer. We therefore took some of the interest cash stream coming from the collateral to pay off a part of the principal value for the A tranche. This adjustment adjusted the ratios—and again all tranches passed all tests. We could then proceed to pay out the coupon as shown in Figure 6-8.

To summarize, coverage tests make certain that the CDO meets credit requirements that are above and beyond the protection that debt seniority assures the different tranches. The O/C test ensures that each tranche has sufficient collateral—in fact, that it is *over*collateralized. The I/C test makes sure that there is a sufficient cash flow coming from the collateral to cover any losses and still make interest payments to the note holders.

Credit Enhancement for Market-Value CDOs

We just looked at coverage tests for a cash-flow CDO. Because a cash-flow CDO does not look at market values, all its tests were fundamentally par-to-par checks where we worked off the principal value of the assets. By contrast, the coverage tests for a market-value CDO look at— not surprisingly, given the name—the market value of all the assets, and not their principal value. This is a natural consequence of the nature of the credit structure, where the cash flow to CDO investors is a combination of cash flow from the underlying collateral and cash flow from trading assets in the CDO portfolio at their market value.

ADVANCE RATES AND OVERCOLLATERALIZATION TESTS

Credit enhancement for market-value CDOs is normally achieved by leaving a margin—or a "cushion"—between the current market value of the collateral and the face value of CDO's obligations. If this cushion becomes negative, CDO managers can sell off parts of the underlying assets, to ensure that they are able to pay the investor's principal and interest. To calculate the margin, CDO managers traditionally use **advance rates** to arrive at adjusted market values, which they then use in overcollateralization tests to make sure the CDO is robust and properly collateralized. (It is worth noting that the **overcollateralization tests** for market-value CDOs, although it shares the same underlying concept, are different from those of cash-flow CDOs; market-value CDOs do not test each tranche separately but test the complete sum of debt tranches at once.) If the CDO does not meet the tests, the manager is required to change the portfolio composition until the tranches do meet the tests again. Being properly overcollateralized gives the CDO a protective buffer against asset price volatility, which might follow, for instance, changes in interest rate movements.

Advance rates are the maximum percentage of the market rate that can be used to issue debt. They take into account the market risk inherent in any underlying reference asset, and thus limit the value that the CDO manager can assign each asset. The advance rate provides the amount that the CDO asset is supposed to be able to support, expressed as a percentage of the asset's market value. Advance rates are thus used to arrive at an **adjusted market value**, also known as a **haircut asset value**. The advance rates themselves, which always mathematically are numbers less than 100 percent, are provided by rating firms and grouped according to the debt's overall rating. The rating firms normally look at three factors to estimate the appropriate advance rate: the securities' price volatility, overall liquidity, and correlation.

After the CDO manager has established the advance rate for each asset, she then carries out the actual overcollateralization test for each tranche. In the test, the sum of all haircut asset values is compared to the sum of all liabilities due to the CDO investors for that tranche. The adjusted asset values should be equal or exceed the liabilities for the tranche to be sufficiently overcollateralized. By liabilities, note that we refer to the debt tranches of the CDO; the nonrated last accrual tranche, which we consistently think of as the equity tranche, is not part of the liabilities. The equity tranche is actually in most instances equal to the cushion or buffer that constitutes the overcollateralization. (The CDO contract may naturally stipulate otherwise—for instance, that only a part of the equity tranche should be counted toward the overcollateralization.)

If the CDO does not pass the overcollateralization—perhaps because of a recent drop in market value—the CDO must sell off assets until it reaches the required overcollateralization ratio again.

A NUMERICAL EXAMPLE USING ADVANCE RATES TO CALCULATE OVERCOLLATERALIZATION RATIOS

To show how advance rates can be used, assume that we have a CDO with underlying assets marked-to-market for a market value of $100 million. The CDO structure builds on four tranches (three debt tranches, A through C, with a fourth equity tranche), as shown in Table 6-7.

Table 6-7 Structure of hypothetical CDO

Tranche Class	Par Value
A	$60 million
B	$10 million
C	$10 million
Equity (D)	$20 million
	$100 million

As Table 6-7 shows, the sum of par (or principal) value for the debt tranches A through C is $80 million, and the par value of the equity tranche D is $20 million.

We now want to make sure that this market-value CDO is properly overcollateralized. For simplicity, we assume that the collateral is composed of only high-yield bonds with an A1 rating. (In reality, the underlying assets would most likely be of varying quality, which automatically complicates the calculations beyond the need of this simple example.)

We start by finding the advance rate for the underlying portfolio. For this, we use the table shown in Table 6-8, which we could have obtained from a rating agency and which shows advance rates against ratings by asset type.

Table 6-8 Hypothetical advance rates against ratings by asset type

Asset Type	Aaa	Aa1	Aa2	Aa3	A1	A2	A3	Baa1	Baa2	Baa3
				Target Rating						
High-Yield Bonds	0.83	0.84	0.85	0.86	0.87	0.89	0.90	0.91	0.92	0.93
High-Yield Loans	0.77	0.79	0.80	0.81	0.83	0.84	0.86	0.87	0.89	0.91
Distressed Bonds	0.62	0.63	0.64	0.65	0.67	0.68	0.69	0.70	0.71	0.72
Distressed Loans	0.48	0.50	0.51	0.52	0.53	0.54	0.56	0.58	0.59	0.60
Distressed Equity	0.40	0.42	0.45	0.47	0.48	0.49	0.50	0.52	0.53	0.55

For high-yield bonds with an A1 rating, the advance rate shown in Table 6-8 is 0.87. We use this advance rate to calculate the adjusted market value of our reference assets.

$$\$100 \text{ million} \times 0.87 = \$87 \text{ million} \qquad [27]$$

We now have the value we need to see if the CDO is properly overcollateralized. We simply compare the adjusted market value to the par value of the debt tranches. If the adjusted market value is higher than the par debt value, the portfolio passes the test. Table 6-9 summarizes the test.

Table 6-9 Initial overcollateralization test of market-value CDO

Par Value of Debt Tranches (A,B,C)	Adjusted Market Value	Overcollateralization Test	Difference, If Failed Test
$80 million	$87 million	Pass	N/A

Suppose that a default event occurs in the reference portfolio. The event naturally affects the value of the portfolio, with the par value dropping as well as the market value. The CDO manager recalculates the market value, and sees that it has dropped 10 percent to $90 million. The portfolio still consists of only A1-rated assets, so the new adjusted market value for the portfolio is then given by

$$\$90 \text{ million} \times 0.87 = \$78.3 \text{ million} \qquad [28]$$

The outstanding debt has not changed, though, and still remains $80 million. Verifying the portfolio, the manager realizes that the CDO no longer is properly overcollateralized, as shown in Table 6-10.

Table 6-10 Overcollateralization test after default event of market-value CDO

Par Value of Debt Tranches (A,B,C)	Adjusted Market Value	Overcollateralization Test	Difference, If Failed Test
$80 million	$78.3 million	Fail	$1.7 million

The adjusted market value of the portfolio is now lower than the par value of the debt tranches. Just as with the cash-flow CDO, the CDO manager now has to pay down debt tranche holders to reestablish the collateralization level. However, unlike the cash-flow CDO, which used the underlying coupon payments to pay down tranches, the market-value CDO manager has to sell off parts of the portfolio to finance the payment.

The difference between the adjusted market value and debt par value— also known as the CDO's **shortfall**—is $1.7 million. It can be shown that the liquidation of assets needs to reach an amount calculated as

$$\text{Collateral to be liquidated} = \frac{\text{Shortfall}}{1 - \text{Advance rate}} \qquad [29]$$

Using the numbers from our example, we arrive then at

$$\text{Collateral to be liquidated} = \frac{\$1.7 \text{ million}}{1 - 0.87} = \$13.08 \text{ million} \qquad [30]$$

The CDO manager thus sells off assets to a value of $13.08 million. The new market value of the collateral then becomes

$$\$90 \text{ million} - \$13.08 \text{ million} = \$76.92 \text{ million} \qquad [31]$$

And the new adjusted market value, given the same advance rate of 0.87, becomes

$$\$76.92 \text{ million} \times 0.87 = \$66.92 \text{ million} \qquad [32]$$

Because the gains from the sale of the assets went to paying down the debt tranches, the par value of the debt, which at the outset was $80 million, has also changed.

$$\$80 \text{ million} - \$13.08 \text{ million} = \$66.92 \text{ million} \qquad [33]$$

Verifying the portfolio, the manager can now see that the CDO again is properly overcollateralized, as shown in Table 6-11.

Table 6-11 Overcollateralization test after default event of market-value CDO

Par Value of Debt Tranches (A,B,C)	Adjusted Market Value	Overcollateralization Test	Difference, If Failed Test
$66.92 million	$66.92 million	Pass	N/A

Pricing a CDO

Using credit enhancement techniques to decrease the credit risk inherent in a CDO naturally influences the price of the CDO. With more credit enhancement in place, the price that a protection seller requests drops.

Exactly how much to price the tranches of a CDO is shown in more detail in the section, "Pricing a CDO: The Theory," in the appendix of this chapter. The appendix does this for the general case, assuming no credit enhancement has been put in place. The reader should note that like the other appendices in this book, it uses a rather advanced level of mathematical analysis.

The CDO Market

The market for collateralized debt obligations has grown continuously over the past ten years, both in absolute and relative market terms. In 2005, it was the second largest credit derivative market after credit default swaps.

Although the CDO market began with cash CDOs, by now, the most commonly traded CDO type is the synthetic CDO that builds on other credit instruments instead of the direct sale of the underlying assets, as shown in Figure 6-9.

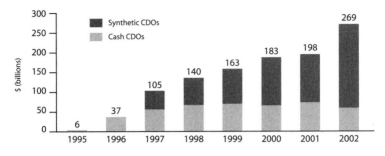

Figure 6-9 CDO growth: synthetic CDOs versus cash CDOs (1995-2002)

Source: Banc of America Securities. Presented on *Credit Magazine* Web site.
    http://db.riskwaters.com/public/showPage.html?page=9439. Accessed July 2005.

The popularity of synthetic CDOs over cash CDOs is in part explained by their feature of allowing the issuer—normally a bank—to maintain the direct relationship with the client, without having to sell or move the loans off his balance sheet. Synthetic CDOs are also attractive for geographic markets where the originator for legal reasons is not allowed to make a full transfer or true sale of assets; the synthetic derivative then provides access to that market's investor community. From an investment perspective, the synthetic CDO also allows a clearer investment opportunity for the buyer: The synthetic CDO only brings credit risk, whereas the cash CDO, with its complete transfer of the asset to the SPV, brings in addition to credit risk all the normal risks associated with owning an asset, such interest rate, prepayment, and currency risk.

If we take the dominant synthetic CDO type and study it according to the motivation of the issuer (either balance sheet or arbitrage driven, as discussed earlier in the section "Motivation for Using CDOs: Balance Sheet or Arbitrage"), we arrive at Figure 6-10.

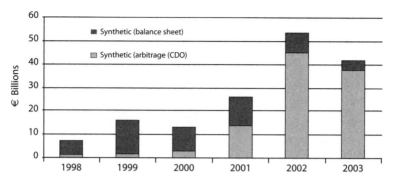

Figure 6-10 CDO growth: balance-sheet CDOs versus arbitrage CDOs

Source: Lehman Brothers. Presented on *Credit Magazine* Web site. http://db.riskwaters.com/
public/showPage.html?page=168501. Accessed July 2005.

Figure 6-10 shows us that arbitrage CDOs have dominated the market
since 2002, although in the origins, most synthetic CDOs were balance
sheet motivated. This can be explained in part by the more diverse set
of market participants that the market now attracts; investors such as
hedge funds, mutual funds, and firms are more prone to look for arbitrage opportunities than the first market participants, the banks.

The growing number of market participants and their respective share
of both the sell-side (protection buying) and buy-side (protection selling) of the market is shown in more detail in Table 6-12.

Table 6-12 Credit derivatives market participants (end of 2003)

Institutions	Protection Buyers	Protection Sellers
Banks	51%	38%
Securities houses	16%	16%
Hedge funds	16%	15%
Corporates	3%	2%
Insurance companies	7%	20%
Mutual funds	3%	4%
Pension funds	3%	4%
Governments	1%	1%
Total	100%	100%

Source: Adapted from British Bankers' Association. "BBA Credit Derivatives Report 2003/2004."

Table 6-12 shows how the same actors play large roles both as protection buyers and protection sellers—especially the banks and insurance companies taken together exceed half the market size no matter which side of the market you study.

Overall, on the sell-side, we find the following typical protection buyers:

- **Banks.** Banks issue CDOs motivated both by balance sheet concerns and arbitrage opportunities. The balance sheet motivation follows to a large extent regulations set by the Bank for International Settlements (BIS). Under the Basel Bank Capital Accord, banks are required to keep their capital reserves at a certain level against notional exposure to cover for any default loss that might occur. Reducing the exposure by issuing cash CDOs helps banks maintain the capital/debt ratio. For other banks, CDO issues help expand the corporate market.

- **Insurance companies.** Insurers become protection buyers for many of the same reasons as banks, as well as looking to decrease risk concentration in different industries and countries.

- **Other participants.** Among the other major CDO sellers, we find hedge funds and other fund managers, attracted to the market by the arbitrage opportunities they perceive.

On the buy-side, protection sellers are driven by investment motivations such as yield and diversification. In addition to the large spectrum of CDOs in terms of return and risk, CDOs also enable investors to invest in credit risk that they for regulatory reasons might not be allowed to invest in directly. Overall, we find the same typical actors on the buy-side as we did on the sell-side:

- **Banks.** Banks buy CDOs to diversify their asset portfolio across industries, credit ratings, and countries in which they don't have customers.

- **Insurance companies.** Most insurance companies seem to prefer CDOs and credit-linked notes over other credit derivative instruments. They typically purchase highly rated tranches, because insurance regulation forces them to treat CDO notes just as, for instance, corporate bonds and Treasury Notes.

- **Other participants.** The motivation for hedge funds, mutual funds, and pension funds to enter the market as protection sellers vary. Hedge funds normally tend to invest in equity and higher-risk mezzanine tranches, looking for a high return, mutual funds tend to buy mezzanine tranches, and pension funds invest in senior tranches.

APPENDIX TO
CHAPTER 6

PRICING A CDO

Just like the credit default swaps we priced in Chapter 5, "Credit Default Swaps," CDOs are by definition multiname credit derivatives, whose price depends on the likelihood of one or more credit events occurring in the underlying collateral. Intuitively, it is easy to see why pricing a multiname product is a difficult endeavor: Not only do you have to find default probabilities for each individual reference asset, but you also have to find out whether their defaults might be linked to each other, which we know from Chapter 5 as default correlation. Default correlation—or **joint default probability**[4]—builds on the idea that two or more defaults might occur in any given time period. A high correlation among default events increases the magnitude of potential losses and is often dependent on macro-economic factors or the general state of an industry or economy. For example, think of two companies that operate in the same industry: They make mechanical calculators. However, the industry for mechanical calculators is going through tough times because everyone has started using electronic calculators. As the industry goes into a severe downturn, many companies are put out of business, and all for the same reason: Nobody is buying their industry's product. The correlation of their bankruptcies is thus a natural consequence of being in the same industry. Other variables can also explain why the default of companies is correlated. Historically, for instance, we can see that companies with the same rating have correlated default patterns.

Assuming we arrive at a default probability for all the reference assets, a fair fee for a CDO is then most easily recognized as a fee that matches

---

the expected loss for the protection seller. Rephrased, the fee paid on the premium leg should match the expected default payment coming off the protection leg of the CDO. Again, this is how we define the fee for a CDS. Unlike the CDS, however, the CDO does not involve just one protection seller. Instead, the transaction takes place between the SPV as the protection buyer and a number of protection sellers in the form of the various CDO tranche investors.

To arrive at a fee, we thus calculate the expected default payment for each tranche, given the underlying assets and the value of loss at default. This is where we also assume a certain default correlation between the underlying assets. Put simply, the correlation tells us how many of the other assets the defaulting asset "brings down" along with itself. Mathematically, there are several ways of handling correlation; in the examples that follow, we use a basic approach to solving systems of linear equations known as **Cholesky decomposition.**

Even with a mathematical approach to handling correlation, the complexity of calculating the expected default payment, which is what we need to arrive at a CDO price, grows exponentially with an increasing number of reference assets. Theoretically, a portfolio composed of N reference assets has a possible combination of joint default events equaling 2^N. Just plug any number into that formula to see how quickly the number of joint default events grows. Add default correlation between the reference assets to that picture, and the complexity increases even more. As it turns out, it is hard to derive a generalized model or formula that handles this complexity while still being practical to use. Instead, the market has turned to using simulations, where computers are put to work to simulate one potential outcome. The simulation produces a random number of defaults during a specified time period among a specified number of reference assets. The simulation is then repeated, for instance, 10,000 or 100,000 times—and based on the total number of outcomes, a loss distribution pattern can be distinguished. Recalling our discussion on loss distribution from Chapter 5, the pattern tells us the probability of default for any level of loss. In other words, we obtain not just one expected default loss, but one for a number of different default probabilities, making it even easier to price the CDO tranches.

As tools in this process, we first need a simulation approach. A common approach to simulate random values coming out of a model is known as a **Monte Carlo simulation**.[5] The simulation process then needs a definition of when default occurs. In our examples that follow, we use the Merton model's definition of default occurring when asset value falls below debt value, but any definition from any other credit risk model—structural or reduced form—could be used.

To summarize, the price of a CDO—the premium fees going across the payment leg—is supposed to match the payments going from the protection seller to the protection buyer—the protection leg—in the case of default. This expected default payment is calculated by looking at the number of default references and loss at default for each tranche, given a certain correlation between the underlying reference assets. The correlation is mathematically handled through a Cholesky composition, and the actual loss distribution is arrived at by running a number of so-called Monte Carlo simulations, which generate at random a number of defaults (as defined by the Merton model) in the underlying assets. In the following sections, we go through the theory behind this pricing model and then illustrate with an actual example.

Pricing a CDO: The Theory

The Protection Leg: Expected Total Default Payment

We'll start by pricing the protection leg of the CDO, or in other words, calculate the expected total payment in case of a default. In the general case, consider a CDO with n reference assets, denoted i, with notional amount V_i and recovery rate δ. The loss given default for each individual asset, L_i, can then be expressed as one minus the recovery rate times the notional amount, or as the following:

$$L_i = (1 - \delta_i)V_i \qquad [34]$$

An asset, i, can have one of two values at any given time, t: It can either be defaulted or it can still be alive. As an indicator for the assets status, we denote $N_i(t)$, which can take as values either 0 (survival) or 1 (default). The definition of default we base on the Merton model, meaning that default occurs when the asset value of a firm drops below the value of its outstanding debt. (Default could be defined by any other model, such as the other structural or reduced form models that we have covered in this book.)

Using this indicator, we can express the total loss given default for the entire portfolio, L(t), as

$$L(t) = \sum_{i=1}^{n} L_i N_i(t) \qquad [35]$$

Now, if default occurs, the total loss should be distributed to each CDO trance in order of seniority. Assume that there are three tranches to a CDO: equity, mezzanine, and senior tranches. With three tranches, we effectively get two attachment points, or thresholds, where one tranche ends and another begins (in this case, between the equity and mezzanine tranche, and then again between the mezzanine and senior tranche; recall our discussion on attachment points earlier in this chapter). We'll refer to these attachment points as C and D, where C is smaller than D, and D in turn has to be smaller than the total sum of all assets in the portfolio, or

$$0 \le C \le D \le \sum_{i=1}^{n} V_i \qquad [36]$$

Given these thresholds, we can express the cumulative loss for each tranche at time t as $M_x(t)$, where x is the tranche. Taken tranche by tranche, the cumulative loss per tranche then becomes

Equity tranche $\quad M_E(t) \quad = L(t),\quad$ if $\quad L(t) \le C,\quad$ or $\qquad [37]$
$\qquad\qquad\qquad\qquad\quad = C,\qquad$ if $\quad L(t) \ge 0$

Mezzanine tranche $\; MM(t) \; = 0,\qquad$ if $\quad L(t) \le C,\quad$ or $\qquad [38]$
$\qquad\qquad\qquad\qquad\quad = L(t) - C,\;$ if $\quad D \ge L(t) \ge C,\quad$ or
$\qquad\qquad\qquad\qquad\quad = D - C,\quad$ if $\quad L(t) \ge D$

Senior tranche $\quad MS(t) \quad = 0,\qquad$ if $\quad L(t) \le D,\quad$ or $\qquad [39]$
$\qquad\qquad\qquad\qquad\quad = L(t) - D,\;$ if $\quad \sum_{i-1}^{n} V_i L(t) \ge D$

To exemplify, picture a CDO based on 10 reference assets, each with a notional amount of $1 million. The CDO consists of three tranches (senior, mezzanine, and equity) with attachment points 10 percent (equal to $1 million) between equity and mezzanine tranches and 40 percent (equal to $4 million) between mezzanine and senior tranches. Assume now that four reference assets default in the first year, and that there is no recovery made on their loss. The cumulative loss on each tranche, using the preceding formulas, can then be calculated as

Equity tranche	$M_E(1)$	= $1 million	[40]
Mezzanine tranche	$MM(1)$	= $3 million	[41]
Senior tranche	$MS(t)$	= $0 million	[42]

The expected total default payment in this case, then, is the $4 million that defaulted, distributed as $1 million to the equity tranche (equal to the whole value of the equity tranche), $3 million to the mezzanine tranche, and nothing for the senior tranche.

After distributing the losses, the mezzanine and senior tranches still continue to exist, and receive a premium payment from the SPV, which now has been adjusted to reflect the loss of principal. It is worth noting that when calculating the expected total default payment, any defaults during the lifespan of the CDO, which does not retire the entire CDO but which does affect tranches and the total notional value, has to be reflected in the original cost calculation. At its core, you then have to remember to incorporate the present value of the remaining notional value, assuming a default occurred.

Please note too that we still have not calculated any default probability for this to occur. So far, we are only concerned with the value of the defaults. We work out the default probabilities, given correlation between the reference assets, a little later. First, though, we look at the other payment stream of this CDO: the premium fee leg.

The Premium Fee Leg

The fee that the protection buyer has to pay the protection seller can be expressed by the following. We let y denote the price, or spread, and

$E^P[\,]$ denote expected value, or premium fee, for each tranche. As an example, using our three-tranche example from earlier, the payment to the holder of the mezzanine tranche can be written as

$$E^P\left[\sum_{i=1}^{m}\Delta_{i-1,i}\times y\times B(0,t_i)\min\left\{\max\left[D-L(t),0\right],D-C\right\}\right] \quad [43]$$

where

- m = All premium payment dates
- D – C = The initial tranche size of mezzanine
- D – L(t) = The outstanding tranche size of mezzanine
- $\Delta_{i-1,i}$ = The period between premium payment dates i – 1 and i
- B(0,t_i) = The discount factor at the period between 0 and t_i

This formula gives us a snapshot of the payment at a certain time, t. If we instead want to look at the payments over time—that is, using continuous time—the present value of the total premium payment for the mezzanine tranche can be written as

$$y\times E^P\left[\int_0^T B(0,t)g(L(t))dt\right] \quad [44]$$

where

$$g(L(t)) = \min\{\max[D-L(t),0],D-C\} \quad [44b]$$

Comparing the Protection Leg and the Premium Leg to Arrive at a Fee

Suppose that premium is a fair spread, which means that total payment to protection seller is equal to total payment to protection buyer. The spread, y, is given by

$$y = \frac{\sum_{i=1}^{k}B(0,t_i)\left[M(t_i)-M(t_{i-1})\right]}{E^P\left[\int_0^T B(0,t)g(L(t))dt\right]} \quad [45]$$

Simulating the Default Outcomes to Arrive at a Price

With the formula in equation 45, we have a theoretical foundation to calculate the spread or price, y. However, it does not tell us how likely defaults are to occur or when they might occur. The formula leaves that question unanswered by incorporating our indicator $N_i(t)$ from equation 35; this indicator simply simulates whether a default has taken place in one of the underlying reference assets. It does this by randomly taking one of two values: 1 for default and 0 for survival of the reference asset. Then, to arrive at an approximation of the total default loss for the whole portfolio over its lifespan, we simply run this simulation over and over again to "copy" what might happen in the real world.

Simulations help us when other analyses are too mathematically complex or too difficult to practically reproduce. Simulations simply imitate a real-life system, and when a value that is required by the system is unknown, it simply draws any random value from a list of allowed values. In the preceding example, the random value is 0 or 1 for the variable of default or no default. We then repeat this simulation over and over to simulate the model, allowing us to observe the results, rather than having to determine them analytically.

Run the simulation we described earlier, but be aware that it takes time (we can run anywhere from 100,000 simulations) and requires special software (in fact, this approach to default simulation was not feasible until the arrival of more powerful computers). That said, anyone with a regular desktop computer can run these sorts of simulations nowadays, especially one of the most common approaches, the Monte Carlo simulation mentioned previously.

Let's quickly show how the simulation works. At its core, it looks at whether a default has occurred in an underlying reference asset. We therefore have to equip ourselves with a definition of default, of which there are numerous (such as structured models, reduced form models, and so on), as we know from earlier chapters. In this case, we choose the Merton approach, where a default occurs when the asset value of a firm is lower than its outstanding debt.

Now, suppose that we have a portfolio where the underlying assets are several loans and that each obligor's asset value is known. Given this, and using the Merton model's determination of default based on the reference asset's value, the simulation can be expressed as

$$V_{t+\Delta t} = V_t \exp\{(r - 0.5\sigma_V^2)\Delta t + \sigma_V \sqrt{\Delta t} \times z\} \qquad [46]$$

where

- V_t = Asset value at time t
- r = Risk-free interest rate
- σ_V = Asset volatility
- t = Time (year)
- z = A random drawn from a standard normal distribution at each instant

The formula indicates the asset value at time $t + \Delta t$. When running the simulation, for each iteration of the formula, the computed asset value is compared to the debt value. If the asset value is smaller than the debt value, a default in the reference asset is considered to have occurred. (Put differently, the indicator for the asset's status denoting $N_i(t)$ from equation 35 becomes 1 for default.) The total expected default payment can then be computed, and any effects this has on tranche allocation are considered, including discounted payments. Consequently, a spread on a tranche can be given by equation 35.

Putting a Value on Correlation: Cholesky Decomposition

Finally, when running our Monte Carlo simulation, we can assume a certain degree of default correlation between the reference assets. Mathematically, we introduce correlation into our simulation using a technique known as Cholesky decomposition, named after the French mathematician André-Louis Cholesky (1875-1918). To exemplify, we use a simple situation with two random variables, X and Y, with correlation ρ. The correlation between the two can be described in a matrix, as done in Table 6-13.

Table 6-13 Correlation between variables X and Y

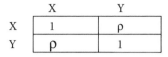

	X	Y
X	1	ρ
Y	ρ	1

In addition to the two random variables, we also include two other independent random numbers, denoted as z_1 and z_2. Now, applying the Cholesky decomposition, we can express the relationship between independent numbers and correlated numbers as follows:

$$\begin{pmatrix} 1 & 0 \\ \rho & \sqrt{1-\rho^2} \end{pmatrix} \begin{pmatrix} z_1 \\ z_2 \end{pmatrix} = \begin{pmatrix} X \\ Y \end{pmatrix} \qquad [47]$$

This two-by-two matrix is referred to as the Cholesky decomposition[6] of the correlation matrix. The preceding matrix equation can be rewritten as

$$X = z_1 \qquad [48]$$

$$Y = \rho \times z_1 + \sqrt{1-\rho^2} \times z_2$$

For example, if $\rho = 0.2$, the correlated number can be given for z_1 and z_2.

$$X = z_1 \qquad [49]$$

$$Y = 0.2z_1 + 0.98 \times z_2$$

Therefore, in the case of the simulation, we first generate several independent random normal distributions and then transform them into correlated random distribution by using equation 48. Although this might seem a very theoretical construct at this point, we show in the following examples how to apply our formulas to price a CDO. The usefulness of a Cholesky decomposition to approximate default correlation should then be more evident.

Pricing a CDO: The Example

We will now exemplify how to price a CDO based on the theoretical foundation we laid earlier. For simplicity, our first example assumes no correlation between the reference assets. We then continue with an example where we assume correlation between the underlying assets; this assumption naturally makes the example more complicated.

Pricing with No Correlation Using a Monte Carlo Simulation

Recall that we are using the Merton model's definition of default: Default occurs when asset value drops below debt value. For our simulations, it is then necessary to establish asset value at maturity time and compare this with the debt value at the same time. To make this evaluation, we use equation 46, which shows us asset value of a reference asset at time $t + \Delta t$.

For our example of pricing with no correlation between reference assets, we make the following assumptions:

- We have a portfolio composed of five reference assets.

- Each reference asset has the same size of $1.0 million and the same recovery rate of 0.4.

- Each reference asset has the same individual default probability as the other reference assets. (This can be calculated as 3.7 percent.[7])

- We consider default and survival of the portfolio during a time horizon of one year.

These assumptions, which become our baseline data for the Monte Carlo simulation, are summarized in Table 6-14.

Table 6-14 Baseline data for the Monte Carlo simulation

Asset value	$1.4 million
Principal value	$1.0 million
Risk-free rate	4%
Asset volatility	20%
Time to maturity	1 year
Recovery rate	0.4

On this portfolio with a total notional value of $5 million, we issue a CDO broken into three tranches. The senior tranche takes $4 million of the underlying assets, whereas the mezzanine and equity tranches take $0.5 million, as shown in Table 6-15.

Table 6-15 CDO tranches

Tranche Name	Notional Amount ($ million)
Senior	4.0
Mezzanine	0.5
Equity	0.5

Note that the attachment points C and D, a concept we introduced in equation 36, then become 0.5 and 1.0, respectively.

Given the preceding information, we now run a Monte Carlo simulation on our portfolio using the Merton model's definition of default. We run the simulation 10,000 times, first for the protection leg and then for the premium leg. For the protection leg of the CDO—the payment for default loss—the simulation steps are as follows:

- Draw five random numbers ($z1$, $z2$, $z3$, $z4$, $z5$) from a standard normal distribution.

- Compute current asset value at maturity time (end of year one) using equation 46 (repeated next for reference) for each reference asset as

$$V_t = V_0 \exp\{(r - 0.5\sigma_V^2) \times t + \sigma_V \times z \times \sqrt{t}\} \qquad [50]$$

where

  - V_t = Asset value at time t
  - V_0 = Initial asset value

- Compare the asset value with debt value. If the asset value is smaller than the debt value, the reference asset defaults. If the asset value is higher than the debt value, the reference asset has not defaulted.

- Sum up any loss payment—that is, take the notional amount times the number of default asset multiplied by 0.6 (= 1 – recovery rate as given in Table 6-14) and allocate the loss into the three tranches in order of seniority. The payment for default loss on a given tranche is discounted by e_{-rt} (where r = risk-free interest rate of 4.0 percent, and t is the maturity date).

- Repeat the preceding steps 10,000 times and compute average of loss payment for each tranche.

Table 6-16 shows the expected default loss payment from the simulation by 10,000 times.

Table 6-16 Expected default loss payment by tranche of CDO

Tranche Name	Expected Default Loss Payment (US $)
Senior	$0.0028
Mezzanine	$0.0213
Equity	$0.0824

The simulation has given us values for the protection leg for each of the tranches. We then turn to the premium fee or payment leg. As we know, to arrive at a fair price or spread for a CDO, the premium leg (or the sum of the premium payments to the tranche holders) should equal the protection leg (or the sum of the expected loss payment from the tranche holders). Using this idea, we simply compute the fair spread— or the premium leg—by calculating the expected discounted total payment on default divided by tranche size, as follows:

Senior tranche: $0.0028 / $4.0   = 0.0007   or   0.07%   [51]

Mezzanine tranche: $0.0213 / $0.5   = 0.0426   or   4.26%   [52]

Equity tranche: $0.0824 / $0.5   = 0.1648   or   16.48%   [53]

Table 6-17 shows the fair spread on three tranches of the CDO.

Table 6-17 Fair spread on three tranches of CDO

Tranche Name	Expected Default Loss Payment (in $)	Tranche Size	Fair Spread (%)
Senior	$0.0028	$4.000	0.07%
Mezzanine	$0.0213	$0.500	4.26%
Equity	$0.0824	$0.500	16.48%

As could be expected, the equity tranche has the highest spread, because it is by far the riskiest of the three tranches. Although the equity tranche's expected loss is less than $0.1 million, the entire principal value of the equity tranche is wiped out if a default event occurs. Given our portfolio, a default of a reference asset would cause a $0.6 million loss ($1 million in reference asset value minus the $0.4 million recovery value), which is greater than the equity tranche. The high spread for the tranche thus reflects more the consequence of a default rather than the expected loss value.

Pricing with Correlation Using a Monte Carlo Simulation

Let's reuse the same portfolio (see Tables 6-14 and 6-15), but this time we assume that there *is* correlation between the reference assets. For simplicity, we assume that each asset has the identical correlation against any other asset at 0.2. This gives the reference assets the asset correlation matrix shown in Table 6-18.

Table 6-18 Correlation matrix for five reference assets

	1	2	3	4	5
1	1.0	0.2	0.2	0.2	0.2
2	0.2	1.0	0.2	0.2	0.2
3	0.2	0.2	1.0	0.2	0.2
4	0.2	0.2	0.2	1.0	0.2
5	0.2	0.2	0.2	0.2	1.0

In addition, we also assume that the probability of a single reference asset to default—or, put differently, of a single name defaulting—does not change with correlation. It remains at 3.7 percent, which was shown in the previous no-correlation example.

For the protection leg, and its payment for default loss, the simulation steps can be outlined as follows:

1. We construct an asset correlation matrix as the one shown in Table 6-18.

2. We then draw five independent random numbers ($z1$, $z2$, $z3$, $z4$, $z5$) from a standard normal distribution.

3. We transform the five independent random numbers into five correlated random numbers ($c1$, $c2$, $c3$, $c4$, $c5$) using the Cholesky decomposition. The Cholesky decomposition generates the 5×5 matrix shown here:

$$\begin{pmatrix} 1.0 & 0 & 0 & 0 & 0 \\ 0.2 & 0.98 & 0 & 0 & 0 \\ 0.2 & 0.16 & 0.97 & 0 & 0 \\ 0.2 & 0.16 & 0.14 & 0.96 & 0 \\ 0.2 & 0.16 & 0.14 & 0.12 & 0.95 \end{pmatrix} \qquad [54]$$

4. The five independent random numbers can then be changed into correlated numbers.

$$\begin{pmatrix} 1.0 & 0 & 0 & 0 & 0 \\ 0.2 & 0.98 & 0 & 0 & 0 \\ 0.2 & 0.16 & 0.97 & 0 & 0 \\ 0.2 & 0.16 & 0.14 & 0.96 & 0 \\ 0.2 & 0.16 & 0.14 & 0.12 & 0.95 \end{pmatrix} \times \begin{pmatrix} z_1 \\ z_2 \\ z_3 \\ z_4 \\ z_5 \end{pmatrix} = \begin{pmatrix} c_1 \\ c_2 \\ c_3 \\ c_4 \\ c_5 \end{pmatrix} \qquad [55]$$

Hence, the correlated numbers can be represented as

$$c_1 = z_1 \qquad\qquad [56]$$
$$c_2 = 0.2 z_1 + 0.98 z_2$$
$$c_3 = 0.2 z_1 + 0.16 z_2 + 0.97 z_3$$
$$c_4 = 0.2 z_1 + 0.16 z_2 + 0.14 z_3 + 0.96 z_4$$
$$c_5 = 0.2 z_1 + 0.16 z_2 + 0.14 z_3 + 0.12 z_4 + 0.95 z_5$$

5. We compute the asset value at maturity time for each reference asset (as we did in equation 46). However, this time, we replace z by c because the random numbers are changed into correlated numbers. The modified equation is written as

$$V_t = V_0 \exp\{(r - 0.5\sigma_V^2) \times t + \sigma_V \times c \times \sqrt{t}\} \qquad [57]$$

6. We then follow the same steps as in the previous simulation.

Table 6-19 shows the expected default loss payment when we have repeated this simulation 10,000 times.

Table 6-19 Expected default loss payment by tranche of CDO (Correlation = 0.2 Among Reference Assets)

Tranche Name	Payment on Default ($ million)
Senior	$0.007
Mezzanine	$0.023
Equity	$0.074

Comparing the default payments from the CDO's protection leg to the payment fee, we can, as in the previous example, calculate a fair spread on each of the three tranches, as shown in Table 6-20.

Table 6-20 Fair spread on three tranches of CDO (Correlation = 0.2)

Tranche Name	Expected Total Payment on Default ($ million)	Tranche Size	Fair Spread (%)
Senior	$0.007	$4.000	0.18%
Mezzanine	$0.023	$0.500	4.60%
Equity	$0.074	$0.500	14.80%

How closely correlated the reference assets are affects the spread of the various tranches. In Table 6-20, we simply assume a default correlation of 0.2. What would happen if the default correlation had been 0.0, 0.2, 0.4, 0.6, 0.8, or 1.0? Figure 6-11 illustrates such a sensitivity analysis of various correlation levels for the three tranches in our sample CDO, running a Monte Carlo simulation 10,000 times.

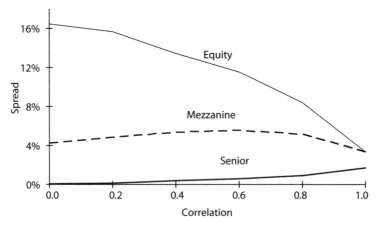

Figure 6-11 Sensitivity analysis of expected fair spread by default correlation

As Figure 6-11 shows, the spreads for the three tranches converge at the higher correlation levels. At these higher levels, the three tranches start acting more like one instrument with the same risk profile, so it is natural that they should share the same spread. However, it may appear strange that the equity tranche *drops* in spread (and conversely increases in price) as the correlation increases. One might expect the spread for equity to remain the same for all correlation levels, with the spreads for the mezzanine and senior tranches rising to the equity spread level for perfect correlation. However, this does not happen; instead, the spread for the equity tranche drops in value. Let's look further into this behavior.

First of all, we recall the assumptions for our simulation portfolio:

- The portfolio consists of five reference assets.

- Each reference asset has the same size of $1.0 million and the same recovery rate of 0.4.

- Each reference asset has the same individual default probability as the other reference assets.

- We consider default and survival of the portfolio during a time horizon of one year.

- The individual default probability is not influenced by correlation.

Under these assumptions, the probability of several defaults—also known as multiname defaults—naturally increases as correlation increases. Also, it should be noted that the probability of no default (which is the same as having all assets surviving) *also* increases as correlation increases. With fewer "in-between" outcomes possible, the probabilities simply start to focus on either of the two extremes. In the case of perfect correlation, there are only these two outcomes possible. Figure 6-12 shows the distribution of default outcomes under perfect correlation for our reference portfolio.

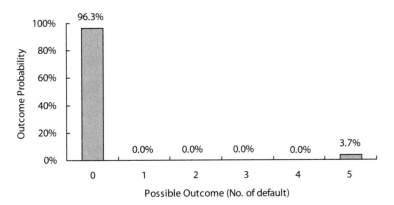

Figure 6-12 Distribution of default outcomes with five assets under perfect correlation

For completeness, we also look at the distribution of default outcomes under zero correlation, as shown in Figure 6-13.[8]

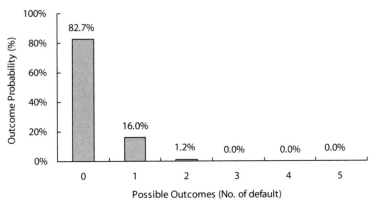

Figure 6-13 Distribution of default outcomes with five assets under zero correlation

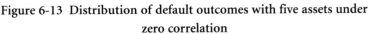

Comparing Figures 6-12 and 6-13, we can see graphically what we previously explained in words: that the probabilities for no default and all default both increase as correlation increases. Table 6-21 summarizes the outcome probability for these two extreme outcomes under zero and perfect correlation.

Table 6-21 Outcome probability under two extreme cases: zero and perfect correlation

Number of Default	Outcome Probability	
	Zero Correlation	Perfect Correlation
No default	82.7%	96.3%
All default	0.0%	3.7%

As Table 6-21 shows, the probability of all default increases from 0.0 percent to 3.7 percent as correlation increases from zero to one. The probability of 3.7 percent at perfect correlation is equal to individual default probability because the portfolio can be regarded as one instrument. In the same way, the probability of no default (or all survival) increases from 82.7 percent for zero correlation to 96.3 percent for perfect correlation. (The default probability at perfect correlation is the same as individual survival probability of 96.3 percent or one minus the individual default probability.)

Let us go back to Figure 6-11 and the question we are trying to answer: Why does the equity tranche drop in spread as correlation increases? The reason is that the probability of no default increases as correlation increases, as we discussed earlier. Simply put, with a lower default risk, the investor asks for less compensation and so the spread drops. To expand on this, Table 6-22 shows the equity tranche holder's payment on default and how it remains the same regardless of the number of default outcomes. In the case of no default, the equity tranche holder doesn't have to make any payment, and so the expected total payment on default decreases as the probability of no default increases.

Table 6-22 Tranche loss allocation by default outcome patterns

Number of Default Outcomes	Total Loss ($ million)	Tranche Loss Allocation ($ million)		
		Equity	Mezzanine	Senior
0	0	0	0	0
1	0.6	0.5	0.1	0
2	1.2	0.5	0.5	0.2
3	1.8	0.5	0.5	0.8
4	2.4	0.5	0.5	1.4
5	3.0	0.5	0.5	2.0

As to the behavior of the mezzanine tranche in Figure 6-11, its spread initially increases as correlation increases, but past a certain point, it actually starts to decrease. The initial growth is easy to understand: The shift from single-name to multiname defaults increases the expected total payment on default (unlike the equity tranche we just discussed). However, if the correlation reaches a higher range (about 0.6 in our example), the increase in no-default probability leads to a decrease of total expected payment on default. The reason for this is the same as for the equity tranche that we just discussed: At this level of correlation, a shift from, for example, two defaults to three defaults does not influence the payment on default (which remains at $0.5 million), but at the same time, the probability of no default increases, which impacts the payment on default and decreases its value after all—hence, the initial rise and then drop in the spread of the mezzanine tranche as correlation increases. It makes the mezzanine tranche behave like a "safe" tranche at low default correlations, with a spread closer to that of the senior tranche than the equity tranche. However, for higher default correlations, the spread on the mezzanine tranche becomes more like that of the equity tranche. Thus, positioned between the senior and equity tranches, the mezzanine tranche takes on the behavior of both tranches at various levels of default correlations.

Finally, unlike the two other tranches, the senior tranche in Figure 6-11 sees its spread continuing to increase with higher correlations. The reason is simple: The higher the number of default outcomes, the greater the payment on default (as shown also in Table 6-22). In fact, the probability of all default increases as correlation increases, which translates into a higher spread for the senior tranche for the higher correlation levels.

An Alternative CDO Pricing Method: The Copula Function

In the previous section, we priced a CDO based on the Merton model using a Cholesky composition to handle correlation. There are several other approaches to pricing CDOs in the market. Among these, the approach that uses a so-called Copula model to handle correlation seems to be emerging as the de facto standard. First presented by David Li in 2000,[9] the mathematics involved in the Copula model are well beyond the scope of this book, which is why we choose to illustrate CDO pricing based on Cholesky and Merton. However, we should note that one of the primary advantages of the Copula approach is that it allows us to capture default timing. For each simulation, the Copula approach only requires finding the underlying asset whose default timing is shorter than each payment date rather than computing default status for each period.

Without going into the mathematics needed to run a Copula simulation, we can still look at the outcomes of the approach, and compare these to other models. As an example, we reuse the same portfolio (recall Table 6-14) and same CDO tranches (recall Table 6-15). We submit this CDO to 10,000 simulations using the Copula approach, and for six different levels of default correlation (0.0, 0.2, 0.4, 06, 0.8, and 1.0). The resulting credit spreads for the various levels are shown in a sensitivity analysis in Figure 6-14.

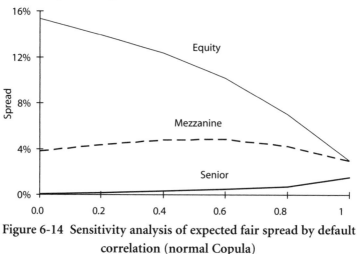

Figure 6-14 Sensitivity analysis of expected fair spread by default correlation (normal Copula)

Using the Copula approach, we arrive at three tranches that behave similarly to the curves in Figure 6-11.

Endnotes

1 SPVs are mostly incorporated in offshore tax havens, such as the Cayman Islands. A number of SPV management companies have sprung up to run SPVs, including providing autonomous boards of directors.

2 Naturally, this credit structure then does not apply to synthetic CDOs where there has been no transfer of the underlying assets to the SPV.

3 The examples on coverage tests draws on the Basel Committee on Banking Supervision, "Credit Risk Transfer," Bank for International Settlements (Basel: 2005), available at www.bis.org/publ/joint13.pdf, accessed July 2005.

4 Although slightly different in its theoretical construct, we will in this book equate the concept of joint default probability with correlation.

5 The Monte Carlo simulation was instituted by Polish-born mathematician Stanislaw Ulam in the 1940s and named after the famous casino in Monaco where random events determine the luck or failure of all participants.

6 Specifically, the Cholesky decomposition can be generalized as follows: If B is a matrix constructed by the Cholesky decomposition, which holds $\Sigma = B^{T}B$, then B can be written as

$$b_{ij} = \frac{a_{ij} - \sum_{k=1}^{j-1} b_{ik} b_{jk}}{\sqrt{1 - \sum_{k=1}^{j-1} b_{jk}^2}} \quad 1 \leq j \leq i \leq n$$

where a_{ij} is element of n dimension matrix Σ.

7 The individual default probability can be given by the Merton model, for example. With the baseline data in Figure 6-10, individual default probability in the previous example can be calculated, using the formula we learned in Chapter 4, "Modeling Credit Risk: Alternative Pricing Approaches," as

$$N(-d_2) = N(\frac{\ln(1.4/1.0) + (0.04 - 0.5 \times 0.2^2) \times 1}{0.2 \times \sqrt{1}}) = 3.7\%$$

8 Theoretically, the distribution of default outcomes follows a binominal distribution, which is what is used for the graph in Figure 6-13. However, we used a Monte Carlo simulation rather than the binominal distribution for the sensitivity analysis in Figure 6-11.

9 For the original paper, see David X. Li, "On Default Correlation: A Copula Function Approach," The RiskMetrics Group, Working Paper Number 99-07, First draft: September 1999, Published April 2000.

INDEX

A

ABSs (asset-backed securities), 192
Acme, Inc., balance sheets, 67
adjusted market value, 216
advance rates, market-value CDOs, 215-216
Altman's initial Z-score paper, 124-125
Altman, Edward I., 121, 125
American option, 72
arbitrage CDOs versus balance-sheet CDOs, 222
arbitrage motivated CDOs, 198-199
arrival rate, 132
arrivals, 131
asset price volatility, 86
asset value
    comparing Black and Cox model and Merton model, 112
    sensitivity analysis of Merton model, 102
asset value models, 66
asset volatility
    comparing Black and Cox model and Merton model, 111
    sensitivity analysis of Merton model, 99-100
asset-backed securities (ABSs), 192
assets, 67
attachment point, 195

B

bad loans, 3
balance sheets
    balance sheet motivated CDOs, 197
    structural credit risk models, 66-69
balance-sheet CDOs versus arbitrage CDOs, 222
Bank for International Settlements (BIS), 58

bankruptcies, 18, 193
    by geography, 37
    U.S. companies, 17
bankruptcy filings, U.S., 14-15
banks, CDOs, 223
barrier function, Black and Cox model, 105-107
basis points, 59
basket CDSs, 156-157
basket credit default swaps, 49
basket default swaps
    loss distribution, 179
    pricing, 176-177, 181-182
        nondefault correlation portfolio, 178-181
        perfect default correlation portfolio, 177-178
BBA (British Bankers' Association), 55, 187
being long, 73
binary CDSs, 154-155
BIS (Bank for International Settlements), 58
Black and Cox model, 70, 104
    barrier function ,105-107
    comparing to Merton model, 110-113
    example of applying extension to Merton model, 107-110
Black, Fischer, 104
Black-Scholes economy
    applying Merton model, 83-84
        assumptions underlying this approach, 86-87
        Black-Scholes formula for call options, 84-85
        Black-Scholes formula for put options, 86
Black-Scholes model, volatility value, 92

bonds, 12
    commercial papers, 13
    corporate bond market, 34
    corporate bonds, 13
    corporate bonds with risk premium, 24
    corporate bonds without risk premium, 23
    government bonds, 13
    public and private bond market debt, U.S., 33
    redemption features, 14
    risk-free bonds, 13
    U.S. Treasury Bonds, 13
    zero-coupon bonds, 14
book value, 128
breaking points, 71
British Bankers' Association (BBA), 55, 187

C

calculating
    credit spread, 25-26
    debt value, Merton model, 89-90
    expected default payment, 226
    risk-neutral default probability, 94-95
call options, 52, 71-72
    Black-Scholes formula, 84-85
cash CDOs, 193, 199
cash flows
    arbitrage motivated CDOs, 199
    basket CDSs, 157
    CDOs, 193
    CDOs of EDS, 204
    digital CDSs, 155
    iTraxx, 163
    plain vanilla CDSs, 153
    portfolio CDSs, 159
    synthetic CDOs, 200
cash settlement, 153
cash-flow CDOs, 205-208
    O/C and I/C, 208-215
cash-flow period, life cycle of CDOs, 197

cash-flow waterfall, cash-flow CDOs, 207
CBOs (collateralized bond obligation), 52, 191
CDO market, 220-223
CDO squared, 202-203
CDO2, 202
CDOs (collateralized debt obligations), 52, 147, 189, 192-195
    arbitrage motivated CDOs, 198-199
    balance sheet motivated CDOs, 197
    balance-sheet CDOs versus arbitrage CDOs, 222
    cash CDOs, 199
    cash flows, 193
    CDO squared, 202-203
    CDOs of EDS, 203-204
    credit enhancement provisions, 205
        cash-flow CDOs, 205-215
        market-value CDO, 205-206
    life cycle, 197
    market-value CDOs. *See* market-value CDOs
    pricing, 220, 225-227
        Cholesky decomposition, 232-233
        comparing protection leg and premium leg to arrive at a fee, 230
        Copula model, 244-245
        with correlation using a Monte Carlo simulation, 237-244
        with no correlation using a Monte Carlo simulation, 234-237
        premium leg, 230
        protection leg, 227-229
        simulating default outcomes to arrive at a price, 231-232
    protection buyers, 223
    protection sellers, 223
    seniority, 194
    synthetic CDOs, 199-201
    tranches, 194-197
CDOs of EDS, 203-204
CDS market, 186-188

CDSs (credit default swap), 48-49, 56, 147-148, 151
  basket CDSs, 156-157
  digital CDSs, 154-155
  indices, 160-163
  interest rate swaps, 148-150
  leg, 165
  multiname CDSs, 156
    pricing, 172-176
  multiname CDSs. *See* multiname CDSs
  plain vanilla CDSs, 152-154
  portfolio CDSs, 158-159
  premium leg, 165
  pricing, 164-165
  pricing swaps, 150-151
  protection leg, 165
  protection sellers, 188
  single-name CDSs, 156
Cholesky decomposition, 226, 232-233
Cholesky, Andre-Louis, 232
CLNs (credit linked notes), 49-51
CLO (collateralized loan obligation), 52, 191
CMOs (collateralized mortgage obligations), 52, 191
collateral, 4, 59
collateralized bond obligation (CBO), 52, 191
collateralized debt, 53
collateralized debt obligations. *See* CDOs
collateralized loan obligation (CLO), 19, 52, 191
collateralized mortgage obligations (CMOs), 19, 52, 191
collateralized products, 52
Colombia Healthcare, 38
commercial papers, 13
companies, defaulting on loans, 15-17
company-specific risk, 7
comparing Black and Cox model and Merton model, 110-113
Copula model, 244-245
corporate bond market, 34

corporate bond with risk premium, 24
corporate bond without risk premium, 23
corporate bonds, sinking fund provision, 13
correlation
  Cholesky decomposition, 232-233
  defaults, 225
  pricing CDOs using a Monte Carlo simulation, 237-244
countries, defaulting on loans, 17
coupon payments, 14
coupons, 10
coverage tests, 206, 209-215
covered option, 118
Cox, J.C., 104
credit
  defined, 10
  types of, 11-14
credit default option, 189
credit default spread premium, 152
credit default swap spread, 152
credit default swaps. *See* CDSs
credit derivatives, 5-6, 44-46
credit derivatives market, 53-54
  market participants, 55-56
  product usage, 56-57
  regional markets, 54
  underlying reference assets, 57-58
credit enhancements provisions
  CDOs, 205
    cash-flow CDOs, 205-215
    market-value CDOs, 205-206
  market-value CDOs, 215
    advance rates and overcollateralization tests, 215-216
    example using advance rates to calculate overcollateralization ratios, 217-220
credit event after merger, 18
credit events, 18
credit exposure, 20
credit linked notes (CLNs), 49-51
credit rating, recovery rate, 42
credit rating agencies, 26-27

credit ratings
    evaluating default probability, 27,
      30-31
    one-year ratings transition
      matrix, 31
credit risk, 3-4
    defined, 9, 20
    measuring through credit spread,
      21-24
    reducing, 5-6
    who suffers from credit risk?, 6
credit risk instruments, 45
credit risk models
    empirical credit risk models, 65
    reduced form models, 65
    structural credit risk models, 65-66
      balance sheet, 66-69
      limitations, 69
      Merton model. See Merton model
      option pricing, 70
      types of, 70
    structure of, 64
credit risk statistics, 33-35
    default rates, 35-38
    recovery rates, 40-43
credit scoring models, 120-121
    Z-score model, 121-123
      Altman's initial Z-score
      paper, 124-125
      example, 126-127
      Z'-score, 128-130
credit spread, 21-22
    calculating, 25-26
    corporate bond with risk premium,
      24
    corporate bond without risk premi-
      um, 23
    determining with Merton model,
      90-91
    irregularities, 97
    risk-free government bond, 23
credit spread options (CSOs), 51-52
credit spread sensitivity
    against maturity time by default
      intensity, Jarrow-Turnbull
      model, 141-142

    against maturity time by recovery
      rate, Jarrow-Turnbull model, 143
credit structures, CDOs, 205
creditors, 10
cross-default provisions, 105
CSOs (credit spread options), 51-52
currency, 11
currency risk, 7

D

debt
    investment grade debt, 26
    junior debt, 19
    junk bonds, 26
    Merton model, 79-81
    mortgage related debt, 34
    non-investment grade, 26
    public and private bond market
      debt, U.S., 33
    risky debt, Merton model, 76
    senior debt, 19
    speculative grade, 26
debt obligations, 12-14
debt value
    calculating with Merton model,
      89-90
    sensitivity analysis of Merton model,
      103-104
debt waterfalls, 19
debtors, 10
default, 6
default correlation, 173, 225
    basket default swaps, 177-178
    multiname CDSs, 173-174
default data, evaluating default
  probability, 27, 30-31
default intensity, 131-133
    credit spread sensitivity against
      maturity time by default intensity,
      Jarrow-Turnbull model, 141-142
    Jarrow-Turnbull model, 138-139
    over time, 133-136
default intensity modeling, 131

default probability, 21, 225
  evaluating, 26-27
    credit ratings and default data, 27, 30-31
    example of difficulty in rating, 31-33
default probablity, 21
default process, 19
default rates, 35-36
  by geography, 36-38
  by industry sector, 38
  for 1994, 30
default remoteness, 193
default risk. *See* credit risk
default timing, Merton model, 104
default-free bonds, 13
default-free rate, 23
defaulting on loans, 14
  companies, 15-17
  countries, 17
  individuals, 14
defaults
  correlation, 225
  credit events, 18
derivatives, 8
diffusion process, 116
digital CDSs, 154-155
distribution, loss distribution, 173
distribution model, 144
Dow Jones CDS indices, 160
Dow Jones iTraxx, 160-161
  cash flows, 163

E

EAD (exposure at default), 20
EBIT/TA (earnings before interest and taxes/total assets), 123
EDS (equity default swaps), 202
  CDOs of EDS, 203-204
empirical credit risk models, 65
empirical models. *See* credit scoring models
equity, 67, 71
  Merton model, 78, 81-82
equity default swaps. *See* EDS

equity value, finding debt value by calculating equity value (Merton model), 89
Euro LIBOR, 162
European options, 72
evaluating default probability, 26-27
  credit ratings and default data, 27, 30-31
  example of difficulty in rating, 31-33
exercise date, 72
expected default payment, protection leg (CDOs), 227-229
expected loss, 22
expiration date, 12
exponential function, 144
exposure at default (EAD), 20
extending Merton model, 104-105
  barrier function, 105-107
  example of applying Black and Cox's extension, 107-110
  Longstaff and Schwartz, 113-114

F

failure to pay, 18
finding
  debt value by calculating equity value, 89
  default intensity, Jarrow-Turnbull model, 138-139
First Passage model. *See* Black and Cox model
first-to-default (FTD), 49
first-to-default (FTD) basket CDSs, 156
fixed-recovery CDSs. *See* digital CDSs
FLP (First-to-Loss Protection), 49
FTD (first-to-default), 49

G

going long, 74
going long the credit, 153
going short the credit, 153
government action, credit events, 18
government bonds, 13
grey zone, 125
guarantees, 4

H-I

haircut asset value, 216

I/C (interest coverage), 207
I/C (overcollateralization), 208-215
IMF (International Monetary Fund), 17
implied volatility, 92
in-the-money, 78
indenture, 118
indices, CDSs, 160-161
    example, 161-163
individuals, defaulting on loans, 14
industries
    default rates, 38
    recovery rate, 42-43
inflation, interest, 11
insurance, 152
insurance companies, CDOs, 223
interest, 10-11
interest cash-flow waterfall, 211
interest coverage (I/C), 207-208
interest coverage test, 208
interest rate risk, 7
interest rate swaps, 148-150
interest rates, 44
    comparing Black and Cox model and
      Merton model, 112
    sensitivity analysis of Merton model,
      100-101
International Monetary Fund (IMF), 17
investment grade, 26
iTraxx, 160-161
    cash flows, 163
iTraxx Europe, 162

J-K

Jarrow-Turnbull model, 130, 137
    credit spread sensitivity against
      maturity time by default intensity,
      141-142
    credit spread sensitivity against
      maturity time by recovery rate, 143
    default intensity, finding, 138-139
    example, 139-140
    sensitivity analysis, 140-141

joint default probability, 225
junior debt, 19
junk bonds, 26

L

leg, 150
    CDSs, 165
liabilities, 67
LIBOR (London Inter Bank Offered
    Rate), 58, 148
life cycle of CDOs, 197
limitations, structural credit risk
    models, 69
loans, 11
    bad loans, 3
    defaulting on loans. See defaulting
      on loans
    mortgages, 12
    non-performing loans, 3
lognormal distribution, 87
London Inter Bank Offered Rate
    (LIBOR), 58
Longstaff and Schwartz model, 113-116
    example of applying, 116-117
    sensitivity analysis, 117
loss distribution, 173
    basket default swaps, 179
    multiname CDSs, 174-176
    portfolio default swap, 184-185

M

marked-to-market, 206
market disruptions, credit events, 18
market participants, credit derivatives
    market, 55-56
market risk, 7
market value, 128
market value of equity/book value of
    total liabilities (MVE/TL), 123
market-value CDOs, 205-206
    credit enhancements, 215
      advance tests and overcollateraliza-
      tion tests, 215-216
      example using advance rates to
      calculate overcollateralization
      ratios, 217-220

markets
    CDO market, 220-223
    CDS market, 186-188
maturity date, 12, 72
measuring credit risk through credit
    spread, 21-24
Merton model, 66, 70, 75-76, 78
    applying in Black-Scholes economy,
        83-84
        *assumptions underlying this
            approach, 86-87*
        *Black-Scholes formula for call
            options, 84-85*
        *Black-Scholes formula for put
            options, 86*
    comparing to Black and Cox model,
        110-113
    debt interpretation, 79-81
    default timing, 104
    equity interpretation, 78, 81-82
    equity payoff as a function of asset
        value, 77
    example, 87-88, 91-94
        arriving at the credit spread, 90-91
        balance sheet, 91
        *calculating debt value directly,
            89-90*
        *finding debt value by calculating
            equity value, 89*
    extending, 104-105
        barrier function, 105-107
        *example of applying Black and
            Cox's extension, 107-110*
        Longstaff and Schwartz, 113-114
    option pricing, 82-83
    payoff of a zero-coupon Treasury
        Bond, 79
    risk-neutral default probability,
        94-95
    risky debt, 76
    sensitivity analysis, 95-98
        asset value, 102
        asset volatility, 99-100
        debt value, 103-104
        interest rates, 100-101

Merton, Robert C., 66, 75
mezzanine tranches, 243
models
    asset value models, 66
    Black and Cox model. *See* Black and
        Cox model
    Copula model, 244-245
    credit risk models. *See* credit risk
        models
    credit scoring models. *See* credit
        scoring models
    default intensity modeling, 131
    empirical models. *See* credit scoring
        models
    Longstaff and Schwartz. *See*
        Longstaff and Schwartz model
    Merton model. *See* Merton model
    reduced form models. *See* reduced
        form models
Money Market, 34
Monte Carlo simulation, 227
    pricing with correlation, 237-244
    pricing with no correlation, 234-237
Moody, credit rating system, 27
moral hazard dilemma, 197
mortgage related debt, 34
mortgages, 12
multiname CDSs, 156
    pricing, 172-173
        basket default swaps, 176-182
        default correlation, 173-174
        loss distribution, 174-176
        *portfolio default swap, 182-184,
            186*
MVE/TL (market value of equity/book
    value of total liabilities), 123

N

naked option, 118
non-investment grade, 26
non-performing loans, 3
nondefault correlation portfolio, basket
    default swaps, 178-181
notional amount, 150
nth-to-default basket CDSs, 156

O

O/C (overcollateralization), 207-215
obligor, 10
option pricing, 66
    Merton model, 82-83
    structural credit risk models, 70
options
    American options, 72
    being long, 73
    call options, 71-72
    covered option, 118
    defined, 71
    equity, 71
    European options, 72
    going long, 74
    naked option, 118
    payoffs for holding options, 73
    payoffs for selling options, 74-75
    put options, 71, 73
    shorting the option 74
OTC (over-the-counter) market, 53
out-of-the-money, 78
over-the-counter (OTC) market, 53
overcollateralization (O/C), 207
overcollateralization tests, 208
    market-value CDOs, 215-216

P

payoffs
    for holding options, 73
    for selling options, 74-75
physical settlement, 153
plain vanilla credit default swaps, 152-154
Poisson distribution, 132
Poisson event, 131
portfolio CDSs, 158-159
portfolio default swap
    loss distribution, 184-185
    pricing multiname CDSs, 182-184, 186
portfolio products, 52
premium leg
    CDOs, 230
    CDSs, 165
    pricing, 165-167

pricing
    CDOs, 220, 225-227
        Cholesky decomposition, 232-233
        comparing protection leg and premium leg to arrive at a fee, 230
        Copula model, 244-245
        premium leg, 230
        protection leg, 227-229
        simulating default outcomes to arrive at a price, 231-232
        with correlation using a Monte Carlo simulation, 237-244
        with no correlation using a Monte Carlo simulation, 234-237
    CDSs, 164-165
        pricing single-name CDSs using the reduced form approach, 171-172
        pricing single-name CDSs using the structural approach, 165-170
    multiname CDSs, 172-173
        basket default swaps, 176-182
        default correlation, 173-174
        loss distribution, 174-176
        portfolio default swap, 182-184, 186
    premium leg, 165-167
    protection leg, 167-168
    swaps, 150-151
principal, 10
principal value of debt, comparing Black and Cox model and Merton model, 113
probability, calculating risk-neutral default probability, 94-95
products, credit derivatives market, 56-57
protection buyers, 153
    CDOs, 223
protection leg
    CDOs, expected total default payment, 227-229
    CDSs, 165
    pricing, 167-168

protection sellers, 46, 153
  CDOs, 223
  CDSs, 188
put options, 71, 73
  Black-Scholes formula, 86

Q

quantitative scores, 120

R

ramp-up period, life cycle of CDOs, 197
random walk, 118
ratings transition matrix, 31
RE/TA (related earnings/total
  assets), 122
recovery rate, 4, 19, 21-22
  credit spread sensitivity against
    maturity time by recovery rate,
    Jarrow-Turnbull model, 143
recovery rates, 40
  by credit rating, 42
  by industry, 42-43
  by seniority, 40
redemption features, bonds, 14
reduced form approach, pricing single-
  name CDSs, 171-172
reduced form models, 65, 130-131
  default intensity, 131-133
    over time, 133-136
reducing credit risk, 5-6
regional markets, credit derivatives
  market, 54
regression analysis, 144
reinvestment period, life cycle of
  CDOs, 197
related earnings, 122
related earnings/total assets
  (RE/TA), 122
replicated swaps, 151
resecuritization, 202
retiring the bond, 13
risk buyer, 153
risk hedger, 153
risk premium, 22
risk-free bonds, 13

risk-free government bond, 23
risk-neutral default probability, calculating, 94-95

S

S&P, credit rating system, 27
S/TA (sales/total assets), 123
safety covenants, 105
sales/total assets (S/TA), 123
second to default (STD), 156
securitization, 192
sellers, protection sellers. *See* protection
  sellers
senior debt, 19
seniority, 19
  CDOs, 194
  recovery rate, 40
sensitivity analysis
  Jarrow-Turnbull Model, 140-141
  Longstaff and Schwartz model, 117
  Merton model. *See* Merton model
shortfall, 219
shorting the option, 74
significant downgrading of credit rating, 18
simulating default outcomes to arrive at
  a price, CDOs, 231-232
single-name CDSs, 156
  pricing using the reduced form
    approach, 171-172
  pricing using the structural
    approach, 165-170
sinking fund provision, 13
SPCs (special purpose companies), 50
speculative grade, 26
SPEs (special purpose entities), 50, 193
SPVs (special purpose vehicle) ,193, 193
stale sources, 32
Standard & Poor's 500 Index, 189
STD (second-to-default), 156
stress scenarios, 22
strike price, 72
structural approach, pricing single-
  name CDSs, 165, 168
  example, 169-170

premium leg, 165-167
protection leg, 167-168
structural credit risk models, 65-66
balance sheet, 66-69
limitations, 69
Merton model. *See* Merton model
option pricing, 70
types of, 70
swaps, CDSs. *See* CDSs
synthetic CDOs, 199-201

T

T-Bills (Treasury Bills), 13
term-to-maturity, 13
the diffusion, 116
the drift, 116
third-to-default, 156
time value, 11
total return swap, 47-48
tranches, 52, 191
CDOs, 194-198
mezzanine tranches, 243
Treasury Bills (T-Bills), 13
types of
credit, 11-14
structural credit risk models, 70

U

U.S.
bankruptcies, companies, 17
bankruptcy filings, 14-15
public and private bond market
debt, 33
U.S. Treasury Bonds, 13
Ulam, Stanislaw, 246
underlying reference assets, credit
derivatives market, 57-58
unwind period, life cycle of CDOs, 197

V

volatility
asset price volatility, 86
asset volatility, sensitivity analysis of
Merton model, 99-100

asset volatility. *See* asset volatility
implied volatility, 92

W

Wal-Mart, 2004 financials, 126
WC/TA (working capital/total
asset), 122
working capital, 122
WorldCom, 32
example of the difficulty in rating, 31-33

Y

yield, 59

Z

Z"-score, 128-130
Z'-score, 128
Z-score model, 121-123
Altman's initial Z-score paper,
124-125
example, 126-127
revised Z-score model, 128-130
zero-coupon bond, 14

Wharton School Publishing

Bernard Baumohl
THE SECRETS OF ECONOMIC INDICATORS
Hidden Clues to Future Economic Trends and Investment Opportunities

Randall Billingsley
UNDERSTANDING ARBITRAGE
An Intuitive Approach to Investment Analysis

Sayan Chatterjee
FAILSAFE STRATEGIES
Profit and Grow from Risks That Others Avoid

Tony Davila, Marc Epstein, and Robert Shelton
MAKING INNOVATION WORK
How to Manage It, Measure It, and Profit from It

Sunil Gupta, Donald R. Lehmann
MANAGING CUSTOMERS AS INVESTMENTS
The Strategic Value of Customers in the Long Run

Stuart L. Hart
CAPITALISM AT THE CROSSROADS
The Unlimited Business Opportunities in Solving the World's Most Difficult Problems

Lawrence G. Hrebiniak
MAKING STRATEGY WORK
Leading Effective Execution and Change

Jon M. Huntsman
WINNERS NEVER CHEAT
Everyday Values We Learned as Children (But May Have Forgotten)

Eamonn Kelly
POWERFUL TIMES
Rising to the Challenge of Our Uncertain World

Doug Lennick, Fred Kiel
MORAL INTELLIGENCE
Enhancing Business Performance and Leadership Success

Vijay Mahajan, Kamini Banga
THE 86 PERCENT SOLUTION
How to Succeed in the Biggest Market Opportunity of the Next 50 Years

Alfred A. Marcus
BIG WINNERS AND BIG LOSERS
The 4 Secrets of Long-Term Business Success and Failure

Robert Mittelstaedt
WILL YOUR NEXT MISTAKE BE FATAL?
Avoiding the Chain of Mistakes That Can Destroy Your Organization

Peter Navarro
THE WELL-TIMED STRATEGY
Managing the Business Cycle for Competitive Advantage

Kenichi Ohmae
THE NEXT GLOBAL STAGE
Challenges and Opportunities in Our Borderless World

Mukul Pandya, Robbie Shell, Susan Warner, Sandeep Junnarkar, Jeffrey Brown
NIGHTLY BUSINESS REPORT PRESENTS LASTING LEADERSHIP
What You Can Learn from the Top 25 Business People of Our Times

C. K. Prahalad
THE FORTUNE AT THE BOTTOM OF THE PYRAMID
Eradicating Poverty Through Profits

Michael A. Roberto
WHY GREAT LEADERS DON'T TAKE YES FOR AN ANSWER
Managing for Conflict and Consensus

Arthur Rubinfeld, Collins Hemingway
BUILT FOR GROWTH
Expanding Your Business Around the Corner or Across the Globe

Scott A. Shane
FINDING FERTILE GROUND
Identifying Extraordinary Opportunities for New Ventures

Oded Shenkar
THE CHINESE CENTURY
The Rising Chinese Economy and Its Impact on the Global Economy, the Balance of Power, and Your Job

David Sirota, Louis A. Mischkind, and Michael Irwin Meltzer
THE ENTHUSIASTIC EMPLOYEE
How Companies Profit by Giving Workers What They Want

Thomas T. Stallkamp
SCORE!
A Better Way to Do Busine$$: Moving from Conflict to Collaboration

Glen Urban
DON'T JUST RELATE — ADVOCATE!
A Blueprint for Profit in the Era of Customer Power

Craig M. Vogel, Jonathan Cagan, and Peter Boatwright
THE DESIGN OF THINGS TO COME
How Ordinary People Create Extraordinary Products

Yoram (Jerry) Wind, Colin Crook, with Robert Gunther
THE POWER OF IMPOSSIBLE THINKING
Transform the Business of Your Life and the Life of Your Business

An Invitation from the Editors:
Join the
Wharton School Publishing Membership Program

Dear Reader,

We hope that you've discovered valuable ideas in this book, which will help you affect real change in your professional life. Each of our titles is evaluated by the Wharton School Publishing editorial board and earns the Wharton Seal of Approval — ensuring that books are timely, important, conceptually sound and/or empirically based and — key for you — implementable.

We encourage you to join the Wharton School Publishing Membership Program. Registration is simple and free, and you will receive these and other valuable benefits:

- **Access to valuable content** — receive access to additional content, including audio summaries, articles, case studies, chapters of forthcoming books, updates, and appendices.
- **Online savings** — save up to 30% on books purchased everyday at Whartonsp.com by joining the site.
- **Exclusive discounts** — receive a special discount on the Financial Times and FT.com when you join today.
- **Up to the minute information** — subscribe to select Wharton School Publishing newsletters to be the first to learn about new releases, special promotions, author appearances, and events.

Becoming a member is easy; please visit Whartonsp.com and click "Join WSP" today.

Wharton School Publishing welcomes your comments and feedback. Please let us know what interests you, so that we can refer you to an appropriate resource or develop future learning in that area. Your suggestions will help us serve you better.

Sincerely,

Jerry Wind
windj@wharton.upenn.edu

Tim Moore
tim_moore@prenhall.com

Become a member today at Whartonsp.com

WW Wharton School Publishing

Understanding Arbitrage
An Intuitive Approach to Financial Analysis
BY RANDALL BILLINGSLEY

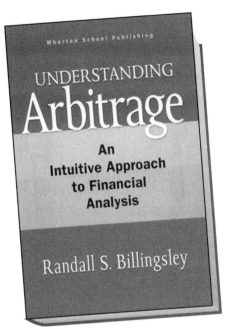

Arbitrage is central both to corporate risk management and to a wide range of investment strategies. Thousands of financial executives, managers, and sophisticated investors want to understand it, but most books on arbitrage are far too abstract and technical to serve their needs. Billingsley addresses this untapped market with the first accessible and realistic guide to the concepts and modern practice of arbitrage. It relies on intuition, not advanced math: readers will find basic algebra sufficient to understand it and begin using its methods. The author starts with a lucid introduction to the fundamentals of arbitrage, including the Laws of One Price and One Expected Return. Using realistic examples, he shows how to identify assets and portfolios ripe for exploitation: mispriced commodities, securities, misvalued currencies; interest rate differences; and more. You'll learn how to establish relative prices between underlying stock, puts, calls, and 'riskless' securities like Treasury bills—and how these techniques support derivatives pricing and hedging. Billingsley then illuminates options pricing, the heart of modern risk management and financial engineering. He concludes with an accessible introduction to the Nobel-winning Modigliani-Miller theory, and its use in analyzing capital structure.

ISBN 0131470205, © 2006, 224 pp., $39.99

The Bible of Options Strategies
The Definitive Guide for Practical Trading Strategies
BY GUY COHEN

In *The Bible of Options Strategies,* options trader Guy Cohen systematically presents today's 60 most effective strategies for trading options: how and why they work, when they're appropriate, and exactly how to use each one—step by step. The only comprehensive reference of its kind, this book will help you identify and implement the optimal strategy for every opportunity, trading environment, and goal. It's practical from start to finish: modular, easy to navigate, and thoroughly cross-referenced, so you can find what you need fast, and act before your opportunity disappears. Cohen systematically covers all five key areas of options strategy: income strategies, volatility strategies, sideways market strategies, leveraged strategies, and synthetic strategies. Even the most complex techniques are explained with unsurpassed clarity—making them accessible to any trader with even modest options experience. This book draws on materials Cohen has presented to thousands of traders via seminars and Web subscriptions that cost $800 and up...now available, for the first time, at a tiny fraction of that price. More than an incredible value, *The Bible of Options Strategies* is the definitive reference to contemporary options trading: the one book you need by your side whenever you trade.

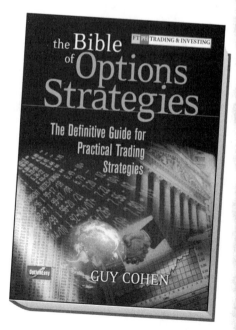

ISBN 0131710664, © 2005, 400 pp., $49.95